Community Search
over Big Graphs

Synthesis Lectures on Data Management

Editor
H.V. Jagadish, *University of Michigan*

Founding Editor
M. Tamer Özsu, *University of Waterloo*

Synthesis Lectures on Data Management is edited by H.V. Jagadish of the University of Michigan.
The series publishes 80–150 page publications on topics pertaining to data management. Topics
include query languages, database system architectures, transaction management, data
warehousing, XML and databases, data stream systems, wide scale data distribution, multimedia
data management, data mining, and related subjects.

Community Search over Big Graphs
Xin Huang, Laks V.S. Lakshmanan, and Jianliang Xu
2019

On Transactional Concurrency Control
Goetz Graefe
2019

Data-Intensive Workflow Management: For Clouds and Data-Intensive and Scalable
Computing Environments
Daniel C.M. de Oliveira, Ji Liu, and Esther Pacitti
2019

Answering Queries Using Views, Second Edition
Foto Afrati and Rada Chirkova
2019

Transaction Processing on Modern Hardware
Mohammad Sadoghi and Spyros Blanas
2019

Data Management in Machine Learning Systems
Matthias Boehm, Arun Kumar, and Jun Yang
2019

Community Search over Big Graphs

Xin Huang, Laks V.S. Lakshmanan, and Jianliang Xu

ISBN: 978-3-031-00746-0   paperback
ISBN: 978-3-031-01874-9   ebook
ISBN: 978-3-031-00101-7   hardcover

DOI 10.1007/978-3-031-01874-9

A Publication in the Springer series
SYNTHESIS LECTURES ON DATA MANAGEMENT

Lecture #61
Series Editor: H.V. Jagadish, *University of Michigan*
Founding Editor: M. Tamer Özsu, *University of Waterloo*
Series ISSN
Print 2153-5418   Electronic 2153-5426

Community Search over Big Graphs

Xin Huang
Hong Kong Baptist University

Laks V.S. Lakshmanan
University of British Columbia

Jianliang Xu
Hong Kong Baptist University

SYNTHESIS LECTURES ON DATA MANAGEMENT #61

ABSTRACT

Communities serve as basic structural building blocks for understanding the organization of many real-world networks, including social, biological, collaboration, and communication networks. Recently, community search over graphs has attracted significantly increasing attention, from small, simple, and static graphs to big, evolving, attributed, and location-based graphs.

In this book, we first review the basic concepts of networks, communities, and various kinds of dense subgraph models. We then survey the state of the art in community search techniques on various kinds of networks across different application areas. Specifically, we discuss cohesive community search, attributed community search, social circle discovery, and geo-social group search. We highlight the challenges posed by different community search problems. We present their motivations, principles, methodologies, algorithms, and applications, and provide a comprehensive comparison of the existing techniques. This book finally concludes by listing publicly available real-world datasets and useful tools for facilitating further research, and by offering further readings and future directions of research in this important and growing area.

KEYWORDS

big data, big graphs, social networks, community detection, community search, dense subgraph, cohesive subgraph, attributed community, geo-spatial community, social circle, k-core, k-truss

To our families:

Chengjin and Weifang

Sarada, Sundaram, Sharada, and Kaavya

Xiaojie and Chen Yi

Contents

Acknowledgments

The materials presented here have been greatly influenced by the research we conducted with many wonderful colleagues, students, and post-doctoral fellows as well as the numerous stimulating discussions we had with them. We would like to express our gratitude to our collaborators, including: Hong Cheng, Yuli Jiang, Ronghua Li, Ye Li, Wei Lu, Qin Lu, Wentao Tian, Jeffrey Xu Yu, Rui Chen, Byron Choi, Haibo Hu, Yafei Li, and Wang-Chien Lee. We would also like to thank Jinbin Huang and Longxu Sun for their careful reading of, and constructive comments on the manuscript, which helped improve our presentation. We acknowledge the support of our research on community search by grants from the National Natural Science Foundation of China under Project No. 61702435, the Research Grants Council of Hong Kong under Project Nos. 12200917, 12200817, and 12201518, and the Natural Sciences and Engineering Research Council of Canada. We thank H.V. Jagadish for encouraging us to write this book and appreciate Diane Cerra and H.V. Jagadish for their assistance throughout the preparation of this manuscript and for their patience. We are grateful to the reviewers for their valuable comments which helped improve the clarity and precision of some of our discussions. Last but not the least, we are indebted to our families whose patience and support throughout this project have been invaluable.

Xin Huang, Laks V.S. Lakshmanan, and Jianliang Xu
July 2019

CHAPTER 1

Introduction

Communities are ubiquitous in nature and society. Since communities serve as fundamental building blocks of networks, significant work has been done on their automatic detection. In contrast to community detection, the aim of community search is to find communities satisfying a given query. Over the last decade, significant strides have been made in the development of community search techniques, which overcome the expensive computation of global community detection by leveraging local network properties and incorporating the constraints in a given query. The main goal of this book is to introduce recent community search models, problems, algorithms, and techniques, and identify important further research that remains open in this important field. We start this chapter by motivating the study of community search using illustrative examples. In addition, we provide some basic concepts and provide an outline of this book.

1.1 GRAPHS AND COMMUNITIES

1.1.1 GRAPHS

Many complex systems in nature and society can be described in terms of graphs (networks) capturing the intricate web of connections among the units they are made of [139]. Graphs have emerged as a powerful model for representing different types of data. For instance, unstructured data (e.g., text documents), semi-structured data (e.g., XML databases), and structured data (e.g., relational databases) can all be modeled as graphs, where the vertices (nodes) are, respectively, documents, elements, and tuples, and the edges can, respectively, be hyperlinks, parent-child relationships, and primary-foreign-key relationships [93]. In addition, graphs naturally arise in application domains such as biological networks, social and information networks, and knowledge graphs, to name but a few.

1.1.2 COMMUNITIES

Community structures naturally exist in numerous real-world networks such as social, biological, collaboration, and communication networks being just a few examples, as shown in Figures 1.1a–1.1d. A question of interest is how to interpret the global organization of such networks in terms of the coexistence of their structural sub-units (communities) associated with more highly interconnected parts [139]. Identifying these *a priori* unknown building blocks (e.g., groups of people [150, 176], industrial sectors [137], and functionally related proteins [142, 158], etc.) is crucial to the understanding of the structural and functional properties of networks [139].

To illustrate, we introduce three notable examples of communities.

Online Social Networks. One type of network where communities are frequently observed is online social networks. Enabled by the Internet and sparked by the recent advent of online social networking sites such as Facebook, Google+, and Twitter [42], research on community discovery over online social networks has been booming. With the ready availability of large-scale social network data, the research has led to the development of many exciting applications, e.g., social circle discovery and influential community search. In addition, due to the prosperity of smart-phone devices, online social networks have led to the rapid growth of geo-social networks (also known as location-based social networks), such as Foursquare, Yelp, Google+, and Facebook Places. In a geo-social network, users are associated with location information (e.g., hometowns and check-in places), and communities consist of users that are closely connected in the social layer as well as spatially proximate in the spatial layer.

Academic Collaboration Networks. A well-known academic collaboration network is the DBLP network, where a vertex represents an author and an edge between two authors indi-cates a collaborative relationship, i.e., they have co-authored publication(s). In addition, vertices can have attributes that represent the authors' areas of expertise. Communities in the DBLP network may represent a group of authors that frequently collaborate with each other and work on similar topics.

Heterogeneous Information Networks. Heterogeneous networks consist of vertices and edges both of different types [159]. For instance, in a healthcare network, vertices can be patients, doc-tors, medical tests, diseases, medicines, hospitals, treatments, and so on. On one hand, treating all the vertices as of the same type may miss important semantic information. On the other hand, treating every vertex as a distinct type may miss the big picture. This is a classic example of a heterogeneous network. Such multiple types of objects, interconnected, heterogeneous but often semi-structured information networks, make the communities over heterogeneous information networks complex and interesting.

1.2   COMMUNITY SEARCH

In this section, we provide some background on community search.

1.2.1   COMMUNITY SEARCH PROBLEM

The community search problem is, given one or more query vertices, to find densely connected communities containing the query vertices [96], as illustrated in Figure 1.1f. Since the commu-nities defined by different vertices in a network may be quite different, community search with query vertices opens up the prospects of user-centered and personalized search, with the poten-tial of producing meaningful answers to a user [54]. As just one example, in a social network,

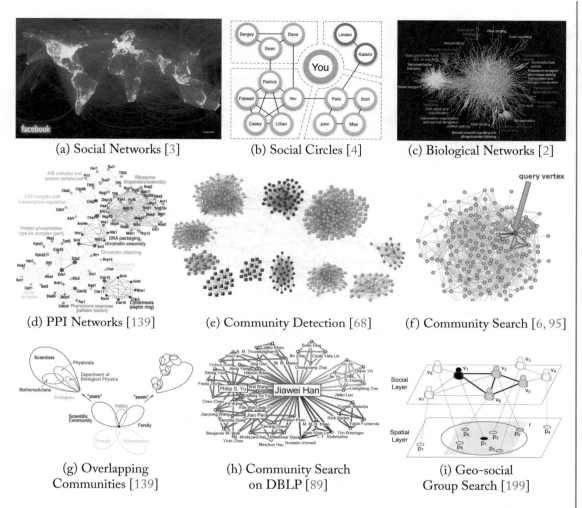

Figure 1.1: **(a)** Facebook social network where two friends have an edge connection. **(b)** Social circles naturally exist in online social networks. **(c)** Different communities in biological networks. **(d)** Different protein complexes in protein-protein-interaction (PPI) networks. **(e)** Community detection is finding all communities over the whole network. Each community is colored differently. **(f)** Community search is to find communities containing the given query nodes in the graph. It is a query-dependent community discovery. **(g)** Communities defined by different nodes in a network may be quite different. **(h)** Five communities containing the author of "Jiawei Han" on DBLP collaboration network. **(i)** Community search on geo-social networks aims at finding densely connected communities within the proximity of given queries.

the community formed by a person's high school classmates can be significantly different from the community formed by his/her family members, which in turn can be quite different from the one formed by his/her colleagues [117], as shown in Figure 1.1g.

1.2.2   A COMPARISON WITH COMMUNITY DETECTION

Community detection, which is to identify all communities in a network shown in Figure 1.1e, is another fundamental and well-studied problem in the literature [6, 46, 68, 133, 135, 139, 144, 154, 183]. Community detection techniques include graph clustering by means of optimizing specific functions (e.g., modularity [135], normalized cut [73, 155], low-conductance cuts [71, 111], personalized pagerank [11, 12, 161]), spectral methods [68, 125, 133, 134], generative models [187, 188, 191], and deep neural networks [193]. Community detection aims at revealing latent community structures from a given network, which provide insight into the underlying interactions and potential functions of networks. Applications include link prediction [34, 100, 115, 156, 164], eradicating social network worms [169], and terrorist group detection [173].

The two problems of community detection and community search have different goals: whereas community detection targets all communities in the entire network and usually applies a global criterion to find qualified communities [89], community search provides personalized community discovery for query vertices in an online manner. Specifically, the following differences between community detection and community search motivate the study of the online community search problem in its own right.

- Community detection finds all communities in a graph in a batched process. In contrast, community search only retrieves query-dependent communities containing the given vertices. To support the online retrieval of communities, the methods of community detection may detect all communities in an offline precomputation stage and construct an index of numerous communities, which is prohibitively costly for massive graphs with million or billions of nodes and edges. For example, Facebook networks had over 800 million nodes and 100 billion links [54] by 2013. As of the third quarter of 2018, Facebook had 2.27 billion monthly active users [1]. Thus, supporting online community detection is very expensive in terms of both space and time.

- Community detection usually uses a global criterion to find all communities in a graph [54], regardless of any notion of query vertices. However, the semantics of discovered communities may vary significantly for different query vertices. For example, in a research collaboration network, the communities of a famous scholar and a junior scholar can be dramatically different in terms of the community size and density. Furthermore, even for a particular researcher, her community w.r.t. her research colleagues can be quite different from her community w.r.t. family and friends, illustrating the difference that query vertices can make.

- It is a challenge for community detection to support dynamically evolving graphs, in which graph vertices and edges can be frequently inserted or deleted. Because it is expensive to re-run the community detection algorithm once the graph changes, the freshness of communities detected cannot be guaranteed [54]. In contrast, online community search provides real-time query services to users.

1.2.3 APPLICATIONS

Community search has many interesting applications in areas such as social network analysis, collaborative tagging systems, query-log analysis, biology, and others [157]. Several representative application scenarios of community search are briefly discussed in the following.

- *Event organization*: Suppose some scientists plan to organize an event like a research workshop. The chances of success of this event would be higher if they can invite a number of well-acquainted scientists that are specialized in this event's topic and with whom they perhaps have even collaborated, possibly together with other participants.

- *Tag suggestion*: In social media websites, many items (photos, videos, and music) are labeled with tags. For instance, in a photo-sharing portal, we can construct a tag-graph as follows: if two tags co-occur frequently in a number of photos, an edge is added between them. Now assume that a new photo is being uploaded, and some initial tags are provided by users. Then the system can suggest a number of additional tags for this new photo. A good suggestion would be the tags that are related to the initial ones and are densely connected to each other.

- *Protein discovery*: A biologist has identified a number of proteins that regulate a gene of interest, and would like to study further a candidate list of other proteins that are likely to participate in the regulation process. Such a candidate set can be obtained by finding a dense subgraph in the protein-protein-interaction network that contains the given proteins [93, 157].

- *Spatial task outsourcing*: Given a set of spatial tasks, each associated with a spatial location, one needs to distribute them to a set of workers, each having a service region. To successfully accomplish the tasks, the service regions of the selected workers should cover all spatial tasks' locations, and the workers are expected to have good collaborative relationships so that the tasks can be efficiently completed. A geo-social community search can address this worker selection problem in spatial task outsourcing, as shown in Figure 1.1i.

Other applications of community search include academic research community discovery [54, 65, 89, 96, 157, 180], influential group search [122], social circle discovery [89, 117], ambiguous name identification [87, 88], analysis of diverse meanings of words [88], and so on. A few examples of networks, communities, and community search are illustrated in Figures 1.1a–1.1i.

1.2.4   DATASETS AND TOOLS

This book introduces five types of real-world graph datasets with ground-truth communities, including simple graphs, attributed graphs, ego social networks, geo-social networks, and public-private collaboration networks. Besides datasets, we also introduce the evaluation metrics and details of query generation, which can be helpful for further study and for evaluating research ideas on community search. Moreover, we list publicly available software tools and demo systems for assisting further study of community search. All these datasets and tools can be found in Chapter 7.

1.3   PREREQUISITE AND TARGET READER

The prerequisite of this book includes basic knowledge of graph theory, network science, data structures and algorithms, and database indexing and query processing. The target reader of this book is anyone who is interested in modeling and searching communities over large graphs, from data mining and data management researchers to practitioners from the industry. Specifically, this book can serve as a textbook for graduate students and as a compact research monograph for a junior researcher to quickly get up to speed and find new research topics on community search. For those new to the area, the book will cover the necessary background material to help understand the topics and offer a comprehensive survey of the state-of-the-art techniques. Moreover, the book aims to provide new perspectives in regards to community search that will be interesting and valuable to the researchers with more experience in the field. For those having worked on classic community detection and graph clustering, we will demonstrate how the problem of community search interacts with commonly used models in terms of algorithmic efficiency and network dynamics, and poses new challenges compared to community detection. For those that have worked on community search, we hope to provide a comprehensive survey of latest work on community search and inspire new research directions by establishing connections with recent developments.

1.4   OUTLINE OF THE BOOK

Community search and its study is the central theme of this book, which consists of eight chapters. On a high level, the book first introduces the basic concepts of communities and networks and then gives an overview of the state-of-the-art research. Community search on different types of networks requires appropriate community models and search algorithms. Each chapter discusses one type of community search on a specific type of networks by presenting detailed community models, the intuition behind them, and the corresponding search algorithms. The presented techniques are illustrated with examples and comparisons are drawn between different community models. We summarize the content of each chapter in what follows.

- **Cohesive Subgraphs.** Chapter 2 presents classical concepts of cohesive subgraphs. In many real applications where information is modeled using graphs, communities are formed by a set of similar entities that are densely connected with certain relationships. Various kinds of cohesive subgraphs, including clique, quasi-clique, k-DBDSG, k-clan, k-club, k-plex, k-core, k-truss, k-vertex-connected, and k-edge-connected, which are widely used in the literature as building blocks for communities in graphs, are introduced.

- **Cohesive Community Search.** Chapter 3 introduces the problem of community search in simple graphs. In simple terms, a graph represents a structure of interactions within a group of vertices. Community models in this class can only leverage the structural characteristics of networks, essentially focusing on the density of the connection structure. Given a set of query vertices, community search is to find a densely connected subgraph containing all query vertices. Recently, several community models based on different dense subgraphs have been proposed, including quasi-clique [54], densest subgraph [180], k-core [18, 55, 122, 157], and k-truss [89, 96]. Our discussion in this chapter covers these various community models.

- **Attributed Community Search.** Chapter 4 discusses the problem of attributed community search in attributed networks, where nodes are associated with attributes or predicates. Many real-world networks contain attributes or predicates on vertices, e.g., a person may have information such as name, interests, and skills. In addition to the network structure, users may aim to search for attribute-related communities, or attributed communities. An attributed community is a group of vertices that are connected with a cohesive structure, and share homogeneous query attributes [65, 93]. The latter property bears some resemblance to keyword search over databases and graphs, but has important differences.

- **Social Circle Discovery.** Chapter 5 presents the problem of social circle discovery in social networks. Online social networks allow users to manually categorize their friends into social circles within their ego-networks (e.g., "circles" on Google+) [117, 170]. As one special kind of community, social circles are communities formed by friends only. The problem of social circles discovery is to automatically identify all social circles for a given user. Social circles can be used for content filtering, privacy protection, or sharing groups of users that others may wish to follow. The number of distinct social contexts also affects the process of information diffusion in social contagion [87, 163].

- **Geo-Social Group Search.** Chapter 6 describes the problem of finding geo-social groups in location-based social networks. In such networks, many users share their locations, which enables a new computing paradigm that explicitly combines the location and social factors to generate useful information for either business or social good. Geo-social group search looks for a group of users densely and closely connected in terms of both social and spatial proximity [123, 124, 199]. Relevant applications include recommending a group of friends for meet up and pushing mobile coupons to a group of close friends in location-based advertisements.

- **Datasets and Tools.** Chapter 7 lists a number of real-world datasets with ground-truth communities for further study in community search. Moreover, software systems implementing the representative community search algorithms presented in this book are also listed.

- **Conclusions.** Chapter 8 concludes this book. Whereas good progress has been made, research on community search is still in its infancy, and there are still many opportunities for further research. We briefly introduce the latest publications that are not covered in the early chapters of this book, discuss open problems, and highlight promising directions.

The content of this book is based on the tutorial entitled "Community Search over Big Graphs: Models, Algorithms, and Opportunities" [94] given by the authors at the 33rd IEEE International Conference on Data Engineering (ICDE) in April 2017. The tutorial slides are available online [95]. While the tutorial slides can serve as a companion to this book, the book includes more comprehensive and in-depth coverage of various community models, community search algorithms, as well as more recent developments in the area. Other supplementary materials of this book can be found at `http://db.comp.hkbu.edu.hk/csbook`.

CHAPTER 2

Cohesive Subgraphs

In many real applications where information is modeled using graphs, communities are formed by a set of similar entities that are densely connected with certain relationships. Massive networks can often be understood and analyzed in terms of these communities [165]. In the literature, several different models for cohesive (dense) subgraphs and communities have been proposed, which we will discuss in Chapters 3–6. Specifically, dense subgraphs of various kinds are often used as building blocks of communities. In this chapter, we will review various kinds of dense/cohesive subgraphs, including clique [31, 45, 166, 182], quasi-clique [162], k-DBDSG [132], k-clan [132], k-club [132], k-plex [165], k-core [19, 44], k-truss [50, 165], k-ecc [38], and densest subgraphs [15, 106]. We also investigate their relationships and compare their structural properties using illustrative examples.

2.1 COMMUNITY SEARCH AND COHESIVE SUBGRAPHS

This book focuses on the community models based on cohesive subgraphs. Unlike community detection, there are three desirable properties for community search models: cohesive structure for high-quality communities, support for easy querying and personalization, and fast algorithms for efficient query processing. The detailed reasons are as follows.

- In real-world applications, communities usually have many kinds of topological structures in different shapes. This brings significant challenges for developing a perfect model to fit all of the variously shaped community structures. However, the intuition that community search shares with community discovery is that community members often have densely connected relationships with members of the same community, and have seldom connections with others beyond this community. This observation naturally motivates the model of community as dense subgraphs. In addition, diameter and connectivity have been considered as important features for modeling communities. Small diameter and high connectivity are proposed as criteria for good communities in [61, 81]. Small diameter guarantees that any two vertices in a community can be found within a short distance of each other. High connectivity ensures the connectivity between vertices in the community is strong and robust.

- Besides good structural properties, high efficiency is highly desirable for community search. This is because community search, being query driven, should be answered in an efficient way, so as to allow the user to interactively modify her query and explore the resulting communities found. There exist several classical dense subgraphs, including clique [31], quasi-clique [162], k-DBDSG [132], k-clan [132], k-club [132], and k-plex [165]. In principle, any of these dense subgraphs could be used as a basis for community search. However, one drawback of these dense subgraph models is that they are NP-hard to discover. Consequently, the search of communities based on such dense subgraphs given a query, is inefficient and intractable for real-time query processing. Recently proposed dense subgraphs k-core [19, 44] and k-truss [50, 165] make real-time retrieval of communities possible, since they can be computed in polynomial time. Moreover, using a single parameter of k, we can get a hierarchical community structure of a query vertex [89]. Polynomial-time complexity for computing cohesive subgraphs of k-core and k-truss is a game-changer in the field of community search, which attracts significant interest in the study of problems related to community search in social and information networks [18, 55, 64, 65, 89, 93, 96, 122–124, 157, 199].

In the following sections, we first introduce the basic concepts of graph theory in Section 2.2. Then, we introduce various kinds of classical dense subgraphs, which are NP-hard to compute, in Section 2.3. Next, we present the definitions of k-core and k-truss, recently widely used in community search, which have a polynomial-time complexity, in Section 2.4. We not only introduce their concepts but also their decomposition algorithms, which are particularly useful in building indexes for speeding up the query processing. Finally, more dense subgraphs including the densest subgraph and k-ecc are introduced in Section 2.5.

2.2   NOTATIONS AND NOTIONS

We start with a brief introduction of the notations and notions used in this book.

2.2.1   GRAPHS AND SUBGRAPHS

A graph $G(V, E)$ is a set of nodes (or vertices) V together with a set of lines (edges) E. Any line of E connects a pair of nodes, say u, v: we denote this as an edge $(u, v) \in E$ and say that u and v are adjacent to each other in G. We also denote the number of vertices and the number of edges, respectively, as $n = |V|$ and $m = |E|$. A self-loop is an edge connecting a node to itself. Unless otherwise specified, all graphs discussed in this book are simple graphs: finite, non-empty, undirected, and having no self-loops. In addition, a complete graph K_p is a graph of p vertices, where every pair of vertices is adjacent to each other.

Figure 2.1 shows an example of graph $G(V, E)$ with 10 nodes and 14 edges, where $|V| = |\{v_1, v_2, \ldots, v_{10}\}| = 10$ and $|E| = 14$. As we can see, G is a simple and undirected graph without self-loops.

A graph $H = (V(H), E(H))$ is a subgraph of graph $G(V, E)$ denoted $H \subset G$, iff $V(H) \subseteq V$ and $E(H) \subseteq E$. In addition, when a graph H is a subgraph of graph G, we say that graph G is a supergraph of H. Furthermore, we give the definition of induced subgraph as follows.

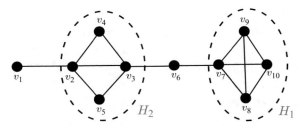

Figure 2.1: An example of graph G with 10 nodes and 14 edges. Two subgraphs H_1 and H_2 of G.

Definition 2.2.1 (Induced Graph) *Given a graph $G(V, E)$ and a vertex set $S \subseteq V$, the induced subgraph of G by S is $G_S = (S, E_S)$ where the edge set $E_S = \{(v, u) : v, u \in S, (v, u) \in E\}$.*

In addition, we define the maximality using supergraphs. A subgraph $H \subseteq G$ satisfying a given property is maximal provided no proper supergraph of H, that is also a subgraph of G, satisfies that property.

In Figure 2.1, the subgraph H_1 of G consists of 4 vertices and 6 edges, i.e., the vertex set $V(H_1) = \{v_7, v_8, v_9, v_{10}\}$, and the edge set $E(H_1) = \{(v_7, v_8), (v_7, v_9), (v_7, v_{10}), (v_8, v_9), (v_8, v_{10}), (v_9, v_{10})\}$. As we can see, for any pair of vertices in H_1, there exists an edge connecting them, indicating H_1 is a complete subgraph of 4 nodes, i.e., a 4-clique. In addition, since we cannot find any supergraph H' containing H_1 to be a clique, H_1 is the maximal complete subgraph K_4 of G.

2.2.2   DEGREE AND NEIGHBORS

The set of neighbors of a vertex v in graph G is denoted by $N_G(v)$, i.e., $N_G(v) = \{u \in V : (v, u) \in E(G)\}$. The degree of a vertex v in G is the number of neighbors (vertices) adjacent to v, denoted by $d_G(v) = |N_G(v)|$. When the context is obvious, we drop the subscript and denote the set of neighbors as $N(v)$ and the degree as $d(v)$. We use $d_{max} = \max_{v \in V} d(v)$ to denote the maximum vertex degree in G. Given a subgraph H of G, we use $N_H(v)$ to represent the set of neighbors to v in the subgraph H only. Similar extensions may be made to degree, path, and other definitions below.

For example, in the graph G shown in Figure 2.1, vertex v_7 has 4 neighbors $N(v_7) = \{v_6, v_8, v_9, v_{10}\}$, thus the degree of v_7 is 4 as $d(v_7) = 4$. In the subgraph H_1 of G, v_7 has 3 neighbors as $N_{H_1}(v_7) = \{v_8, v_9, v_{10}\}$ and $d_{H_1}(v_7) = 3$.

2.2.3   PATH, CYCLE, CONNECTIVITY, AND DIAMETER

A path, connecting two vertices v, u of a subgraph H, consists of a series of vertices $v, w_1, w_2, \ldots, w_{l-1}, u \in V(H)$, such that $(v, w_1) \in E(H)$, $(w_i, w_{i+1}) \in E(H)$ for $1 \le i < l-1$, and $(w_{l-1}, u) \in E(H)$. The length l of a path is given by the number of its edges.

A cycle C_l of length l is a path of length l, where $u = v$. A triangle in G is a cycle of length 3. We denote a triangle involving vertices $u, v, w \in V$ as $\triangle_{uvw}$.

Consider the graph G in Figure 2.1 and two vertices v_8, v_9, one path P connecting v_8 and v_9 can be $P =< v_8, v_7, v_9 >$ which consists of two edges (v_8, v_7) and (v_7, v_9). The length of P is 2. Moreover, the cycle formed by vertices v_7, v_8, v_9 is a triangle $\triangle_{v_7 v_8 v_9}$.

A subgraph H of G is connected if every pair of vertices $u, v \in H$ is connected by a path in H. W.l.o.g we assume in this book that the graph G we consider is connected. Note that this implies that $m \geq n - 1$.

Furthermore, we give the definition of the shortest path. For two nodes $u, v \in G$, we denote by $\text{dist}_G(u, v)$ the length of the shortest path between u and v in G, where $\text{dist}_G(u, v) = +\infty$ if u and v are not connected. Based on the concept of the shortest path, we can define graph diameter as follows. The diameter of a graph G is defined as the maximum length of a shortest path in G, i.e., $\text{diam}(G) = \max_{u,v \in G}\{\text{dist}_G(u, v)\}$. One well-known relation will be frequently used in this book, that is, if H is a subgraph G, then for every pair of vertices $v, u \in H$, $\text{dist}_G(u, v) \leq \text{dist}_H(u, v)$. In other words, the distance between any two vertices in a subgraph of G cannot be shorter than their distance in G itself.

Continuing the above example in Figure 2.1, we know that the shortest path between v_8 and v_9 is the edge (v_8, v_9) of length as 1, thus the path $P =< v_8, v_7, v_9 >$ is not the shortest path as $|P| = 2$. Considering the graph G, the shortest path between v_1 and v_{10} has 5 edges, $\text{dist}_G(v_1, v_{10}) = 5$, which is the longest shortest path in G. As such, the diameter of G is $\text{diam}(G) = \max_{v,u \in G}\{\text{dist}_G(v, u)\} = 5$. In addition, consider the subgraph $H = H_1 \cup H_2$, the distance between v_2 and v_7 in graph H is $\text{dist}_H(v_2, v_7) = +\infty$.

2.3   CLASSICAL DENSE SUBGRAPHS

A community (group) is usually regarded as a set of members that are interconnected with dense substructures. For example, in social networks, there are several concepts associated with communities that indicate various types and configurations of social groups, such as social circles, peer groups, coteries, and so on [132]. To effectively represent such more or less closely knit groups, several definitions of subgraphs are developed with the help of graph theory and network science. A well-known concept of peer group is the clique: a group all members of which are in contact with, or are friends with, or know each other. However, relaxed concepts of cliques are also necessary to denote less loosely knit, yet significantly homogeneous social groups, e.g., for every pair of members, even if they are not in mutual contact, have multiple common third contacts [132].

There is a large body of work on mining dense subgraph patterns, including clique [31, 45, 166, 182], quasi-clique [162], k-DBDSG, k-clan, k-club, k-core [19, 44], k-truss [50, 165, 192], dense neighborhood graph [168], to name a few. In the following, we first introduce cliques and their relaxed variants.

2.3.1   CLIQUE AND QUASI-CLIQUE

We start with the well-known notion of k-cliques.

Definition 2.3.1 (k-Clique) *A k-clique is a complete subgraph of k vertices, where every pair of vertices is adjacent.*

A k-clique is the densest graph among all k-node graphs. Let G be the graph shown in Figure 2.2, with subgraphs H_1 (Figure 2.2a) and H_2 (Figure 2.2b). H_1 is a 4-clique, while H_2 misses being one by just one edge. Nevertheless, the vertices of H_2 form a closely knit cohesive subgraph. Another dense subgraph called γ-quasi-k-clique has been introduced for capturing subgraphs that are "close" to being cliques, based on the notion of edge density, defined next.

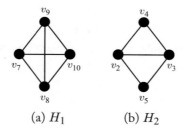

(a) H_1 (b) H_2

Figure 2.2: Examples of k-clique as H_1 and γ-quasi-k-clique as H_2 where $k = 4$ and $\gamma = 0.8$.

Definition 2.3.2 (Edge Density) *Given a graph $G(V, E)$, the edge density of G is defined as* $\mathsf{den}(G) = \frac{2|E|}{|V|(|V|-1)}$.

By tuning the edge density of the graph using a parameter γ, a generalization of k-clique, called γ-quasi-k-clique is defined as follows.

Definition 2.3.3 (γ-Quasi-k-Clique) *A γ-quasi-k-clique is a graph of k vertices with at least* $\lfloor \gamma \frac{k(k-1)}{2} \rfloor$ *edges where $0 \leq \gamma \leq 1$.*

In Figure 2.2, H_2 has 4 vertices and 5 edges, and the edge density of H_2 is $\mathsf{den}(H_2) = \frac{2*5}{4*(4-1)} = \frac{5}{6} = 0.833$. Thus, H_2 is a 0.8-quasi-4-clique where $\mathsf{den}(H_2) \geq 0.8$.

Clique and quasi-clique enumeration methods include the classical algorithm [31], the external-memory H^*-graph algorithm [45], redundancy-aware clique enumeration [166], maximum clique computation using MapReduce [182], and optimal quasi-clique mining [162].

2.3.2 k-DBDSG, k-CLAN, k-CLUB, AND k-PLEX

Other kinds of dense subgraphs proposed in the literature include k-DBDSG, k-clan, k-club, and also k-plex.

Definition 2.3.4 (k-distance bounded dense subgraph [132]) *A k-distance bounded dense subgraph (k-DBDSG) is a loose definition of a clique on n vertices. Specifically, a k-DBDSG of a graph G is a maximal subgraph $H \subseteq G$ such that every pair of vertices $u, v \in V(H)$ is at most a distance k apart in G, i.e.,* $\text{dist}_G(u, v) \le k, \forall u, v \in V(H)$.

Note that, due to the maximality of H, for each node $x \in V(G) \setminus V(H)$, there exists a node $v \in V(H)$ with $\text{dist}_G(x, v) > k$.

From this definition, it can be seen that the k-DBDSG is a global notion, in that it is based on the overall structure of the network, i.e., based on the entire graph and reflected in its distance matrix. We note that k-DBDSG was originally defined in [132], where the term n-clique was used to describe it, where n is the bound on the distance between pairs of nodes. Owing to the obvious confusion this may cause with the standard notion of k-clique, we have changed the terminology to k-DBDSG.

Notice that the bound k is on the distance between vertices of H, where the distance is measured in the original graph G. Consequently, the diameter of H may exceed k. For example, consider the graph G in Figure 2.3a, and the two subgraphs H_1 and H_2 of G presented in Figures 2.3b and 2.3c. First, both subgraphs are 2-DBDSG's, as $\text{dist}_G(u, v) \le 2$ holds for any pair of vertices u, v in H_1 and H_2. However, the diameter of H_1 is 3 as the shortest path connecting v_4 and v_5 passes through vertices v_2 and v_3. On the other hand, the diameter of H_2 is 2.

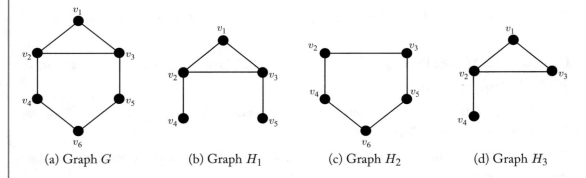

(a) Graph G (b) Graph H_1 (c) Graph H_2 (d) Graph H_3

Figure 2.3: Several examples of k-DBDSGs, k-clans, k-clubs, and also k-plexes. Here $k = 2$. H_1 is a k-DBDSG of G, but not a k-clan. H_2 is a k-DBDSG, a k-clan, a k-club, and also a 3-plex with 5 vertices. H_3 is a k-club, but not a k-DBDSG or a k-clan.

Definition 2.3.5 (k-clan [132]) *A k-clan H of a graph G is a k-DBDSG of G such that for every pair of vertices v, u in H, the distance in H is at most k, i.e.,* $\text{dist}_H(v, u) \le k$.

In the above example, H_1 is not a 2-clan, since the distance $\text{dist}_{H_1}(v_4, v_5) = 3 > 2$. In contrast, H_2 is a k-clan and k-DBDSG for $k = 2$. Notice that since a k-clan is a 2-DBDSG, it is required to be maximal.

Consequently, a k-clan H of G satisfies the following conditions:
(1) for all vertices $u, v \in V(H)$: $\mathrm{dist}_H(u, v) \leq k$; and
(2) for all vertices $w \in V(G) \setminus V(H)$, there exist a vertex $u \in V(H)$ with $\mathrm{dist}_G(u, w) > k$.

It is easy to see that a k-clan is a stronger notion than a k-DBDSG. By definition, k-clans are k-DBDSGs of diameter at most k in H.

Definition 2.3.6 (k-club [132]) *A k-club H of a graph G is a maximal subgraph of G with diameter at most k, i.e., $\mathrm{diam}(H) \leq k$.*

k-clan **v.s.** k-club While the definitions of k-club and k-clan look very similar, their maximality conditions are issued on different distance constraints. The distance function of k-club focuses on the local subgraph H, which requires the maximal subgraph achieving $\mathrm{dist}_H(v, u) \leq k$. On the other hand, a k-clan H is first a k-DBDSG by definition. Thus, the distance function of k-clan focuses on the global graph G, which requires the maximal subgraph achieving $\mathrm{dist}_G(v, u) \leq k$. The following example shows the difference of k-clan and k-club.

Example 2.3.1 *Consider the subgraph H_3 in Figure 2.3d of graph G in Figure 2.3a. H_3 is a k-club ($k=2$), since $\mathrm{diam}(H_3) = 2$ and there exists no supergraph H' of H_3 with $\mathrm{diam}(H') = 2$. On the other hand, H_3 is not a 2-DBDSG ($k=2$) since it violates the maximality constraint; as a supergraph of H_3, H_1 is a 2-DBDSG ($k=2$). Hence, H_3 is not k-clan ($k=2$) by definition.*

The notion of k-plex relaxes the degree of each vertex within a clique of n vertices from $(n-1)$ to $(n-k)$ [165].

Definition 2.3.7 (k-plex) *A k-plex of size n is a subgraph H of size n where each vertex is adjacent to at least $n - k$ vertices in H.*

For example, H_2 in Figure 2.3c is a 3-plex of size 5, as each vertex has at least $(5 - 3) = 2$ neighbors in H_2.

Comparisons and Algorithms. All the above-mentioned cohesive subgraphs are relatively small substructures in a graph. The basic ones are the cliques (i.e., complete subgraphs) and maximal cliques. As the definition of clique is often too rigid, more relaxed forms of cohesive subgraphs have been studied. The k-DBDSG relaxes the distance between any two vertices in a clique from 1 to k. The k-clan is the same as the k-DBDSG except for imposing a constraint on the diameter. The k-club removes the k-DBDSG requirement from the k-clan. The k-plex relaxes the degree of each vertex within a clique of n vertices from $n - 1$ to $n - k$. The quasi-clique can be either a relaxation on the density or the degree. However, the computation of all the above cohesive subgraphs is NP-hard [132, 162, 165].

The algorithms typically need to enumerate the subgraphs corresponding to all subsets of vertices for finding all maximal cliques, quasi-cliques, k-DBDSGs, k-clans, k-clubs, and k-plexes [132].

2.4 k-CORE **AND** k-TRUSS

In this section, we introduce two common dense subgraph definitions of k-core and k-truss. In addition, we present algorithms for core decomposition and truss decomposition on graphs, which can efficiently find k-core and k-truss for any possible value k.

2.4.1 k-CORE

The k-core of a graph G is the largest subgraph of G in which every vertex is adjacent to at least k other vertices within the subgraph. In other words, we can define k-core as follows.

Definition 2.4.1 *[K-Core] Given a graph G and an integer k, a k-core H of G is the largest subgraph such that $\forall v \in V(H)$, $\deg_H(v) \geq k$.*

If a vertex v is present in the k-core subgraph, but not in the $(k + 1)$-core subgraph, we say the core number of v is k. We next give the formal definition of *core number*.

Definition 2.4.2 *[Core Number] The* core number *of a vertex $v \in V$, denoted $\varphi(v)$, is the maximum integer k for which there exists a k-core of G that contains v.*

We denote the maximum core number of any vertex in a graph as $c_{\max}$. Based on the core number of vertices, we can partition vertices into different classes. The k-class of G, $\Psi(k)$, is defined as $\Psi(k) = \{v : v \in V, \varphi(v) = k\}$.

We illustrate the concepts of k-core and k-class using an example. Consider the graph G in Figure 2.4. The whole graph G is a 1-core, since each vertex has degree at least 1. The 1-class $\Psi(1) = \{v_1\}$, 2-class $\Psi(2) = \{v_2, v_3, v_4, v_5, v_6\}$, and 3-class $\Psi(3) = \{v_7, v_8, v_9, v_{10}\}$. In this example, the largest core number of any vertex is $c_{\max} = 3$. The 3-core is formed by the subgraph of G induced by $\Psi(3)$, and the core number of vertex v_7 is $\varphi(v_7) = 3$.

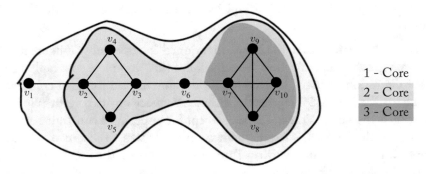

Figure 2.4: An example of k-core in graph G where $1 \leq k \leq 3$. There exists no 4-core in G.

Core decomposition. The problem of core decomposition of a graph G is to find all possible k-cores of G, for $k = 0, 1, \ldots, c_{\max}$, where $c_{\max}$ is the maximum core number of any vertex

Algorithm 2.1 Core Decomposition

Input: $G = (V, E)$
Output: $\varphi(v)$ for each $v \in V$

1: sort the vertices in G in ascending order of their degree;
2: **while** (G is not empty)
3:      let d be the minimum vertex degree in G;
4:      **while** (there exists a vertex v with degree of at most d)
5:          $\varphi(v) \leftarrow d$;
6:          remove v and all edges incident to v from G;
7:          update the vertex degrees and reorder the remaining vertices in ascending order of their degree;
8: **return** $\varphi(v)$ for each $v \in V$;

in G. Equivalently, the problem is to find all k-classes of G for $k = 0, 1, \ldots, c_{\max}$. Given the core decomposition of G, we can easily obtain the k-core of G for any k, as the subgraph of G induced by the vertex set $\bigcup_{k \le i \le k_{\max}} \Psi(i)$.

Algorithm. For the sake of exposition, we describe a basic core decomposition algorithm [19] that computes the *core number* of each vertex in G. The skeleton of core decomposition is outlined in Algorithm 2.1. It is a simple bottom-up method that computes the k-class from smaller to larger values of k [44].

The algorithm first sorts the vertices in G in ascending order of their degrees. Then the algorithm iteratively removes from G a vertex v with the minimum degree, together with all the edges incident to it, and assigns d, the current minimum degree in G, as its core number $\varphi(v)$. Upon the removal of v, we also update the degrees of the remaining vertices and reorder them according to their new degrees. The algorithm terminates when all vertices are removed from G. In this way, we can compute the core numbers of all vertices in G.

Batagelj and Zaversnik [19] apply bin-sort to order the vertices, leading to an overall running time complexity of $O(m)$ for the algorithm.

Clearly, k-cores constitute dense subgraphs, since each vertex is required to have degree at least k. On the other hand, a k-core may be disconnected, e.g., consider a graph G consisting of two isolated 4-cliques shown in Figure 2.5a. Then the 3-core of the graph G is the union of the two disjoint 4-cliques. However, in the application of community detection and search, it is critical that the community be connected. This motivates the following.

Definition 2.4.3 *[Connected K-Core] Given a graph G and an integer k, a connected k-core is a connected subgraph $H \subseteq G$, such that $\forall v \in V(H)$, $\deg_H(v) \ge k$.*

Figure 2.5b shows a subgraph H of G in Figure 2.5a. H is a connected 3-core, since every vertex has a degree of 3 in H and H is connected.

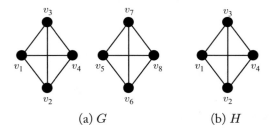

(a) G   (b) H

Figure 2.5: An example of classical k-core G and connected k-core H. Here $k = 3$.

2.4.2 k-TRUSS

Recall that the k-core of a graph is the largest subgraph such that each vertex has degree at least k in this subgraph. Similar to the definition of k-core, the k-truss, as a definition of cohesive subgraph of a graph G, requires that each edge be contained in at least $(k-2)$ triangles within this subgraph. Consider the graph G in Figure 2.6; in the subgraph of the whole grey region (i.e., excluding the nodes v_1 and v_6), each edge is contained in at least one triangle. Thus, the subgraph is a 3-truss. It is well known that most of the real-world social networks are triangle-based, in the sense that connections are induced by triangle closures, which always have a high local clustering coefficient.[1] Triangles are also known as the fundamental building blocks of networks [165]. In a social network, a triangle indicates two friends having a common friend, which shows a strong and stable relationship among the three friends. Intuitively, the more common friends two people have, the stronger their relationships. In a k-truss, every pair of friends is "endorsed" by at least $(k-2)$ common friends. Thus, a k-truss with a large value of k signifies strong interconnections between members of the subgraph.

We use the notation $\triangle_{uvw}$ to denote a triangle over u, v, w, i.e., a subgraph over the vertices $\{u, v, w\}$, every pair of which is adjacent. Given an edge $e(u, v) \in E$ in G, the *support* of edge e, is defined as the number of triangles containing e, denoted $sup_G(e) = |\{\triangle_{uvw} : w \in V\}|$. When the context is obvious, we drop the subscript and denote the support as $sup(e)$. Based on the definition of support, we formally define the k-truss as follows.

Definition 2.4.4 *[K-Truss] Given a graph G and an integer k, a k-truss H of G is the largest subgraph such that $\forall e \in E(H)$, $sup_H(e) \geq (k-2)$.*

Note that just like the k-core, the k-truss may be disconnected. For example, consider the graph G in Figure 2.6: the 3-truss consists of two components, viz., the subgraphs of G induced by vertex sets $\{v_2, v_3, v_4, v_5\}$ and $\{v_7, v_8, v_9, v_{10}\}$. Similar to the definition of k-core in Definition 2.4.3, we define a connected k-truss based on the definition of k-truss [50, 165] as follows.

---

[1]The local clustering coefficient of a vertex v in a graph measures how close its neighborhood is to being a clique: $L_v := \frac{2|\{(v,w) \in E | v, w \in N(v)\}|}{|N(v)|(|N(v)|-1)}$.

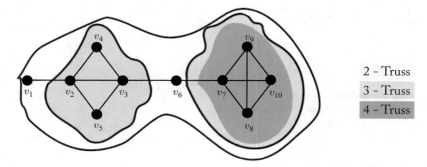

Figure 2.6: An example of k-truss in graph G where $2 \leq k \leq 4$. There exists no 5-truss in G.

Definition 2.4.5 *[Connected K-Truss] Given a graph G and an integer k, a connected k-truss is a connected subgraph $H \subseteq G$, such that $\forall e \in E(H)$, $\sup_H(e) \geq (k-2)$.*

Intuitively, a connected k-truss is a connected subgraph such that each edge (u, v) in the subgraph is "endorsed" by $k - 2$ common neighbors of u and v [50]. In a connected k-truss graph, each node has degree at least $k - 1$ and a connected k-truss is also a connected $(k - 1)$-core [19]. Next, we define the *trussness* of a subgraph, an edge, and a vertex.

Definition 2.4.6 *[Trussness] The trussness of a subgraph $H \subseteq G$ is the minimum support of an edge in H plus 2, i.e., $\tau(H) = 2 + \min_{e \in E(H)}\{\sup_H(e)\}$. The trussness of an edge $e \in E(G)$ is $\tau(e) = \max_{H \subseteq G \wedge e \in E(H)}\{\tau(H)\}$. The trussness of a vertex $v \in V(G)$ is $\tau(v) = \max_{H \subseteq G \wedge v \in V(H)}\{\tau(H)\}$.*

Consider the graph G in Figure 2.6 as an example. The trussness of the edge $e(v_2, v_3)$ is $\tau(e) = 3$, since the edge $e(v_2, v_3)$ is present in a 3-truss, but not in a 4-truss.

Truss Decomposition. The problem of truss decomposition is to find all possible k-trusses of the graph for $k = 0, 1, \ldots, k_{tmax}$, where k_{tmax} is the maximum truss number of any edge in G. Equivalently, the problem is to find the trussness of all edges of G. For any k, we can easily see that the edge set of the k-truss of G is $\{e : e \in E, k \leq \tau(e) \leq k_{tmax}\}$.

The basic idea of truss decomposition is similar to the core decomposition, that is, to successively remove the edge with the smallest support in each iteration.

We present the truss decomposition algorithm proposed in [165]. Invoked on a graph G, it computes the trussness of each edge. As outlined in Algorithm 2.2, after the initialization, for each k starting from $k = 2$, the algorithm iteratively removes a lowest support edge $e(u, v)$ with $\sup(e) \leq k - 2$. We assign the trussness of the removed edge as $\tau(e) = k$. Upon removal of e, we decrement the support of all other edges that form a triangle with e, and reorder them according to their new supports. This process continues until all edges with support less than or equal to $(k - 2)$ are removed. In this way, we can compute the trussness of all edges in G, and complete the truss decomposition of G.

Algorithm 2.2 Truss Decomposition

Input: $G = (V, E)$
Output: $\tau(e)$ for each $e \in E$

1: $k \leftarrow 2$;
2: compute $sup(e)$ for each edge $e \in E$;
3: sort all the edges in ascending order of their support;
4: **while**($\exists e$ such that $sup(e) \leq (k - 2)$)
5:    let $e = (u, v)$ be the edge with the lowest support;
6:    assume, w.l.o.g, $\deg(u) \leq \deg(v)$;
7:    **for** each $w \in N(u)$ **and** $(v, w) \in E$ **do**
8:       $sup((u, w)) \leftarrow sup((u, w)) - 1$;
         $sup((v, w)) \leftarrow sup((v, w)) - 1$;
9:       reorder (u, w) and (v, w) according to their new support;
10:   $\tau(e) \leftarrow k$, remove e from G;
11: **if**(*not* all edges in G are removed)
12:    $k \leftarrow k + 1$;
13:    **goto** Step 4;
14: **return** $\{\tau(e)|e \in E\}$;

The algorithms of core decomposition and truss decomposition presented in this and previous sections are both in-memory algorithms, i.e., they assume that the whole graph can fit in main memory. Various studies have been done on core decomposition and truss decomposition in different settings, including in-memory [19, 50, 192], external-memory [44, 165], and MapReduce [51]. In addition, [89, 192] design incremental algorithms for updating a k-truss w.r.t. edge insertions/deletions.

2.5   MORE DENSE SUBGRAPHS

The dense subgraphs are often interpreted as "communities" [40], based on a basic assumption that the connections inside a community are much denser than those between communities. The problem of finding the dense subgraphs of a graph is an important primitive in data analysis, with wide-ranging applications from community mining to spam detection and to the discovery of biological network modules [15]. In Section 3.4, we will introduce one community search model based on the densest subgraph.

In this section, we first give an introduction to densest subgraphs, and then briefly describe other types of dense subgraphs.

2.5.1   DENSEST SUBGRAPHS

Definition 2.5.1 (Classical Edge Density) *Given a graph $G(V, E)$ and a vertex set $S \subseteq V$, the density $\rho(S)$ is defined as $\rho(S) = \frac{|E(S)|}{|S|} = \sum_{v \in S} \frac{\deg_{G_S}(v)}{2|S|}$.*

With these two definitions, the problem of finding the densest subgraph with the maximum edge density can be formulated as follows [15, 106].

Definition 2.5.2 (Densest Subgraph) *Given a graph G, we find a vertex set S^* such that the induced subgraph $G_{S^*} \subseteq G$ has the maximum edge density, i.e., $S^* = \arg\max_{S \subseteq V}\{\rho(S)\}$. Then, the induced subgraph G_{S^*} is the densest subgraph of G.*

It is well known that finding a subgraph with the maximum edge density can be solved optimally using the parametric flow or linear programming relaxation [15]. We denote the problem of finding the densest subgraph as DS-Problem. However, given a positive integer k, finding the maximum density of a subgraph G_S containing at least k vertices is NP-hard [106]. We denote the problem of computing the maximum edge density with at least k vertices as DalK-Problem. Specifically, the problem can be formulated as follows [15, 106].

Definition 2.5.3 (DalK-Problem) *Given a graph G and a positive integer $k > 0$, the DalK-Problem is to find a vertex set $S^*_{\geq k}$ such that $S^*_{\geq k} = \arg\max_{S \subseteq V, |S| \geq k}\{\rho(S)\}$. Then, the induced subgraph $G_{S^*_{\geq k}}$ is the densest subgraph of k vertices.*

For example, consider the graph G in Figure 2.1, the subgraph H_1 is the densest subgraph of 4 vertices.

Approximation. For $\alpha \geq 1$, we say that an algorithm achieves an α-approximation to a maximization (minimization) problem P with objective function f, provided on every input instance with optimal solution $A*$, the algorithm outputs a feasible answer A such that $f(A) \geq f(A^*)/\alpha$ (resp., $f(A) \leq \alpha \times f(A^*)$).

Algorithms. In the literature, various algorithms have been proposed to address the DS-Problem and the DalK-Problem. For the DS-Problem, there exist several exact algorithms [15] to find the densest subgraph of an arbitrary size, including parametric flow [113] and linear programming relaxation [39]. Kortsarz and Peleg [107] and Charikar [39] independently propose 2-approximation algorithms for the DS-Problem. On a high level, the combinatorial approximation algorithm proposed by Charikar [39], iteratively removing the worst node (w.r.t. degree) from the graph in each iteration, is similar to the core decomposition algorithm. For the DalK-Problem, Andersen and Chellapilla [10] apply a similar idea of core decomposition to achieve a 3-approximation to the DalK-Problem. In addition, Khuller and Saha [106] further develop a greedy algorithm to obtain a 2-approximation solution for the DalK-Problem. In the following, we present an algorithm, Algorithm 2.3, called FindLargeDenseSubgraph, which achieves 3-approximation to the DalK-Problem [10].

The algorithm is outlined in Algorithm 2.3. It starts from the original graph G as H_i and proceeds in passes. In each pass, the vertex with the smallest degree is removed. We output one of the intermediate subgraphs $\{H_{|V|}, H_{|V|-1}, \ldots, H_k\}$ with at least k vertices and the largest edge density to form an approximation to the DalK-Problem.

Algorithm 2.3 FindLargeDenseSubgraph

Input: $G = (V, E), k$
Output: an induced subgraph of G with at least k vertices

1: Let $i \leftarrow |V|$ and $H_i \leftarrow G$;
2: $d \leftarrow 0$; $H^* \leftarrow \emptyset$;
3: **while** $(i \geq k)$
4:     $\rho(H_i) = \frac{E(H_i)}{V(H_i)}$;
5:     if $\rho(H_i) \geq d$ then
6:         $d \leftarrow \rho(H_i)$; $H^* \leftarrow H_i$;
7:     let v be a vertex with the minimum degree in H_i;
8:     remove v and all edges incident to v from H_i;
9:     $H_{i-1} \leftarrow H_i$;
10:    $i \leftarrow i - 1$;
11: **return** H^*;

In terms of time complexity analysis, Algorithm 2.3 runs in time $O(m + n)$ in a graph G with n vertices and m edges. The approximation ratio of Algorithm 2.3 is shown in the following theorem.

Theorem 2.5.1 *FindLargeDenseSubgraph(G, k) of Algorithm 2.3 is a 3-approximation algorithm for the* DalK-Problem *[10].*

Theorem 2.5.1 shows that the approximation ratio of Algorithm 2.3 is 3, which indicates the discovered subgraph H^* by Algorithm 2.3 has at least 1/3 of the density of an optimal solution OPT for the DalK-Problem, i.e., $\rho(H^*) \geq \rho(\text{OPT})/3$.

2.5.2 k-ECC **AND** k-VCC

In this section, we introduce two kinds of dense subgraphs, namely k-edge-connected component (k-ecc) [38, 197] and k-vertex-connected component (k-vcc) [126, 178], which, respectively, enforce the constraints of edge connectivity and vertex connectivity. We start with the definition of k-edge-connected graphs.

Definition 2.5.4 (k-edge-connected) *A graph $G(V, E)$ is k-edge-connected if G is still connected after removing fewer than k edges from G. In other words, if $G'(V, E \setminus X)$ is connected for any $X \subseteq E$ where $|X| < k$, then G is k-edge-connected.*

Consider the graphs in Figure 2.3. Graph G in Figure 2.3a is 2-edge-connected, as G remains connected if any one edge is removed from G. On the other hand, graph H_1 in Figure 2.3b is 1-edge-connected, since H_1 will become disconnected if the edge (v_2, v_4) is removed from H_1.

Definition 2.5.5 (k-edge-connected component (k-ecc) [38]) *A subgraph $H \subseteq G$ is a k-edge-connected component of graph G, if (i) H is k-edge-connected and (ii) any proper supergraph of H in G is not k-edge-connected.*

Consider the graph H_1 in Figure 2.3b. H_1 is 1-edge-connected. The triangle $\triangle_{v_1 v_2 v_3}$ is a subgraph of H_1, and $\triangle_{v_1 v_2 v_3}$ is 2-edge-connected. Moreover, $\triangle_{v_1 v_2 v_3}$ is a 2-edge-connected component of H_1, since any supergraph of $\triangle_{v_1 v_2 v_3}$ in H_1 is 1-edge-connected.

Using Definition 2.5.5, in the following we show several properties of k-edge-connected components. First, a k-edge-connected component is an induced subgraph of G. Second, a k-edge-connected component is maximal in that adding any vertices and their incident edges into the component would make the new graph no longer k-edge-connected. Third, the k-edge-connected components of a graph are pairwise disjoint. The problem of computing all k-edge-connected components is to decompose a graph G into a set of disjoint k-edge-connected components. To this end, Chang et al. [38] propose a novel graph decomposition paradigm to iteratively decompose a graph G.

Similar to k-edge-connected graphs, k-vertex-connected graphs can be defined as follows [178].

Definition 2.5.6 (k-vertex-connected) *A connected graph G is said to be k-vertex-connected if it has more than k vertices and remains connected whenever fewer than k vertices are removed.*

Notice that by definition, when a vertex is removed, all edges incident on the vertex are removed as well. For example, consider the graph G and H_1, respectively, in Figures 2.3a and 2.3b. According to Definition 2.5.6, G is 2-vertex-connected, since the removal of vertices v_4 and v_5 would make vertex v_6 disconnected from the remaining vertices in G. On the other hand, the removal of any one vertex from graph G leaves G connected. Thus, G is 2-vertex-connected.

The notion of k-vcc can be defined analogously to k-ecc. It is easy to see that the k-vertex-connected components, i.e., maximal k-vertex-connected subgraphs, of a given graph may be overlapping. Wen et al. [178] propose a polynomial-time algorithm to enumerate all k-vertex-connected components of a graph by recursively partitioning the graph into overlapping subgraphs. We note that between k-vcc and k-ecc, k-ecc has been studied more extensively in the literature on dense subgraphs and community search. In our subsequent discussion, we thus focus more on k-ecc. Exploration of community models based on k-vcc may be interesting future work.

2.5.3 OTHER DENSE SUBGRAPHS

Besides the above-mentioned dense subgraphs, there are other types of dense subgraphs. For example, Wang et al. [168] define a dense neighborhood graph based on common neighbors, which is a connected subgraph in which the lower bound on the number of triangles of edges is locally maximized. Their definition renders the problem NP-hard and their proposed solution is approximate [165]. Gibson et al. [74] study dense bipartite subgraphs that are pairs of subsets $A, B \subseteq V$ such that the nodes of A are densely connected with the nodes of B.

2.6   SUMMARY

We close this chapter by comparing the computational efficiency and structural cohesiveness of four representative dense subgraphs: k-clique, k-ecc, k-core, and k-truss. Among them, k-core, k-truss, and k-ecc are often used in community models, since they have decomposition algorithms with a polynomial-time complexity. On the other hand, k-clique is a typical dense subgraph that is NP-hard to compute. Similar dense subgraphs include k-plex, k-clan, k-club, and γ-quasi-k-clique. We compare them in terms of theoretical analysis and experimental evaluation.

Theoretical Efficiency. In terms of theoretical computational efficiency of finding them, the four subgraphs can be ordered as follows: k-core is the most efficient, then k-ecc and k-truss, and k-clique is the most inefficient. This is because the algorithm of core decomposition takes $O(n + m)$ time and $O(n + m)$ space, for a given graph with n nodes and m edges [19]. While the decomposition of k-ecc for a specific k takes $O(hlm)$ time and $O(n + m)$ space, where h and l are often bounded by constant numbers for real-world graphs [38]. As for k-truss decomposition, it has an $O(m^{1.5})$ time complexity [165], which is more expensive than the decomposition of k-core and k-ecc. Finally, due to the NP-hardness of the Maximum Clique problem, the decomposition problem, i.e., finding all k-clique's takes exponential time in the graph size [31].

Theoretical Cohesiveness. In terms of cohesiveness analysis, the structural cohesiveness ranking among these four subgraphs is: k-clique has the most cohesive structure, followed by k-truss, k-ecc, and k-core. Obviously, a k-clique is a complete subgraph of k nodes, which has the smallest diameter of 1 and the highest density of 1. Moreover, k-clique has the following properties: (1) each node has at least $k - 1$ neighbors; (2) the graph remains connected after deleting fewer than $(k - 2)$ edges; and (3) each pair of nodes has at least $k - 2$ neighbors. Thus, k-clique is a subgraph of $(k - 1)$-core, $(k - 2)$-ECC, and $(k - 2)$-truss, indicating its strongest cohesiveness. In addition, k-truss and k-ecc both are subgraphs of $(k - 1)$-core, obtained by filtering the disqualified subgraphs based on cohesiveness constraints. Moreover, k-truss has the triangle support constraint for each edge and naturally satisfies the edge connectivity of k-ecc. As a result, the decreasing order of cohesiveness among the four subgraphs is as mentioned above.

Experimental Comparison. We have conducted experiments to compare the four dense subgraph models: k-core, k-ecc, k-truss, and k-clique. We report the running time (in seconds) for comparing their efficiency and various structural metrics for comparing their cohesiveness quality.

First, we compare the decomposition algorithms of k-core [19], k-ecc [38], k-truss [165], and k-clique [56]. We tested five real-world graph datasets: Email-Enron, Google, Livejournal,[2]

---

[2]Email-Enron, Google, Liverjournal are available at https://snap.stanford.edu/data/index.html.

Wise,[3] and UK-2002.[4] Table 2.1 reports the statistics of these datasets and the running time results of the decomposition algorithms. As expected, k-core is the most efficient method on all datasets; k-ecc is faster than k-truss and k-clique; not surprisingly, k-clique is the worst of all.

Table 2.1: Efficiency comparison for four dense subgraph decomposition algorithms. Here, **K**$= 10^3$ and **M**$= 10^6$.

Datasets	$|V|$	$|E|$	k-core [19]	k-ecc [38]	k-truss [165]	k-clique [56]
email-Enron	36.7 K	183.8 K	0.2 s	0.8 s	5 s	201 s
Google	876 K	5.1 M	8.9 s	40.8 s	65 s	>24 h
Livejournal	4.8 M	69 M	85 s	854 s	1,726 s	>24 h
Wise	58.6 M	265.1 M	553 s	5,764 s	32,221 s	>24 h
UK-2002	18.6 M	298.1 M	387 s	5,967 s	18,830 s	>24 h

Second, we perform the quality comparison on the Livejournal network. We compare the cohesiveness of the four dense subgraph models with the same parameter $k = 6$. We randomly select 100 query nodes and find the corresponding connected subgraphs of k-clique, k-core, k-truss, and k-ecc that contain the query nodes. We evaluate six structural metrics of those discovered subgraphs: the number of vertices, the number of edges, diameter, density, average degree, and clustering coefficient. Given a subgraph $H \subseteq G$, the average degree is defined as $\frac{2|E(H)|}{|V(H)|}$; and the clustering coefficient is a measure of the degree to which the nodes in a graph tend to cluster together.[5] The quality results are reported in Table 2.2. Obviously, k-clique achieves the best quality with the highest density and clustering coefficient, and has the smallest diameter and graph size. In terms of density, average degree, and clustering coefficient, k-truss performs better than k-core and k-ecc, which is consistent with the theoretical quality analysis.

Note that a k-truss has a good robustness of connectivity. A connected k-truss remains connected when fewer than $(k - 1)$ edges are removed from the graph. For example, consider the 4-truss of G in Figure 2.6, the 4-truss remains connected whenever any 2 edges are moved from the 4-truss.

In summary, all discussed dense subgraphs are generally useful for community models, but also have their own disadvantages on either efficiency or quality. In the following chapters, we present different community search problems based on these models.

---

[3]Wise is available at `http://www.wise2012.cs.ucy.ac.cy/challenge.html`
[4]UK-2002 is available at `http://law.di.unimi.it/datasets.php`.
[5]`https://en.wikipedia.org/wiki/Clustering_coefficient`

Table 2.2: Quality comparison for k-core, k-ecc, k-truss, and k-clique on Livejournal dataset. Here, $k = 6$.

Quality Metrics	k-core	k-ecc	k-truss	k-clique
The number of vertices	1,894,460	1,880,000	1,164,210	6
The number of edges	29,924,900	29,777,900	20,834,200	21
Diameter	17	15	18	1
Density	1.67×10^{-5}	1.69×10^{-5}	3.07×10^{-5}	1.0
Average degree	31.59	31.69	35.79	5
Clustering coefficient	0.303	0.298	0.434	1.0

CHAPTER 3

Cohesive Community Search

This chapter discusses the problem of community search in simple graphs, and focuses on just the structural characteristics of networks. In this simplest setting, a graph represents a structure of interactions within a group of vertices. We consider an undirected, unweighted simple graph $G = (V(G), E(G))$ with $n = |V(G)|$ vertices and $m = |E(G)|$ edges. Community models in this class can only leverage the structural characteristics of networks, essentially focusing on the density of the connection structure. Given a set of query nodes, community search is to find a densely-connected subgraph containing all query nodes. Community search has attracted a great deal of attention, motivated by applications such as social circle discovery, advertising and viral marketing, content recommendation, and team formation [55]. Several different criteria to assess the goodness of a community have been proposed recently, based on dense subgraphs such as quasi-clique, k-core, k-truss, and densest-subgraph.

In the following sections, we introduce representative community models in detail. Associated with each community model is its corresponding community search problem. Specifically, we present four kinds of community search models based on quasi-clique, k-core, k-truss, and densest-subgraph respectively. Section 3.1 introduces the k-clique-based community search models, which aim at finding highly cohesive communities. However, finding k-clique [139] and even γ-quasi-k-clique [54] have been proven to be NP-hard, which imposes a severe computational bottleneck. The heuristic algorithms reduce the complexity, but cannot give a theoretical guarantee of the approximation quality [54]. Section 3.2 presents the community search models based on k-core, which has polynomial time complexity for computing the k-core subgraph and makes the k-core-based community search computationally tractable and efficient [18, 55, 122, 157]. Section 3.3 presents the community models based on k-truss, which unlike k-core considering simple edge connections only, requires each edge connection to be contained within at least $k - 2$ triangles [89, 96]. Section 3.4 studies the densest-subgraph-based community model, which uses the technique of random walk for detecting communities with highest query-biased densities [180]. For most of these community search problems, queries consisting of one or more vertices have been studied. Section 3.5 summarizes all community models introduced in this chapter.

3.1 QUASI-CLIQUE COMMUNITY MODELS

In this section, we first introduce a *clique*-based community model. Recall that a k-clique is a complete graph of k vertices where every pair of nodes is connected by an edge (see Definition 2.3.1). Then, we generalize it to a *quasi-clique*-based community model and formulate its corresponding community search problem.

3.1.1   CLIQUE-BASED COMMUNITY DETECTION

In a clique, every pair of vertices is adjacent. Clique is a widely accepted structure of communities where a group of vertices are densely connected to each other. The clique percolation method (CPM) is a well-known approach for analyzing overlapping communities in networks [139]. The high-level idea of CPM is to first find a k-clique as a seed and then expand it to a community. This approach works well on small-scale networks, but has a poor performance on large-scale networks, due to the expensive computation of k-clique enumeration.

Algorithm. The CPM method builds up the communities in a bottom-up manner. It starts from the k-cliques, i.e., complete subgraphs of k vertices. Two cliques are adjacent if they share $k - 1$ vertices. Based on the definitions of k-clique and clique adjacency, a community is defined as the maximal union of k-cliques where each pair of k-clique subgraphs can be reached from each other via a series of adjacent k-cliques.

For example, given the graph G in Figure 3.1 and a parameter $k = 4$, the subgraphs of G induced by $\{v_1, v_2, v_3, v_5\}$ and $\{v_1, v_3, v_4, v_5\}$ are both k-cliques, respectively, denoted H_1 and H_2 shown in Figures 3.2a and 3.2b. The k-cliques H_1 and H_2 are adjacent since they share $(k - 1) = 3$ vertices $\{v_1, v_3, v_5\}$—see Figure 3.2c. Finally, the CPM method finds one community formed by vertices $\{v_1, v_2, v_3, v_4, v_5\}$ (Figure 3.2d). The community is the union of all k-cliques (H_1 and H_2) that can be reached from each other through a series of adjacent k-cliques.

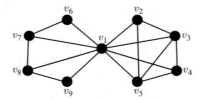

Figure 3.1: An example of graph G.

Overlapping Communities. Intuitively, given a query vertex q, there may exist several communities containing q. k-clique communities naturally form the overlapping communities of q. Figure 3.3 shows four different k-clique communities, highlighted in different colors, detected by CPM where $k = 4$ [139]. Note that two 4-cliques are adjacent if they share 3 vertices, and any k-clique can be reached only from the k-cliques of the same community through a series of adjacent k-cliques. The yellow community shares a single vertex with the blue one, whereas it overlaps with the green one in three vertices and one edge. These overlapping parts are highlighted in red.

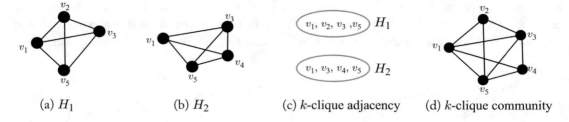

(a) H_1 (b) H_2 (c) k-clique adjacency   (d) k-clique community

Figure 3.2: An example of applying the CPM method for $k = 4$ on graph G in Figure 3.1. H_1 and H_2 are 4-cliques and share 3 vertices $\{v_1, v_3, v_5\}$, thus H_1 and H_2 are adjacent as $3 \geq (k - 1)$.

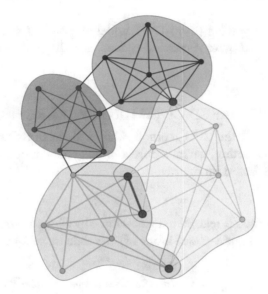

Figure 3.3: An example of k-clique communities detected by the clique percolation method (CPM) [139]. Here, $k = 4$. Used with Permission.

Limitations of clique-based community model. Intuitively, the CPM method requires to locate all maximal cliques, which is known to be an NP-hard problem. Even though this approach has already been applied successfully for analyzing networks with a few million nodes, the running time complexity is exponential in k in the worst case and it is not practical for very large values of k. Besides its high running time complexity, the definition of communities based on cliques is a restrictive notion, which limits opportunities for locating communities in real data. First, *every* pair of vertices in a k-clique must be connected, allowing no missing edges. For example, consider the graph G in Figure 3.1 and the parameter $k = 4$, graphs H_3 and H_4 shown in Figures 3.4a and 3.4b are not 4-cliques, which implies that the CPM method would miss the community C_1 shown in Figure 3.4d. Second, two k-cliques are considered adjacent iff they share as many as $k - 1$ vertices, and there is no flexibility in the amount of overlap allowed between k-cliques. This is another source of rigidity in the definition of clique-based communities.

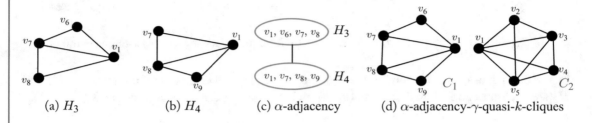

(a) H_3 (b) H_4 (c) α-adjacency   (d) α-adjacency-γ-quasi-k-cliques

Figure 3.4: An example of applying (α, γ)-OCS model on graph G in Figure 3.1. Here, $k = 4$, $\gamma = 0.8$, and $\alpha = 3$. H_1 and H_2 are γ-quasi-k-cliques, and they are α-adjacent as they share at least α vertices.

3.1.2   QUASI-CLIQUE-BASED COMMUNITY SEARCH

To address the limitations of the CPM method, Cui et al. relax its two constraints of clique and adjacency [54]. In this section, we introduce a more general model of **O**nline **C**ommunity **S**earch, called (α, γ)-OCS, based on their work.

Problem Formulation
First, the constraint of k-clique is relaxed to quasi-clique by allowing some missing edges within the subgraph. The concept of quasi-clique is one of several dense subgraphs defined in Chapter 2 (see Definition 2.3.3).

Definition 3.1.1 (γ-quasi-k-clique) *Given a positive integer number k and a number $0 \leq \gamma \leq 1$, a γ-quasi-k-clique is a graph of k vertices with at least $\lfloor \gamma \frac{k(k-1)}{2} \rfloor$ edges.*

Second, the adjacency constraint is relaxed. In (α, γ)-OCS, two γ-quasi-k-cliques are considered adjacent if they share at least α vertices, where $1 \leq \alpha \leq k - 1$. It is defined as α-adjacency.

Definition 3.1.2 (α-adjacency) *Given two γ-quasi-k-cliques G_1 and G_2, they are considered adjacent if they share at least α vertices, where $1 \leq \alpha \leq k - 1$.*

Based on the definitions of γ-quasi-k-clique and α-adjacency, the quasi-clique-based community is defined as follows.

Definition 3.1.3 (Quasi-clique based Community) *Given a graph G and three parameters k, α, and γ, an α-adjacency-γ-quasi-k-clique is the maximal connected subgraph such that every pair of γ-quasi-k-cliques can be reached from each other via a series of α-adjacent γ-quasi-k-cliques.*

The problem of (α, γ)-OCS is formulated as follows.

Problem 3.1.1 (((α, γ)-OCS [54]) *Given a query vertex q and three parameters k, α, and γ, the problem of (α, γ)-OCS is to find all α-adjacency-γ-quasi-k-cliques containing q.*

For example, given the graph G in Figure 3.1, consider the (α, γ)-OCS model on G with query vertex $q = v_1$, and parameters $k = 4$, $\gamma = 0.8$, and $\alpha = 3$. The subgraphs H_3, H_4 shown in Figures 3.4a and 3.4b are both γ-quasi-k-cliques, as H_3 and H_4 both have edge density as $\frac{5}{6} \geq \gamma = 0.8$. In addition, the γ-quasi-k-cliques H_3 and H_4 are adjacent as they share $(k-1) = 3$ vertices $\{v_1, v_7, v_8\}$, see Figure 3.4c. By Definition 3.1.3, H_3 and H_4 are merged into a single α-adjacency-γ-quasi-k-clique C_1 formed by vertices $\{v_1, v_6, v_7, v_8, v_9\}$; see Figure 3.4d. Moreover, it is easy to verify that subgraph C_2 shown in Figure 3.4d is also an α-adjacency-γ-quasi-k-clique containing v_1. Finally, the (α, γ)-OCS model returns two communities C_1 and C_2 as answers to the community search with the above parameters.

Query Processing Algorithms

In this section, we first introduce an exact and straightforward solution to solving (α, γ)-OCS. After that, a more efficient approximation algorithm is presented. The core idea of the efficient algorithm for finding (α, γ)-OCS is finding a γ-quasi-k-clique and meanwhile checking the adjacency constraint for pruning disqualified candidates for speed-up. Similar to CPM, this approach works well on small-scale networks, but not real large-scale networks, due to the expensive computation of γ-quasi-k-clique enumeration.

A Naive Method. The basic algorithm is outlined in Algorithm 3.4, which consists of two major stages. In the first stage, initially the query vertex q is added into a unvisited list S. Then, for each unvisited vertex, we find all γ-quasi-k-cliques that contain the vertex, and the unvisited new vertices of these γ-quasi-k-cliques are added to S. We repeat this procedure until no new vertex can be seen among the γ-quasi-k-cliques found. In the second stage, we calculate the clique adjacency for all γ-quasi-k-cliques found in the first step. Finally, we return all clique components as the resulting communities.

An Improved Algorithm. Cui et al. [54] point out that the decision version of (α, γ)-OCS problem, which determines whether there are any k-cliques containing the query vertex, is NP-hard. The naive algorithm needs to enumerate an exponential number of γ-quasi-k-cliques for a candidate community, which is clearly inefficient. Even worse, many such γ-quasi-k-cliques do not belong to a valid community. To avoid such wasteful computation, the adjacency constraint can be checked when a γ-quasi-k-clique is enumerated. Following this strategy, Cui et al. [54] propose an improved algorithm, shown in Algorithm 3.5. The algorithm runs iteratively. In each iteration it finds an unvisited γ-quasi-k-clique containing the query vertex using the procedure of *Next-Quasi-Clique*. If such a γ-quasi-k-clique exists, we *Expand* the γ-quasi-k-clique to find an α-adjacency-γ-quasi-k-cliques community by following the constraint of α-adjacency.

Algorithm 3.4 Naive (α, γ)-OCS

Input: A graph $G = (V, E)$, a query vertex q, numbers k, γ, and α.
Output: α-adjacency-γ-quasi-k-cliques containing q.

1: //Stage 1. Find all the candidate γ-quasi-k-cliques;
2: $S \leftarrow \{q\}$.
3: **while** S is not empty **do**
4:    **for all** unvisited vertex $v \in S$ **do**
5:        mark v as visited;
6:        find all γ-quasi-k-cliques containing v;
7:        Add unvisited new vertices into S;
8: //Stage 2. Calculate clique adjacency;
9: Calculate the adjacency matrix of candidate γ-quasi-k-cliques;
10: Return α-adjacency-γ-quasi-k-cliques containing q;

Algorithm 3.5 Improved (α, γ)-OCS

Input: A graph $G = (V, E)$, a query vertex q, numbers k, γ, and α.
Output: α-adjacency-γ-quasi-k-cliques containing q.

1: $R \leftarrow \emptyset$;
2: **while true do**
3:    $seed \leftarrow Next\text{-}Quasi\text{-}Clique(q, \{q\})$;
4:    **if** $seed = \emptyset$ **then break**;
5:    $C \leftarrow Expand(seed)$;
6:    $R \leftarrow R \cup \{C\}$;
7: **return** R;

In the following, we detail the implementations of the procedures: *Next-Quasi-Clique* and *Expand*.

Next-Quasi-Clique.

Finding a γ-quasi-k-clique is computationally hard. A brute-force method needs to enumerate all k-sized subsets for identifying a valid γ-quasi-k-clique. Cui et al. [54] propose a procedure using depth-first search strategy with backtracking, shown in Algorithm 3.6. The method *Next-Quasi-Clique(u, S)* starts from a candidate vertex set S by exploring vertex $u's$ neighborhood. It iteratively adds a new vertex into S until an unvisited γ-quasi-k-clique G_S is found (lines 3–4). The backtracking has two significant advantages. First, it speeds up the search process by pruning impossible candidates (lines 7–9). Second, it selects a new vertex v from the neighbors of the current vertex u (lines 10–12), which ensures the answer G_S is a connected subgraph. Given a vertex set $S \subseteq V$, the maximum number of edges in a γ-quasi-k-clique that contains G_S is

$$f(S) = |E(G_S)| + \frac{(k - |S|)(k + |S| - 1)}{2}, \tag{3.1}$$

Algorithm 3.6 Next-Quasi-Clique (u, S)

Input: a vertex u, a candidate vertex set S.
Output: a γ-quasi-k-clique containing u.

1: $ans \leftarrow \emptyset$;
2: **if** $|S| = k$ **then**
3:     **if** G_S is an unvisited γ-quasi-k-clique **then**
4:         **return** G_S;
5:     **else**
6:         **return** ans;
7: $f(S) = |E(G_S)| + \frac{(k-|S|)(k+|S|-1)}{2}$;
8: **if** $f(S) < \gamma\frac{k(k-1)}{2}$ **then**
9:     **return** ans;
10: **for** $v \in N(u) - S$ **do**
11:     $ans \leftarrow$ Next-Quasi-Clique $(v, S \cup \{v\})$;
12:     **if** $ans \neq \emptyset$ **then break**;
13: **return** ans;

Algorithm 3.7 Expand (C)

Input: a γ-quasi-k-clique C.
Output: an α-adjacency-γ-quasi-k-clique containing C.

1: $ans \leftarrow C$;
2: **for** $S \subset C, |S| = \alpha$ **do**
3:     $f(S) = |E(G_S)| + \frac{(k-|S|)(k+|S|-1)}{2}$;
4:     **if** $f(S) < \gamma\frac{k(k-1)}{2}$ **then continue**;
5:     **for** $S' \subset V, |S'| = k - \alpha$ **do**
6:         $C' \leftarrow S \cup S'$;
7:         **if** C' is an unvisited γ-quasi-k-clique **then**
8:             $ans \leftarrow ans \cup$ Expand (C');
9: **return** ans;

---

where $|E(G_S)|$ is the number of edges existing in G_S, and $\frac{(k-|S|)(k+|S|-1)}{2}$ results from the maximum number of candidate edges. $\frac{(k-|S|)(k+|S|-1)}{2} = (k - |S|)|S| + \frac{(k-|S|)(k-|S|-1)}{2}$ is formed by two parts: the first part is $(k - |S|)|S|$ edges between the vertices in S and the $(k - |S|)$ vertices in γ-quasi-k-clique that are not in S; the second part is $\frac{(k-|S|)(k-|S|-1)}{2}$ edges among those $(k - |S|)$ vertices. Obviously, if $f(S) < \gamma\frac{k(k-1)}{2}$, we can certainly prune the candidate S (lines 8–9).

Expand. The procedure *Expand*(C) for finding an α-adjacency-γ-quasi-k-clique containing C via α-adjacency is outlined in Algorithm 3.6. The key idea is to find a subset S of size $|S| = \alpha$ and then find another subset S' from the local neighborhood subgraph of C so that the combined subgraph $S \cup S'$ is a valid α-adjacency-γ-quasi-k-clique (lines 2–8). Note that it is not needed to enumerate S' from the entire vertex set V (line 5). The induced graph $G_{S \cup S'}$ is always connected, thus, in the worst case, we just need to explore the $|S'|$-hop-neighborhood of S, which contains all vertices at most $|S'|$ hops away from any vertex in S [54].

Duplication Detection of γ-quasi-k-cliques. In both procedures *Next-Quasi-Clique* and *Expand*, we may generate the same γ-quasi-k-clique from different search paths. Hence, we need to identify whether a γ-quasi-k-clique has ever been generated before, i.e., visited. For this purpose, a hash table is used to store the visited γ-quasi-k-cliques, allowing for querying a visited clique in constant time. Consider the following hash function:

$$h(C) = \left(\sum_{v \in C} ID(v) \times a^{ID(v)} \right) \quad \mod b \tag{3.2}$$

where a, b are two large primes and $ID(v)$ is the id of v. Hashing each k-sized γ-quasi-k-clique takes $O(k)$ time. Applying the DFS strategy, the complexity of such hashing computation can be further reduced to $O(1)$ [54].

Limitations of (α, γ)-**OCS model.** Next, we analyze the limitations of the (α, γ)-OCS model.

- First, γ as an average density measure may not necessarily guarantee a cohesive community structure. Consider the graph in Figure 3.5 which is a 0.8-quasi-7-clique containing query vertex q. However, q is only connected with one vertex in the community, thus it is obviously not a cohesive community for q.

- Second, there are three parameters α, γ, k in this model, the setting of which may vary significantly for different query vertices. For example, in a research collaboration network, the communities of a famous scholar and a junior scholar can be dramatically different in terms of the community size and density. Thus, it is difficult to choose proper values for the three parameters given an arbitrary query vertex.

- Third, finding α-adjacency-γ-quasi-k-clique has been proven to be NP-hard [54], which imposes a severe computational bottleneck. The approximate algorithms for clique enumeration and expansion proposed in [54] reduce the complexity, but they cannot give a theoretical guarantee on the approximation quality since it is NP-hard to approximate maximum cliques.

3.2   CORE-BASED COMMUNITY MODELS

In this section, we present community models built upon the dense subgraph of k-core. Recall that a k-core is the largest subgraph of graph G such that every vertex has degree at least k within this subgraph (see Definition 2.4.1). There exist several k-core-based community models such as Global-Core and Constrained-Core [157], Local-Core [55], Minimum-Core [18], and

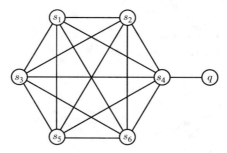

Figure 3.5: A 0.8-quasi-7-clique containing q.

k-Influential [122]. We summarize these works into three types of community models and introduce them in detail. The first one is maximum-core community model. It aims at maximizing the density of community, i.e., find a connected k-core with the largest k. The second one is minimum-sized k-core community model, which finds a k-core community with the smallest vertex size. The third one is k-Influential community model, which finds k-Influential communities with the largest influence scores.

3.2.1   MAXIMUM-CORE COMMUNITY SEARCH

Global-Core **Community Search**

Sozio and Gionis [157] propose one of the widely known formulations of k-core-based community search model. The problem is to find a connected subgraph that contains all query nodes and maximizes the minimum degree in this subgraph. This problem, termed Global-Core, is defined as follows.

Problem 3.2.1 (Global Core) *Given a graph $G(V, E)$ and a set of query nodes $Q \subseteq V$, find an induced subgraph $H = (V_H, E_H)$ of G, such that:*

(i) *H is a connected subgraph containing the query nodes ($Q \subseteq H$); and*

(ii) *the minimum degree of H is maximized.*

Sozio and Gionis [157] show that the Global-Core can be solved in linear time in the size of the input graph. The core idea is to adapt the peeling strategy of core decomposition by removing the weakest nodes, and finally obtaining a connected community with the largest coreness. Specifically, the algorithm applies the idea of core decomposition to remove a node having the minimum degree along with its incident edges in each iteration. The algorithm stops when the remaining connected subgraph containing the query nodes becomes disconnected. This process generates a set of immediate subgraphs. Among these subgraphs, the connected subgraph containing all query nodes and having the maximum minimum degree is returned as the answer.

Example 3.2.1 *Consider the graph G in Figure 3.6. For query vertices $Q = \{v_3, v_7\}$, the* Global-Core *community containing Q is shown in Figure 3.7. It is a connected k-core containing Q with the largest k = 2. Notice that the 3-core, shown in Figure 3.6, is disconnected, even though it contains the query nodes.*

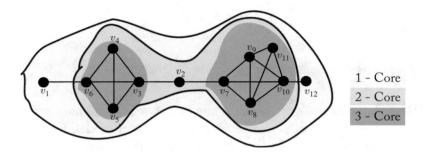

Figure 3.6: An example graph G for k-core-based community models.

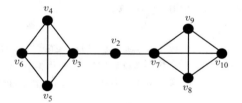

Figure 3.7: A Global-Core community for query vertices $Q = \{v_3, v_7\}$.

In addition, Global-Core tends to find quite large solutions. The large communities may involve redundant nodes or free-riders that are far away and irrelevant to the query nodes. This negatively affects the accuracy of the discovered communities. To address this issue, Sozio and Gionis [157] present a constrained version of community search problem where an upper bound on the size of the output community and an upper bound on the total distance between community members are imposed. In the following, we present the constrained version of the community search problem as Constrained-Core [157].

Constrained-Core **Community Search**

Two constraints, namely the size constraint and the distance constraint, are introduced in the Constrained-Core model. For the size constraint, it requires that the vertex size of a desired community H be not greater than a user-specified threshold. The distance constraint is defined as follows. First, denote by $\text{dist}_G(v, q)$ the length of the shortest path between v and q in G, where $\mathrm{dist}_G(v,q) = +\infty$ if v and q are not connected. Given a node v in the graph G, the distance of v from the query nodes Q is defined to be $D_Q(G,v) = \sum_{q \in Q} \mathrm{dist}_G(v,q)^2$, and $D_Q(G) = \max_{v \in V(G)}\{D_Q(G,v)\}$ is defined as the distance of the farthest node from the query nodes. For defining $D_Q(G,v)$, other alternatives are also possible, for instance, using max instead of $\sum$ or not using square.

Based on the Global-Core community model, the size constraint, and the distance constraint, the Constrained-Core community model is formulated as follows.

Problem 3.2.2 (Constrained Core) *Given a graph $G(V,E)$, a set of query nodes $Q \subseteq V$, a number d (distance constraint), and an integer s (size constraint), find an induced subgraph $H = (V_H, E_H)$ of G, such that:*

(i) *H is a connected subgraph containing the query nodes ($Q \subseteq H$);*

(ii) *$D_Q(H) \le d$;*

(iii) *$|V_H| \le s$; and*

(iv) *the minimum degree of H is maximized.*

Condition (i) ensures that the query nodes Q do not belong to different connected components. Condition (ii) is the distance constraint, which can avoid the pathological situations of attaching communities that are far away from the query nodes. Condition (iii) requires that H has at most s nodes. In addition, the objective function to maximize is the density measure, i.e., minimum degree in H.

Example 3.2.2 *Let us consider the graph G in Figure 3.6, and apply the definition of Constrained-Core community model on graph G, with query vertices $Q = \{v_3, v_7\}$, distance parameter $d = 100$, and size parameter $s = 8$. One answer of Constrained-Core community is shown in Figure 3.8. The number of vertices is 8, which satisfies the size constraint. The whole community is a connected k-core with the largest $k = 2$, which satisfies the distance and size constraints. It is smaller than the Global-Core community in Figure 3.7, as it prunes away those vertices far away from the query nodes.*

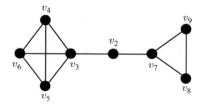

Figure 3.8: A Constrained-Core community for query vertices $Q = \{v_3, v_7\}$. Here, the distance parameter $d = 100$ and the size parameter $s = 8$.

Algorithm Greedy-Fast. A well-known combinatorial optimization problem is the *Minimum Steiner Tree* problem, defined as follows: given a graph $G = (V, E)$ with non-negative edge weights and a subset of vertices $S \subseteq V$, find a tree T in G that spans S and has the minimum total weight. T may involve vertices in $V \setminus S$. The minimum Steiner tree problem is well known to be NP-hard. From this, it follows that the problem of finding a minimum-degree-based community is also NP-hard. Thus, a heuristics method Greedy-Fast is proposed in [157] to find communities with a bounded size by achieving good quality and optimization efficiency. Specifically, Greedy-Fast performs a preprocessing phase to shrink the input graph to the s' closest nodes to the query nodes, where s' is a minimum number such that the resulting graph remains connected and contains at least s nodes. The intuition of this preprocessing phase is that the closer nodes are more likely to be the nodes that belong to their community. Next, the algorithm applies a greedy strategy to iteratively remove the nodes with the smallest degree and ensures the discovered community satisfies the distance and size constraints.

Local-Core Community Search

Cui et al. [55] study the same problem of Global-Core for the special case with a single query vertex, i.e., $|Q| = 1$.

Problem 3.2.3 (Local Core) *Given a graph $G(V, E)$ and a query vertex q, find an induced subgraph $H = (V_H, E_H)$ of G containing q, such that:*

(i) *H is a connected subgraph containing the query vertex ($q \in H$); and*

(ii) *the minimum degree of H is maximized.*

Example 3.2.3 *Consider the graph G in Figure 3.6. Applying the definition of the Local-Core community model on G with query vertex $q = v_7$, Figure 3.9 shows the Local-Core community, a connected 3-core containing q.*

Figure 3.9: A Local-Core community for query nodes $Q = \{v_7\}$.

Algorithm. Since the methods for Global-Core and Constrained-Core both need to visit the entire input graph, their computation can be expensive over large graphs. Cui et al. [55] propose a local-search algorithm to improve the efficiency of the Global-Core algorithm. This algorithm iteratively expands the neighborhood of the (unique) query vertex, until a subgraph that is guaranteed to contain an optimal solution has been built. Then, this subgraph is used as a reduced version of the input graph to retrieve the optimal solution. The worst-case time complexity of the Local-Core is still linear in the size of the whole input graph, but Local-Core has been shown to achieve better efficiency than Global-Core in practice. The detailed algorithm can be found in [55].

3.2.2 MINIMUM-SIZED k-CORE COMMUNITY SEARCH

Problem Formulation

Definition 3.2.1 (Minimum-Core) *Given a graph G and a set of query nodes Q, H is a* Minimum-Core *community, if H satisfies the following two conditions.*

(1) Connected k-core. *H is a connected k-core containing Q with the largest k, i.e., $Q \subseteq H \subseteq G$ and $\forall v \in V(H)$, $\deg_H(v) \geq k$.*

(2) Smallest Size. *H is a subgraph with the smallest number of vertices satisfying condition (1). That is, $\nexists H' \subseteq G$, such that $|V(H')| < |V(H)|$, and H' satisfies condition (1).*

Example 3.2.4 *Consider the graph G in Figure 3.6, and apply the definition of the* Minimum-Core *community model on G with query vertices $Q = \{v_3, v_7\}$. Figure 3.10 shows the* Minimum-Core *community for query Q. The community consists of 7 vertices and is a connected 2-core, which has minimum vertex size.*

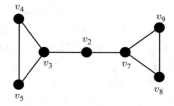

Figure 3.10: A Minimum-Core community for query vertices $Q = \{v_3, v_7\}$.

Consider the three different models Global-Core, Constrained-Core, *and* Minimum-Core. *Their query results in the above examples for the same query vertices $Q = \{v_3, v_7\}$ in graph G are, respectively, shown in Figure 3.7, Figure 3.8, and Figure 3.10. We can see that all three communities are connected 2-cores containing the query vertices Q. However, the* Constrained-Core *model is able to shrink the* Global-Core *community into a smaller one, while the* Minimum-Core *model is most stringent in finding the most compact community.*

Algorithm

Barbieri et al. [18] propose an index-based approach to solve the Minimum-Core community search effectively and efficiently. The high-level idea of Minimum-Core community search algorithms is firstly constructing an index for keeping the structural information of all k-cores, and then developing an efficient heuristic strategy to connect all query nodes into a candidate community and refine it. The approach is composed of two phases: preprocessing and query processing. In the preprocessing phase, a Shell-Index is constructed in order to precompute and store some useful information for query processing. The query processing phase consists of two sub-phases: a retrieval phase, where the proper information computed/stored during the preprocessing is retrieved from the Shell-Index, and an online processing phase, where the information retrieved is further processed in order to obtain an answer to the query. In the following, we first introduce the Shell-Index.

Shell-Index. The index is constructed for the maintenance of maximal connected k-cores in graphs. The idea is to apply the core decomposition on graph G and precompute all maximal connected k-cores. Further, all maximal connected k-cores are organized into a tree-shaped structure to easily retrieve any maximal connected k-core that contains the given query vertices. This tree-shaped structure is called Shell-Index.

The data structure of Shell-Index T for graph G is defined as follows. Suppose that the maximum core number in G is $c_{\max}$. Then T has $c_{\max}$ different levels of tree nodes. We use S_i^k to denote the i-th tree node at level k of T, $1 \le k \le c_{\max}$. Each tree node S_i^k consists of a set of k-class vertices whose core number is k, i.e., $S_i^k \subseteq \Psi(k)$. Moreover, the subtree of T rooted at S_i^k corresponds to a maximal connected k-core in G. For example, consider the graph G in Figure 3.6. The largest core number of G is 3. It consists of three class sets $\Psi(1) = \{v_1, v_{12}\}$, $\Psi(2) = \{v_2\}$, and $\Psi(3) = \{v_3, v_4, v_5, v_6, v_7, v_8, v_9, v_{10}, v_{11}\}$. As we can see the Shell-Index T shown in Figure 3.11. T has three levels of tree nodes. At the level 1, it has a node $S_1^1 = \{v_1, v_{12}\}$ indicating vertices v_1 and v_{12} have core number 1. The subtree of T rooted at S_1^1 corresponds to a maximal connected 1-core. First, the subtree has four tree nodes and $S = S_1^1 \cup S_1^2 \cup S_1^3 \cup S_2^3 = V$, and the induced subgraph G_S is the whole graph, which is the maximal connected 1-core. Similarly, it can be easily verified that the subtrees of G rooted at S_1^3 and S_2^3 correspond, respectively, to the maximal connected 3-cores in Figure 3.6. We note that if graph G is disconnected, the Shell-Index of G will be a forest consisting of multiple trees, where each tree represents a connected component in G.

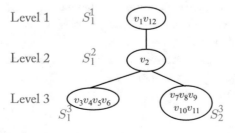

Figure 3.11: The Shell-Index for graph G in Figure 3.6.

Algorithm 3.8 Shell-Index Construction

Input: A graph $G = (V, E)$.
Output: Shell-Index of G.

1: Apply the core decomposition on G using Algorithm 2.1;
2: Let c_{max} be the maximum core number in G;
3: Tree-shaped structure $T \leftarrow \emptyset$;
4: Graph $H \leftarrow \emptyset$;
5: **for** $k \leftarrow c_{max}$ to 1 **do**
6:     Let k-class set $\Psi(k) = \{v : v \in V, \varphi(v) = k\}$.
7:     Let k-edge set $E_k = \{(v, u) \in E : \varphi(v) \geq k, \varphi(u) \geq k, \min\{\varphi(v), \varphi(u)\} = k\}$;
8:     Adding the subgraph $H'(\Psi(k), E_k)$ into H to find all maximal connected k-cores $\{C_1, \ldots, C_r\}$ using Union-Find forest;
9:     **for** $i \leftarrow 1$ to r **do**
10:        Add a tree node S_i^k where $S_i^k = \Psi(k) \cap C_i$, denoted by the i-th node at the k-th level of Tree T;
11:        **if** $\exists S_j^{k'} \subseteq C_i$ where $k < k' \leq c_{max}$ **and** $S_j^{k'}$ has no parent in T **do**
12:           Add a relationship <parent, child> between nodes S_i^k and $S_j^{k'}$ in tree T.
13: **return** tree-shaped structure T as Shell-Index of G;

Shell-Index **Construction.** Algorithm 3.8 presents a method of constructing Shell-Index for a graph G. The basic idea is to compute all maximal connected components and then organize them into a tree-shaped structure, based on an inclusion rule that the $(k + 1)$-core is a subgraph of the k-core, for all k. However, for each vertex v with core number $\varphi(v) = l$, v may be present in many maximal connected k-cores for $1 \leq k \leq l$. To avoid duplicate information and save storage cost, each vertex v is stored only once to indicate the maximal connected k-core with the largest k, that contains v. In this way, Shell-Index is organized in an elegant tree structure. The algorithm starts by applying the core decomposition on G using Algorithm 2.1 (line 1). Then, we obtain all core numbers of vertices and let c_{max} be the maximum one (line 2). We construct the Shell-Index T from scratch level-by-level in a bottom-up manner (lines 3–12). In other words, we first create the k-th-level tree nodes and then create the $(k - 1)$-th-level tree nodes. At the level k (lines 6–12), we define a set of nodes with core number k, as $\Psi(k) = \{v : v \in V, \varphi(v) = k\}$ and the k-edge set $E_k = \{(v, u) \in E : \varphi(v) \geq k, \varphi(u) \geq k, \min\{\varphi(v), \varphi(u)\} = k\}$ (lines 6–7). We add the subgraph $H'(\Psi(k), E_k)$ into H to find all maximal connected k-cores $\{C_1, \ldots, C_r\}$ (line 8). Then, for each maximal connected k-core C_i, we create a subtree of T rooted by S_i^k (lines 9–12). The tree nodes S_i^k are formed by a set of k-class vertices in C_i, i.e., $S_i^k = \Psi(k) \cap C_i$. Then, we add tree edges between S_i^k and $S_j^{k'}$ where $k' > k$, indicating that each vertex present in the subtree of T rooted at $S_j^{k'}$ also belongs to the maximal connected k-core C_i. Finally, the algorithm returns T as Shell-Index (line 13).

Example 3.2.5 *Figure 3.12 shows a special case of tree edges that are between S_i^k and $S_j^{k'}$, where $k' > k + 1$. Consider the graph G in Figure 3.12a, and the corresponding* Shell-Index *of graph G is* *shown in Figure 3.12b. The induced subgraph of G by the vertex set $\{v_7, v_8, v_9, v_{10}, v_{11}\}$ is a connected 4–core, thus vertices $\{v_7, v_8, v_9, v_{10}, v_{11}\}$ are stored in the tree node S_2^4 at the level–4 of Shell-Index. The vertex v_{12} can present in a connected 2–core, but does not belong to any 3–core. Thus, v_{12} is stored in the tree node S_1^2 at the level 2 of Shell-Index. Due to the edge (v_{12}, v_7), we add a tree edge between S_1^2 and S_2^4, indicating that a maximal connected 4–core rooted at S_2^4 belongs to a maximal connected 2–core rooted at S_1^2.*

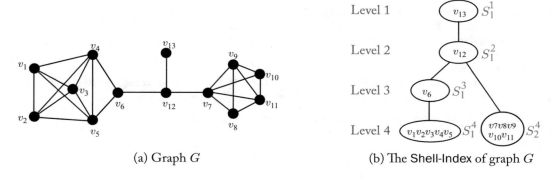

(a) Graph G (b) The Shell-Index of graph G

Figure 3.12: An example of Shell-Index.

Now, based on the Shell-Index, we are ready to present the query processing phase in detail. This phase consists of two steps: *retrieval* of the information computed from Shell-Index, and *online processing* of this information to obtain the final query answer.

Retrieval from Shell-Index. Given a set of query vertices Q, the retrieval phase aims at finding a maximal connected k-core H^* with the largest k containing all query vertices Q. To retrieve H^* from Shell-Index, the problem is turned into one of finding a subtree of T rooted at a k-th level node with the largest k. This is a classical problem of finding the lowest-common-ancestor (LCA). In the worst case, for every vertex $q \in Q$, we may visit each tree node S containing q all the way to the root, and finally find the lowest-common-ancestor. The time complexity is $O(|Q|c_{\max} + |H^*|)$. The well-known Tarjan's offline lowest common ancestors (LCA) algorithm can also be applied to store Shell-Index, which enables constant time online retrieval [69].

Online processing. The retrieval phase described above finds the set H^* containing all solutions to Global-Core for a given query Q. The goal of the online processing phase is to further refine H^* to extract a solution that is as small as possible. Since the Minimum-Core community search problem is NP-hard, Barbieri et al. [18] propose an efficient heuristic algorithm called Greedy-Connection. The idea of Greedy-Connection is as follows. A solution to Minimum-Core needs to satisfy two constraints: (a) the query vertices are connected, and (b) the solution has minimum degree no less than the core number of any vertex in H^*. Among all possible solutions satisfying these constraints, the goal is to output a community with the smallest vertex size. The main intuition of Minimum-Core is to look at constraints (a) and (b) one by one. In particular, one may first find a solution that satisfies constraint (a) only, and then refine this solution in order to make it satisfy constraint (b) too. The motivation is that in real-world graphs with power-law-like degree distribution, the minimum degree of a community is typically small (i.e., in the order of a few tens or even less); thus, it is likely that any solution that satisfies (only) constraint (a) needs just a very few additional vertices to satisfy constraint (b) too. As a result, Barbieri et al. [18] apply a bottom-up method to find a connected subgraph using as few more vertices as possible. After that, they perform a sequential procedure that first ensures connection among the query vertices, and then aims at satisfying the constraint on the minimum degree. They apply the Steiner Tree algorithm [108] to connect all query vertices Q.

3.2.3   INFLUENTIAL COMMUNITY SEARCH

Motivation. In all previous studies on community detection and search, a community is defined as a densely connected subgraph. This ignores another important aspect, namely the "influence" (or importance) of a community. In many applications, we are interested in finding the most influential communities. For example, consider the following two scenarios. Suppose that Alice is a database researcher. She may want to identify the most influential research groups from the co-authorship network of the database community, so as to be aware of the recent trends of database research by the "movers and shakers," which can be modeled using those influential groups and following their publications and blogs. Another example is the influential communities in the social network. A user Bob may intend to follow the most influential groups of three different topics "technology," "investments," and "politics," so that he can track the recent activities from those three influential groups and may conduct further analytics on that activity data. Both of the above applications motivate the identification of the most influential communities within a network [122].

Note that [122] proposes to measure the influence of a community by counting the minimum value of influential importance among all nodes in the community. The node influence is different from influential edges in social networks, which are based on independent cascade (IC) model or linear threshold (LT) model [28, 42, 75, 105, 127]. Several studies of influential community search [120, 184] have recently been conducted using diffusion models, which leave the study of influential community search under diffusion models such as IC and LT models as an open problem.

Problem Formulation
In this section, we describe k-Influential community search, the problem of finding influential communities in large networks. For this, Li et al. [122] propose a new community model called k-Influential community based on the well-known concept of connected k-core, where the importance of nodes is taken into account. To find the k-Influential community, the key ideas of the proposed solutions are building an index that incorporates the importance of nodes and

the structure of k-core, and developing an index-based online query processing algorithm for quickly identifying the k-Influential community containing query nodes. In the following, we introduce the problem setting using several new definitions.

Graph with node weights. Consider an undirected graph $G = (V, E)$ and a node weight function w, such that each node v in G is associated with a non-negative weight $w(v)$, denoting the influence (or importance) of the node v. Such weight can be computed using the PageRank algorithm [138], centrality, degree, expected spread computed using a standard diffusion model [105], or other user-defined ranking functions. Additionally, without loss of generality, we assume that the weight of each node is distinct. Note that if that is not the case, we can break ties using node identity whenever $w(v_i) = w(v_j)$, for distinct nodes v_i and v_j [122]. The influence score of a subgraph is defined as follows.

Definition 3.2.2 (Influence Score) *Given a subgraph H of graph G, the influence score of H is the minimum weight of the vertices in H, i.e., $f(H) = \min_{v \in V_H} w(v)$.*

Example 3.2.6 *Consider the weighted graph G in Figure 3.13 where each vertex has a weight, shown in red color, e.g., vertex v_6 has weight 6. The subgraph $H_1 \subseteq G$ shown in Figure 3.14a has weight $f(H_1) = \min_{v \in \{v_5, v_7\}} w(v) = 5$. Similarly, the subgraphs H_2 and H_3 in Figures 3.14b and 3.14c both have weight $f(H_2) = f(H_3) = 5$.*

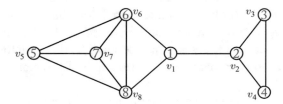

Figure 3.13: An example of weighted graph G (the numbers in red denote the node weights).

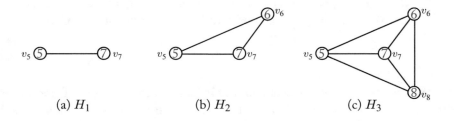

(a) H_1 (b) H_2 (c) H_3

Figure 3.14: An example of k-Influential community H_3 where $k = 2$. H_1 and H_2 are not k-Influential communities for any $k \in \{1, 2, 3\}$.

Based on the definitions of k-core and influence score, a k-Influential community is defined as follows.

Definition 3.2.3 (K-Influential Community) *Given a graph G and a parameter k, the k-Influential community is defined as a maximal connected k-core H such that there exists no other connected k-core H' having $f(H') = f(H)$ and $H \subset H'$.*

In the k-Influential community model, the parameter k measures the cohesiveness of the community. Note that a maximal connected k-core H must be an induced subgraph of G, thus the requirement of induced subgraph is redundant and is removed from the definition of k-Influential community [122].

Example 3.2.7 *Consider the graph G in Figure 3.13 and $k = 2$. The subgraph H_3 is a k-Influential community, since it is a maximal connected 2-core such that each vertex in H_3 has degree at least 2 and $f(H_3) = 5$. On the other hand, H_1 and H_2 are not 2-influential communities. H_1 is not even a connected 2-core, since each vertex has degree only 1. On the other hand, although H_2 is a connected 2-core, H_2 violates the maximal property (see Definition 3.2.3). H_2 is not a maximal connected 2-core with $f(H_2) = 5$, since $H_2 \subset H_3$ and $f(H_2) = f(H_3) = 5$. Notice that H_3 is also a maximal connected 3-core with influence score $f(H_3) = 5$, and is thus also a k-Influential community for $k = 3$.*

Intuitively, a good influential community should not only be a strongly cohesive induced subgraph, but also have a large influence value. In many practical applications, we are typically interested in the most influential communities whose influence values are larger than those of other influential communities. Based on these motivations, the definition of k-Influential community search is given as follows.

Problem 3.2.4 (k-Influential) *Given a graph $G = (V, E)$, a weight function w, and parameters k and r, find the top-r k-Influential communities with the highest influence scores.*

Example 3.2.8 *Consider the graph G in Figure 3.13 and parameters $k = 3$ and $r = 1$. The solution for k-Influential on G is the k-Influential community H_3 in Figure 3.14c, since H_3 has the highest influence score $f(H_3) = 5$. However, if we modify the parameters to $k = 2$ and $r = 1$, then the solution will be the subgraph of G by induced by the vertices $\{v_6, v_7, v_8\}$, since $\triangle_{v_6 v_7 v_8}$ is the 2-core with the highest influence score $f(\triangle_{v_6 v_7 v_8}) = 6$.*

It is important to note that although we define the influence score of a community as the minimum weight of a node in the community, we could also in principle aggregate the weights in other ways, e.g., MAX, by defining the influence score as the maximum weight of the nodes in the community. The techniques proposed in [122] (e.g., ICP-Index to be introduced in Section 3.2.3) can be easily extended to process queries for the MAX aggregation of influence scores. In place of minimum weight, we could aggregate node weights using other aggregate functions such as MAX or AVG in order to define the influence score of a community. In this case, some simple modifications to the proposed techniques are needed to solve this more general k-Influential community search problem.

DFS-Based Query Processing Algorithm

We first make some observations of k-Influential communities from the example graph G in Figure 3.13.

Observation 3.1   Given a graph G and any k-core H of G, each maximal component of H is a k-Influential community. For example, the 2-core of graph G in Figure 3.13 is itself; G is the maximal component of G, and is thus a 2-Influential community. Its influence score is 1.

Observation 3.2   For any k-Influential community H, let v be the vertex that has the smallest weight in H, i.e., $v = \arg\min_{v \in V(H)} w(v)$. Let us first remove the vertex v and all its incident edges from H. Since the remaining graph may have vertices with degree less than k, we then continue removing these unqualified vertices and their incident edges until the remaining graph is empty or all remaining vertices have degree at least k in H. As a result, each maximal connected component of the remaining graph H is a k-Influential community. For example, consider the graph G from Figure 3.13. As seen above, it is a 2-influential community, and the vertex v_1 has the smallest weight of 1. Let us remove the vertex v_1 and its incident edges from G. The remaining graph satisfies the k-core property and contains two maximal connected components R_2 and R_3 (see Figures 3.15b and 3.15c), which are k-Influential communities.

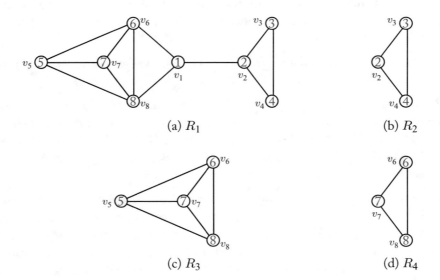

Figure 3.15: All k-Influential communities $\{R_1, R_2, R_3, R_4\}$ of graph G in Figure 3.13. Here, $k = 2$.

Algorithm 3.9 The DFS-based algorithm

Input: A graph $G = (V, E)$, a weight function w, and parameters k and r.
Output: The top-r k-Influential communities.

1: Find k-core H of G using the core decomposition in Algorithm 2.1;
2: $l \leftarrow 0$;
3: **while** $H \neq \emptyset$ **then**
4:    $l \leftarrow l + 1$;
5:    $v^* \leftarrow \arg\max_{v \in V(H)} w(v)$;
6:    Let H_{v*} be the maximal connected component of H containing v^*;
7:    $R_l \leftarrow H_{v*}$; // H_{v*} is a k-Influential community;
8:    Delete v^* and its incident edges from H;
9:    Maintain k-core property of H by iteratively removing vertex v with $\deg_H(v) < k$ and its incident edges;
10: **if** $l \geq r$ **then**
11:    **return** $\{R_l, ..., R_{l-r+1}\}$;
12: **else**
13:    **return** $\{R_l, ..., R_1\}$;

Algorithm. Based on the above observations, we are ready to present an efficient algorithm for k-Influential community search in Algorithm 3.9. The key idea is largely similar to that for k-core decomposition. First, for the given parameter k, we find the k-core H of graph G using the core decomposition in Algorithm 2.1 (line 1). Then, we iteratively invoke the following procedure until the resulting graph H becomes empty (lines 3–9). The procedure has two steps. The first step is to find a vertex v^* with the smallest weight in H. Based on Observation 3.1, the maximal connected component of H containing v^*, denoted H_{v*}, is a k-Influential community. We have the influence score $f(H_{v*}) = w(v^*)$ and add H_{v*} to our list of k-Influential communities (lines 4–7). The second step is to remove $v*$ and its incident edges from H and maintain k-core property in the remaining graph H, i.e., each vertex in H has degree at least k (lines 8–9). Finally, if the number of discovered k-Influential communities is less than r, we return all k-Influential communities the algorithm found; otherwise, we return the top-r k-Influential communities $\{R_l, \ldots, R_{l-r+1}\}$ with the highest influence scores.

Example 3.2.9 *We apply Algorithm 3.9 on the graph G in Figure 3.13 with parameters $k = 2$ and $r = 1$. The whole graph G is 2-core, H is identical to G (line 1). In the first iteration, we identify the vertex $v^* = v_1$ with the smallest weight of 1 and obtain the k-Influential community $R_1 = G$ in Figure 3.15a. After the removal of vertex v_1, the remaining graph consists of two components as shown in Figures 3.15b and 3.15c. In the second iteration, we identify the vertex $v^* = v_2$ and obtain the maximal connected component $H_{v*} = R_2$ in Figure 3.15b. After removing v_2 from the graph, vertices v_3 and v_4 will be also deleted for violating the property of k-core. Repeating the above process, in the third and fourth iterations, k-Influential communities R_3 and R_4 in Figures 3.15c and 3.15d are obtained. Finally, for $r = 1$, the algorithm returns $\{R_1\}$ as the (top-r) answer.*

Complexity Analysis. The time complexity and space complexity is $O(m + n)$, which is the same as the complexity of core decomposition algorithm.

ICP-Index-**Based Query Processing Algorithm**

Although Algorithm 3.9 takes linear time in graph size, an index-based algorithm can further improve efficiency for query processing. The basic idea is to first precompute all k-Influential communities for every k, then use a space-efficient structure called ICP-Index to keep track of all k-Influential communities in memory. Based on ICP-Index, the algorithm produces all top-r results in optimal time.

A novel ICP-Index. We first introduce ICP-Index using the Example 3.2.9. Assume $k = 2$ and consider all k-Influential communities $\{R_1, R_2, R_3, R_4\}$ of graph G, as shown in Figure 3.13. The k-Influential communities R_1, R_2, R_3, R_4 have increasing influence scores. Moreover, R_2 and R_3 are subgraphs of R_1 and recursively R_4 is a subgraph of R_3. We define an inclusion relationship on k-Influential communities as follows. Given two k-Influential communities A and B with $A \subset B$, we say A is a sub-k-Influential community of B. Based on such an inclusion relationship, all k-Influential communities can be organized in a tree-shaped (more generally, a forest-shaped) structure. However, instead of storing all communities explicitly, which is expensive, we can represent them compactly. We only store those nodes of a k-Influential community H that are not included in any sub-k-Influential communities of H. For example, in the k-Influential community R_1, the vertex v_1 does not belong to any sub-k-Influential communities R_2, R_3, or R_4. Thus, in the ICP-Index in Figure 3.16b (for $k = 2$), we create an isolated tree node $S_{v_1} = \{v_1\}$ containing v_1. It can be seen in a similar way that the node corresponding to S_{v_5} in Figure 3.16b only needs to store the vertex v_5. The tree of ICP-Index rooted at S_{v_1} corresponds to the k-Influential community R_1, i.e., the union of the vertex sets of all tree nodes in Figure 3.16b is $V = S_{v_1} \cup S_{v_2} \cup S_{v_5} \cup S_{v_6}$. Similarly, the tree of ICP-Index rooted by S_{v_5} corresponds to the k-Influential community R_3.

ICP-Index **Construction.** The ICP-Index construction algorithm is outlined in Algorithm 3.10. The general idea is to repeatedly run Algorithm 3.9 for finding all k-Influential communities for any k. More precisely, it consists of two steps: *generating tree nodes* and *generating tree edges*. First, it invokes Algorithm 3.9 $c_{\max}$ times, where $c_{\max}$ is the maximum core number in G. That is, for each $1 \leq k \leq c_{\max}$, it applies Algorithm 3.9 to generate isolated tree nodes in the tree T_k for k-Influential communities. Second, it invokes a procedure of tree construction that adds edges between tree nodes generated in Step 1, in order to build ICP-Index.

Generating Tree Nodes. In the procedure of tree node generation, after the deletion of v^*, all vertices removed because of violation of the k-core property in H must be stored in a tree node (lines 10–13 of Algorithm 3.10). Notice that the vertex v^* with the smallest weight is also included in the tree node S_{v^*}. The reason is that all these deleted nodes are excluded in any sub-k-Influential communities $H' \subset H$. For example, consider the second iteration of Al-

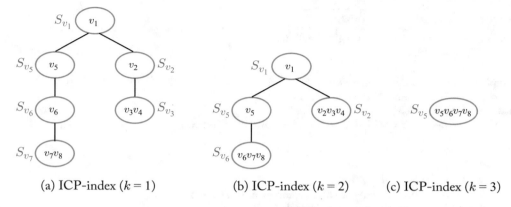

(a) ICP-index ($k = 1$)   (b) ICP-index ($k = 2$)   (c) ICP-index ($k = 3$)

Figure 3.16: Tree organization of all the k-Influential communities of graph G in Figure 3.13.

gorithm 3.10 for $k = 2$ and vertex $v^* = v_2$. The corresponding tree node is $S_{v_2} = \{v_2, v_3, v_4\}$. After removal of vertex v_2, vertices v_3 and v_4 are deleted due to the violation of the k-core property.

Generating Tree Edges. After generating all tree nodes in the previous step, the procedure ConstructTree adds the edges by connecting tree nodes for each tree T_k, $1 \leq k \leq c_{\max}$. First, we treat each isolated node of T_k as a single-node tree. Then, we iteratively "merge" two trees into one and finally obtain the tree (or forest) structure as ICP-Index. Here the merge operation between two trees P_1 and P_2 is defined as follows. Let S_1 and S_2 be the roots of subtrees P_1 and P_2, respectively. Assume that $f(S_1) < f(S_2)$ where $f(S_i) = \min_{u \in S_i} w(u)$ for $i = 1, 2$. Then, the merge operation between S_1 and S_2 is to add an edge between S_1 and S_2 indicating S_2 is a child node of S_1. We note that such a bottom-up tree construction algorithm for all k can be done by traversing the graph once, in decreasing order of node weights (lines 3–13).

Query Processing Algorithm. Based on the ICP-Index, the query processing algorithm is straightforward. To find the top-r k-Influential communities with the highest influence scores for a given k, we first identify the tree T_k in the ICP-Index. Given any tree node $S \in T_k$, denote the subtree of T_k rooted at S as T_k^S, which corresponds to a k-Influential community. In other words, let the vertex set be $C = \cup_{x \in T_k^S} x$, then the induced subgraph G_C is a k-Influential community. Thus, we then generate answers by returning r subtrees T_k^S with the highest weights, where the weight of a tree node is the minimum weight of nodes in its root vertex, i.e., $f(T_k^S) = \min_{x \in T_k^S, v \in x} w(v)$. The time complexity of the ICP-Index based query processing algorithm is linear in the size of the answer, which is optimal.

Algorithm 3.10 ICP-Index Construction

Input: A graph $G = (V, E)$ and a weight function w.
Output: ICP-Index of G.

1: Apply the core decomposition on G using Algorithm 2.1;
2: Let $c_{\max}$ be the maximum core number in G;
3: **for** $k \leftarrow 1$ to $c_{\max}$ **do**
4:     Compute k-core H of G based on the core numbers of vertices;
5:     $T_k \leftarrow \emptyset; l \leftarrow 0$;
6:     **while** $H \neq \emptyset$ **then**
7:         $l \leftarrow l + 1$;
8:         $v^* \leftarrow \arg \max_{v \in V(H)} w(v)$;
9:         Let H_{v^*} be the maximal connected component of H containing v^*;
10:        Delete v^* and its incident edges from H;
11:        Maintain k-core property of H by iteratively removing vertex v with $\deg_H(v) < k$ and its incident edges;
12:        Let S_{v^*} be the set of vertices removed from H at this loop and $v^* \in S$;
13:        Add an isolated node S_{v^*} into tree T_k;
14: **return** ConstructTree();

15: **Procedure** ConstructTree()
16: // This procedure adds the connecting edge between vertices in each tree T_k;
17: **for all** node u in G sorted in decreasing order of $w(u)$ **do**
18:     **for** $\forall v \in N(u)$ with $w(v) > w(u)$ **do**
19:         **for** $i \leftarrow 1$ to $\min c_u, c_v$ **do**
20:             $S_u \leftarrow$ the root of a tree containing u in T_i;
21:             $S_v \leftarrow$ the root of a tree containing v in T_i;
22:         **if** $S_u \neq S_v$ **then**
23:             Add an edge between S_u and S_v indicating that S_v is a child of S_u;
24: **return** $\{T_1, ..., T_{c_{\max}}\}$;

Discussion

Li et al. [122] study another problem formulation of k-Influential using a *non-containment* constraint. It is defined as follows. Given a k-Influential community H, H satisfies the non-containment constraint if and only if there exists no k-Influential community $H' \subset H$ such that $f(H') > f(H)$ holds. Thus, H is called a *non-contained k-Influential community*. The problem of non-contained k-Influential is to find the top-r non-contained k-Influential communities with the highest influence scores [122]. Since there is no inclusion relationship among the top-r non-contained k-Influential communities, no redundant results are included. To solve the problem of non-contained k-Influential, a slight modification needs to be made to Algorithm 3.9, by adding one more check. For a k-Influential community H, we conclude H is a non-contained k-Influential community provided H does not contain a k-core, upon removing the node with the smallest weight from H.

Table 3.1: Comparison of state-of-the-art k-core-based methods [18]. The ratings of the first four methods Global-Core, Constrained-Core, Local-Core, and Minimum-Core for Empirical Efficiency and Quality are from [18]. k-Influential is rated by us, based on the linear running time of graph size and high quality of specific communities with the maximum influence score.

Methods	Empirical Efficiency	Quality	Query Vertices	Parameter-Free
Global-Core [157]	+	+	Multiple	Yes
Constrained-Core [157]	+	+ +	Multiple	No
Local-Core [55]	+ +	+ +	Single	Yes
Minimum-Core [18]	+ + +	+ + +	Yes	Yes
k-Influential [122]	+ + +	+ + +	No	No

3.2.4 COMPARISON OF VARIOUS k-CORE COMMUNITY MODELS

A comparison of the state-of-the-art k-core-based methods is provided in Table 3.1, which is extended from the comparison table in [18] by additionally including k-Influential in the comparison. We compare all methods in terms of empirical efficiency, quality, the number of query vertices, and whether they are parameter-free.

In terms of empirical efficiency, the method of Constrained-Core is the worst. The problem of Constrained-Core is shown to be NP-hard, and Sozio and Gionis [157] devise heuristics that perform even worse than the known heuristics for standard Global-Core. Besides the efficiency limitations, the available algorithms for Constrained-Core also suffer from providing no guarantee w.r.t. the optimal minimum degree. The Local-Core method deals with the same problem as Global-Core for the special case of a single query vertex. In terms of improving efficiency and quality, Local-Core is proposed for searching for communities in the local graph structure and speeds up the search processing by avoiding global search.

Another problem proposed in [55] and [18] is to find a k-core with the smallest size that contains a set of given query vertices Q. Cui et al. [55] define this problem for the case of a single query vertex, i.e., $|Q| = 1$, and they do not propose algorithms. They show that this problem is NP-hard. Barbieri et al. [18] extend this result to the general case where $|Q| \geq 1$ by using a reduction from the minimum Steiner tree problem and propose a general approach called Minimum-Core to find k-core-based communities containing multiple query vertices. This method improves the efficiency of the above methods and also offers a method for finding Local-Core proposed by Cui et al. for the special case of a single query vertex. Moreover, k-Influential method address a different problem from the above. The time complexity of ICP-Index based query processing algorithm is optimal w.r.t. the answer size.

3.3   TRUSS-BASED COMMUNITY MODELS

Motivation. In social networks, it is quite typical that pairs of friends have several common friends, thus forming many triangles [60]. Indeed, triangles are regarded as the fundamental building blocks of networks and lead to a high clustering coefficient [20, 136, 165, 174, 177]. In a social network, a triangle indicates that two friends have a common friend "endorsing" their friendship, which shows a strong and stable relationship among the three friends. Intuitively, the more common friends two people have, the stronger their relationship.

In this section, we discuss community models based on the dense subgraphs of k-truss. Given a graph G, the k-truss of G is the largest subgraph in which every edge is contained in at least $(k-2)$ triangles within the subgraph [50] (see Definition 2.4.4). The k-truss is a type of cohesive subgraph defined based on triangles which model stable relationships among three nodes. However, the k-truss subgraph may be disconnected, for example, the subgraph shown in Figure 3.17a, consisting of the two shaded regions, forms the 4-truss which is obviously disconnected. Thus, the classical k-truss subgraph may not correspond to a meaningful community. To address this issue, Huang et al. [89, 96] propose two different constraints to build up densely-connected community models. One truss community model is based on the triangle connectivity such that every pair of edges of a truss community should be connected to each other via a series of triangles. The high-level idea of finding triangle-connected communities is to build an index, incorporating the triangle connectivity and k-truss structure. An index-based truss community search algorithm is proposed to find answers in optimal time. Another truss community model is based on the k-truss with the smallest diameter. The core idea of closest community search is to find a k-truss connecting all query nodes and then shrink the community to reduce the diameter as much as possible. In the following, we will introduce in detail these two truss community models, based on (i) triangle connectivity and (ii) diameter.

3.3.1   TRIANGLE-CONNECTED TRUSS COMMUNITY SEARCH

An *triangle connectivity* constraint is imposed on top of the k-truss, that is, any two edges in a community either belong to the same triangle, or are reachable from each other through a series of adjacent triangles. Here two triangles are said to be *adjacent* if they share a common edge. The triangle connectivity requirement ensures that a discovered community is connected and cohesive. This defines *triangle-connected truss community model*.

Notions and Notations
In the following, we give a series of definitions and then formulate the model. A triangle in G is a cycle of length 3. Let $u, v, w \in V$ be the three vertices on the cycle. We denote this triangle by $\triangle_{uvw}$. Then the *support* of an edge is defined as follows.

Definition 3.3.1 (Support) *The support of an edge $e(u, v) \in E$ in G, denoted $sup(e, G)$, is defined as $|\{\triangle_{uvw} : w \in V\}|$. When the context is obvious, we replace $sup(e, G)$ by $sup(e)$.*

We write $e \in \triangle$ to indicate that the edge e belongs to the triangle $\triangle$. We next define *triangle adjacency* and *triangle connectivity*.

Definition 3.3.2 (Triangle Adjacency) *Given two triangles* $\triangle_1, \triangle_2$ *in G, they are adjacent if* $\triangle_1$ *and* $\triangle_2$ *share a common edge, which is denoted by* $\triangle_1 \cap \triangle_2 \neq \emptyset$.

Definition 3.3.3 (Triangle Connectivity) *Given two triangles* $\triangle_s, \triangle_t$ *in G,* $\triangle_s$ *and* $\triangle_t$ *are triangle connected, if there exist a series of triangles* $\triangle_1, \ldots, \triangle_n$ *in G, where* $n \geq 2$, *such that* $\triangle_1 = \triangle_s$, $\triangle_n = \triangle_t$ *and for* $1 \leq i < n$, $\triangle_i \cap \triangle_{i+1} \neq \emptyset$.

For the graph G in Figure 3.17a, $e(q, p_4)$ is contained in $\triangle_{qp_3p_4}$ and $\triangle_{qp_2p_4}$, thus its support $sup(e(q, p_4)) = 2$. $\triangle_{qp_3p_4}$ and $\triangle_{qp_2p_4}$ are triangle adjacent as they share a common edge $e(q, p_4)$. $\triangle_{tp_3p_4}$ and $\triangle_{qp_2p_4}$ are triangle connected through $\triangle_{qp_3p_4}$ in G.

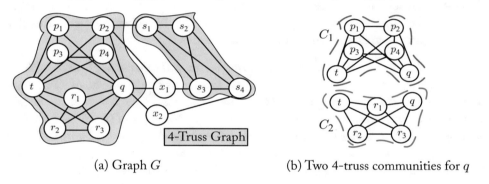

(a) Graph G (b) Two 4-truss communities for q

Figure 3.17: k-truss community example.

Problem Formulation

Based on the definitions of support and triangle connectivity, we define the model of triangle connected truss community in the following. For simplicity, we also call the *triangle connected k-truss community* as *k-truss community* for short, and use both of them interchangeably in this book.

Definition 3.3.4 (K-Truss Community) *Given a graph G and an integer* $k \geq 2$, G' *is a k-truss community, if* G' *satisfies the following three conditions.*

(1) K-Truss. G' *is a subgraph of G, denoted as* $G' \subseteq G$, *such that* $\forall e \in E(G')$, $sup(e, G') \geq (k - 2)$.

(2) Triangle Connectivity. $\forall e_1, e_2 \in E(G')$, $\exists \triangle_1, \triangle_2$ *in* G' *such that* $e_1 \in \triangle_1$, $e_2 \in \triangle_2$, *then either* $\triangle_1 = \triangle_2$, *or* $\triangle_1$ *is triangle connected with* $\triangle_2$ *in* G'.

(3) Maximal Subgraph. G' *is a maximal subgraph satisfying conditions (1) and (2). That is,* $\nexists G'' \subseteq G$, *such that* $G' \subset G''$, *and* G'' *satisfies conditions (1) and (2).*

Actually the largest subgraph that satisfies condition (1) is exactly the k-truss definition used in the literature [50, 165]. However, the k-truss condition itself is insufficient to define a cohesive and meaningful community due to the following two reasons. First, a k-truss subgraph can be disconnected, thus does not represent a cohesive community. For example, as seen earlier, in Figure 3.17a, the subgraph consisting of the two shaded regions is the 4-truss, which is disconnected. So this 4-truss subgraph does not correspond to a meaningful community. Second, for a fixed k value, any vertex can belong to at most one k-truss subgraph. This limitation cannot deal with a common scenario that a user can participate in multiple communities.

With these considerations, the triangle connectivity requirement is imposed in condition (2) to ensure that the discovered communities are connected and cohesive. The rationale is that a triangle represents a strong and stable relationship among three vertices. If any two edges in a subgraph are reachable from each other through a series of adjacent triangles, the subgraph must be connected, and have a cohesive structure among all involved vertices. This definition also allows a vertex to participate in multiple communities.

Example 3.3.1 *Two 4-truss communities containing vertex q are shown in Figure 3.17b as C_1 and C_2. We can verify that every edge in C_1 is contained in at least two triangles, any two edges in C_1 are reachable through adjacent triangles, and C_1 is maximal. Thus, C_1 is a 4-truss community. These properties also hold for another 4-truss community C_2. Notice that C_1 and C_2 are connected with, i.e., reachable from, each other, although they are not triangle connected with each other. If we had defined a k-truss community based on classical notion of connectivity, the union of the graphs C_1 and C_2 would be regarded a k-truss community. However, as the edges in C_1 cannot reach the edges in C_2 through adjacent triangles, C_1 and C_2 cannot merge as one large community. This is very reasonable, as there is no direct connection between the two vertex sets $\{p_1, p_2, p_3, p_4\}$ and $\{r_1, r_2, r_3\}$. Finally, we can see that vertices q and t participate in both communities C_1 and C_2.*

Problem Definition Given a graph $G(V, E)$, a query vertex $v_q \in V$, and an integer $k \geq 2$, find all k-truss communities containing v_q.

Why K-Truss Community?

To help appreciate the benefits of the k-truss community model, let us compare it with one of the most recent proposals for a community model, namely the α-adjacency-γ-quasi-k-clique model [54]. Compared with that model, the k-truss community model has three significant advantages: stronger guarantee on cohesive structure, fewer parameters, and lower computational cost. These nice properties, which are inherited from the k-truss subgraph [50], not only lead to the discovery of more cohesive and meaningful communities, but also enable the design of more efficient, scalable, and easier-to-use algorithms for community search. We elaborate these properties below.

Bounded Diameter in K-Truss Community. As shown in [50], the diameter of a k-truss community C with $|C|$ vertices is no larger than $\lfloor \frac{2|C|-2}{k} \rfloor$. This property guarantees that the shortest distance between any two vertices in a community is bounded, which has been considered as an important feature of a good community in [61]. As an example, consider the 4-truss community C_1 in Figure 3.17b. The diameter of C_1 is 2, which matches the diameter upper bound $\lfloor \frac{2 \times 6 - 2}{4} \rfloor = 2$.

(K-1)-Edge-Connected Graph. A graph is $(k - 1)$-edge-connected if it remains connected whenever fewer than $k - 1$ edges are removed [72]. A k-truss community is guaranteed to be $(k - 1)$-edge-connected [50]. This property ensures a high connectivity of a community, which has been proposed as a criterion for a good community in [81]. In contrast, the γ-quasi-k-clique is not $(k - 1)$-edge-connected whenever $\gamma < 1$. For example, the 0.8-quasi-7-clique in Figure 3.5 becomes disconnected when just one edge is removed.

Fewer Parameters. In the k-truss community model, we only need to specify the trussness value k, which controls the diameter, the triangle connectivity, and the edge support in a community. In contrast, the α-adjacency-γ-quasi-k-clique model requires three parameters, the adjacency parameter α, the density γ, and the clique size k. Arguably, one advantage of having more parameters may give more control over the properties of the community. On the other hand, it is much more difficult to set proper values for different parameters.

Polynomial Time Complexity. There exist polynomial time algorithms [50, 165] for computing k-truss subgraphs. By applying such algorithms, one can compute the k-truss subgraphs for all k. The precomputed results enable to design compact index structures and efficient algorithms for querying k-truss communities. In contrast, finding γ-quasi-k-cliques has been proven to be NP-hard [54], which imposes a severe computational bottleneck.

A Simple Index-Based Query Processing Algorithm

In the following, we discuss how to process a k-truss community query on a graph. We begin by describing a simple k-truss index and use it to develop a simple k-truss community search algorithm (Figure 3.18). We will subsequently analyze the limitations of this simple approach.

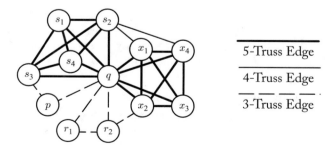

Figure 3.18: An example graph for k-truss community search.

Algorithm 3.11 Query Processing Using K-Truss Index

Input: $G = (V, E)$, an integer k, query vertex v_q
Output: k-truss communities containing v_q

1: $visited \leftarrow \emptyset; l \leftarrow 0;$
2: **for** $u \in N(v_q)$ **do**
3:    **if** $\tau((v_q, u)) \geq k$ **and** $(v_q, u) \notin visited$
4:       $l \leftarrow l + 1; C_l \leftarrow \emptyset; L \leftarrow \emptyset;$
5:       $L.push((v_q, u)); visited \leftarrow visited \cup \{(v_q, u)\};$
6:       **while** $L \neq \emptyset$
7:          $(x, y) \leftarrow L.pop(); C_l \leftarrow C_l \cup \{(x, y)\};$
8:          **for** $z \in N(x) \cap N(y)$ **do**
9:             **if** $\tau((x, z)) \geq k$ **and** $\tau((y, z)) \geq k$
10:                **if** $(x, z) \notin visited$
11:                   $L.push((x, z)); visited \leftarrow visited \cup \{(x, z)\};$
12:                **if** $(y, z) \notin visited$
13:                   $L.push((y, z)); visited \leftarrow visited \cup \{(y, z)\};$
14: **return** $\{C_1, \ldots, C_l\};$

A Simple K-Truss Index Construction First, a truss decomposition algorithm [165] is applied to compute the trussness of all edges in G. Then, for each vertex $v \in V$, we sort its neighbors $u \in N(v)$ in descending order of the edge trussness $\tau(e(u, v))$. For each distinct trussness value $k \geq 2$, we mark the position of the first vertex u in the sorted adjacency list where $\tau(e(u, v)) = k$. This supports efficient retrieval of v's incident edges with a given trussness value. We also use a hashtable to maintain all the edges and their trussness values. This is the simple k-truss index.

Query Processing Algorithm 3.11 outlines the procedure for processing a k-truss community query based on the simple index. Given an integer k and a query vertex v_q, the algorithm checks every incident edge on v_q to search k-truss communities. If there exists an unvisited edge (v_q, u) with $\tau((v_q, u)) \geq k$, (v_q, u) is used as the seed edge to form a new community C_l. By definition, all the other edges in C_l should be reachable from (v_q, u) through adjacent triangles. So we push (v_q, u) into a queue L and perform a BFS traversal to search for other edges for expanding C_l, i.e., edges which have trussness no less than k and form triangles with edges already in C_l (lines 6–13). When L becomes empty, all edges in C_l have been found. Then the algorithm checks the next unvisited incident edge of v_q for forming a new community C_{l+1}. This process iterates until all incident edges of v_q have been processed. Finally, a set of k-truss communities containing v_q are returned.

The correctness of Algorithm 3.11 is apparent since the algorithm essentially computes k-truss communities by following the definition, that is, exploring triangle-connected edges with trussness no less than k in a BFS manner. We next show the complexity of the simple k-truss index construction and query processing by Algorithm 3.11.

Theorem 3.3.1 *The construction of the simple k-truss index takes $O(\sum_{(u,v)\in E} \min\{d(u), d(v)\})$ time and $O(m)$ space. The index size is $O(m)$. Algorithm 3.11 takes $O(d_{Amax}|Ans|)$ time to process one query, where $Ans = C_1 \cup \ldots \cup C_l$ is the union of the produced k-truss communities, $|Ans|$ is the number of edges in Ans and d_{Amax} is the maximum vertex degree in Ans.*

Proof. The truss decomposition algorithm (Algorithm 2.2) takes $O(\sum_{(u,v)\in E} \min\{d(u), d(v)\})$ time and $O(m)$ space for computing the trussness of all edges. Sorting the adjacency lists of all vertices in G can be done in $O(m)$ time and $O(m)$ space, using binsort, similarly to using the sorted degree array in [19, 37]. Building an edge hashtable costs $O(m)$ time and $O(m)$ space. Thus, the construction of the k-truss index takes $O(\sum_{(u,v)\in E} \min\{d(u), d(v)\})$ time and $O(m)$ space. The index size is $O(m)$.

In k-truss community search, for each edge (u, v) in the generated communities, Algorithm 3.11 accesses the common neighbors of u and v, i.e., $N(u) \cap N(v)$ (lines 7–9), whose size is bounded by d_{Amax}. Thus, the query time complexity is $O(d_{Amax}|Ans|)$. □

Example 3.3.2 *Suppose we want to query the 4-truss communities containing vertex q in the graph in Figure 3.18. Algorithm 3.11 first visits edge (q, s_1) with $\tau((q, s_1)) = 5 \geq 4$, and adds it into L. The algorithm pops (q, s_1) from L and inserts it into a new community C_1. Then the algorithm checks the common neighbors of q and s_1 and the edges between them. Consider a common neighbor s_2 as an example. As $\tau((q, s_2)) \geq 4$ and $\tau((s_1, s_2)) \geq 4$, both edges (q, s_2) and (s_1, s_2) are then inserted into C_1 and also pushed into L for further expansion. This BFS expansion process continues until L becomes empty and the 4-truss community C_1 is the subgraph induced by the vertex set $\{q, s_1, s_2, s_3, s_4, x_1, x_2, x_3, x_4\}$.*

TCP-Index-Based Query Processing Algorithms

In this section, we introduce a compact and elegant structure, called *Triangle Connectivity Preserving Index* (TCP-Index), and a highly efficient algorithm to process a k-truss community query. We first discuss the limitations of the simple k-truss index.

Limitations of Simple K-Truss Index Algorithm 3.11 has two drawbacks in its query processing mechanism of using the simple k-truss index. Specifically, in lines 8–13, for any edge (x, y) that has already been included in C_l, the algorithm needs to access adjacent edges (x, z) and (y, z) for each common neighbor z of x and y. The following two cases lead to unnecessary and excessive computational overhead.

1. **Unnecessary access of disqualified edges**: If $\tau((x, z)) < k$ or $\tau((y, z)) < k$, then $(x, z), (y, z)$ will not be included in C_l, thus accessing and checking such disqualified edges is clearly *wasteful* and should be avoided.

2. **Repeated access of qualified edges**: For each edge (u, v) in C_l, it is accessed at least $2(k - 2)$ times in the BFS traversal, which is a huge *overhead*, but avoidable. This is because $\tau((u, v)) \geq k$, (u, v) is contained in at least $(k - 2)$ triangles by definition. For each such

triangle denoted $\triangle_{uvw}$, (u, v) will be accessed twice when we do BFS expansion from the other two edges (u, w), (v, w). It follows that the query time of Algorithm 3.11 is lower bounded by $\Omega(k|Ans|)$.

TCP-Index In view of these two drawbacks, Huang et al. [89] design a novel Triangle Connectivity Preserving Index, or TCP-Index for short, which avoids the computational issues of Algorithm 3.11 outlined above. Remarkably, the TCP-Index supports the k-truss community query in $O(|Ans|)$ time, which is essentially optimal. Meanwhile, the TCP-Index can be constructed in $O(\sum_{(u,v)\in E} \min\{d(u), d(v)\})$ time and stored in $O(m)$ space, which has exactly the same complexity as the simple k-truss index.

TCP-Index Construction

We first present some observations from the example in Figure 3.18.

Observation 3.3   Consider $\triangle_{pqs_3}$ in which the three edge trussness values are 5, 3, and 3. Then $\triangle_{pqs_3}$ can appear in a 3-truss community, but not in 4- or 5-truss communities. To generalize, a triangle $\triangle_{xyz}$ can appear only in k-truss communities where $k \le \min\{\tau((x, y)), \tau((x, z)), \tau((y, z))\}$.

Observation 3.4   Consider the subgraph in Figure 3.19a, extracted from the graph in Figure 3.18. By definition, vertices x_1, x_2, x_3, x_4 all belong to the same 5-truss community containing q (see Figure 3.18), as each involved edge has trussness 5, and $\triangle_{qx_1x_2}$ and $\triangle_{qx_1x_3}$ are adjacent via edge (q, x_1). $\triangle_{qx_1x_2}$ and $\triangle_{qx_1x_3}$ are triangle connected. Similarly, $\triangle_{qx_1x_2}$, $\triangle_{qx_1x_3}$, $\triangle_{qx_1x_4}$, $\triangle_{qx_2x_3}$, $\triangle_{qx_2x_4}$ and $\triangle_{qx_3x_4}$ all are triangle connected. Thus, we can use a compact representation for vertex q as depicted in solid line in Figure 3.19b, which preserves the trussness and triangle connectivity information for community search. Note that there is no need to include edges (x_2, x_3), (x_2, x_4), and (x_3, x_4), as the tree-shaped structure clearly indicates that x_2, x_3, x_4 belong to the same 5-truss community as x_1 by triangle connectivity.

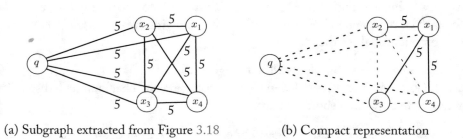

(a) Subgraph extracted from Figure 3.18   (b) Compact representation

Figure 3.19: Compact representation of a community with query vertex q.

Algorithm 3.12 TCP-Index Construction

Input: $G = (V, E)$
Output: TCP-Index $\mathcal{T}_x$ for each $x \in V$

1: Perform truss decomposition for G;
2: **for** $x \in V$ **do**
3:      $G_x \leftarrow \{(y, z) | y, z \in N(x), (y, z) \in E\}$;
4:      **for** $(y, z) \in E(G_x)$ **do**
5:           $w(y, z) \leftarrow \min\{\tau((x, y)), \tau((x, z)), \tau((y, z))\}$;
6:      $\mathcal{T}_x \leftarrow N(x)$;
7:      $k_{\max} \leftarrow \max\{w(y, z) | (y, z) \in E(G_x)\}$;
8:      **for** $k \leftarrow k_{\max}$ to 2 **do**
9:           $S_k \leftarrow \{(y, z) | (y, z) \in E(G_x), w(y, z) = k\}$;
10:          **for** $(y, z) \in S_k$ **do**
11:              **if** y and z are in different connected components in $\mathcal{T}_x$
12:                  add (y, z) with weight $w(y, z)$ in $\mathcal{T}_x$;
13: **return** $\{\mathcal{T}_x | x \in V\}$;

Observation 3.5   From Figure 3.18, we can see the two 5-truss communities $\{q, x_1, x_2, x_3, x_4\}, \{q, s_1, s_2, s_3, s_4\}$ involving vertex q are contained in the 4-truss community $\{q, x_1, x_2, x_3, x_4, s_1, s_2, s_3, s_4\}$, which is in turn contained in the 3-truss community, which is the whole graph.

Based on the above observations, Algorithm 3.12 outlines the procedure of constructing the TCP-Index. For each vertex $x \in V$, we build a graph G_x, where $V(G_x) = N(x)$, and $E(G_x) = \{(y, z) | (y, z) \in E(G), y, z \in N(x)\}$. For each edge $(y, z) \in E(G_x)$, we assign a weight $w(y, z) = \min\{\tau((x, y)), \tau((x, z)), \tau((y, z))\}$, which indicates that $\triangle_{xyz}$ can appear only in k-truss communities where $k \leq w(y, z)$, based on Observation 3.3. The TCP-Index for vertex x is a tree structure, denoted as $\mathcal{T}_x$, which is initialized to be the node set $N(x)$. Then in lines 8–12, for each k from the largest weight $k_{\max}$ to 2, we iteratively collect the set of edges $S_k \subseteq E(G_k)$ whose weight is k. For each $(y, z) \in S_k$, if y, z are still in different components of $\mathcal{T}_x$, we add the edge (y, z) with a weight $w(y, z)$ into $\mathcal{T}_x$. Essentially, $\mathcal{T}_x$ is the maximum spanning forest of G_x. The trees $\mathcal{T}_x$ for all $x \in V$ form the TCP-Index of graph G.

Example 3.3.3 *Figure 3.20 shows the TCP-Index for vertex q in the graph in Figure 3.18. $\mathcal{T}_q$ is initialized to be $N(q)$. Figure 3.20a shows the tree structure when we add edges whose weights are 5. According to Observation 3.4, when the edges (x_1, x_2) and (x_1, x_3) are added into $\mathcal{T}_q$, the edge (x_2, x_3) will not be added into $\mathcal{T}_q$, as x_2, x_3 are already connected in $\mathcal{T}_q$ and we know that x_2, x_3 belong to the same 5-truss community by triangle connectivity. This is essential to keep $\mathcal{T}_q$ as a compact forest. The complete TCP-Index for q is shown in Figure 3.20c. According to the community containment relationship in Observation 3.5, it is sufficient to use a single structure $\mathcal{T}_q$ for all trussness levels from $k_{\max}$ to 2.*

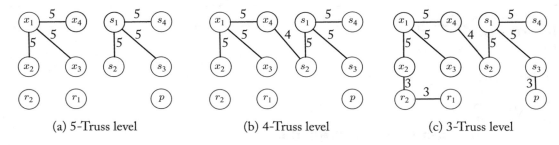

(a) 5-Truss level   (b) 4-Truss level   (c) 3-Truss level

Figure 3.20: TCP-Index construction of vertex q.

Theorem 3.3.2 *The TCP-Index of graph G can be constructed in $O(\sum_{(u,v)\in E} \min\{d(u), d(v)\})$ time and $O(m)$ space by Algorithm 3.12. The index size is $O(m)$.*

Proof. The first step costs $O(\sum_{(u,v)\in E} \min\{d(u), d(v)\})$ time. For a vertex $x \in V$, it takes $O(\sum_{y\in N(x)} \min\{d(x), d(y)\})$ time to list all triangles containing x to obtain G_x in line 3. The number of edges $|E(G_x)|$ is $O(\sum_{y\in N(x)} \min\{d(x), d(y)\})$, thus $\mathcal{T}_x$ can be computed in $O(\sum_{y\in N(x)} \min\{d(x), d(y)\})$ time by Kruskal's algorithm. For all vertices in V, it takes $O(\sum_{x\in V} \sum_{y\in N(x)} \min\{d(x), d(y)\})$ time in total to build the TCP-Index. Thus, the time complexity of Algorithm 3.12 is $O(\sum_{(u,v)\in E} \min\{d(u), d(v)\})$.

For a vertex $x \in V$, G_x, as a subgraph of G, takes $O(m)$ space, which can be released after obtaining $\mathcal{T}_x$. $\mathcal{T}_x$, as a spanning forest on the vertex set $N(x)$, takes $O(|N(x)|)$ space. Thus, the TCP-Index size for all vertices is $O(\sum_{x\in V} |N(x)|) = O(m)$. □

We remark that the *arboricity* of a graph is the minimum number of spanning forests needed to cover the edges of the graph. According to [47], $O(\sum_{(u,v)\in E} \min\{d(u), d(v)\}) \subseteq O(\rho m)$ where ρ is the arboricity of a graph G. $\rho \leq \min\{\lceil \sqrt{m} \rceil, d_{\max}\}$ holds for any graph. Thus, the TCP-Index construction takes $O(\sum_{(u,v)\in E} \min\{d(u), d(v)\}) \subseteq O(\rho m) \subseteq O(m^{1.5})$ time.

Query Processing Using TCP-Index

We first illustrate query processing through an example, before we formally present the algorithm. According to the design of the TCP-Index, if two vertices are connected through a series of edges with weight $\geq k$ in $\mathcal{T}_x$ for $x \in V$, these two vertices belong to the same k-truss community via a series of adjacent triangles. Consider $\mathcal{T}_q$ in Figure 3.20c. As x_2, x_3 are connected through two edges with weight 5, they belong to the same 5-truss community. Thus, we first define the k-*level connected vertex set* on a tree $\mathcal{T}_x$ to find all such vertices that belong to a k-truss community.

Definition 3.3.5 (K-Level Connected Vertex Set) *For $x \in V$ and $y \in N(x)$, we use $V_k(x, y)$ to denote the set of vertices which are connected with y through edges of weight $\geq k$ in $\mathcal{T}_x$. We adopt the convention that y also belongs to this set, i.e., $y \in V_k(x, y)$.*

Example 3.3.4 *If we want to query 5-truss communities containing a query vertex q, we first visit an incident edge on q, say (q, x_1), where $\tau((q, x_1)) = 5$. From $\mathcal{T}_q$ we retrieve the vertex set $V_5(q, x_1) = \{x_1, x_2, x_3, x_4\}$ as they are connected through edges with weight 5. According to Observation 3.4, these four vertices belong to the same 5-truss community with q. As $V_5(q, x_1) \subset N(q)$, we can construct part of the community as shown in Figure 3.21a.*

At this stage, we still miss the edges between the four vertices, for example, $(x_2, x_3), (x_3, x_4)$, etc. This is because $\mathcal{T}_q$, which is a spanning forest, does not keep all the edges between the vertices. To fully recover all the edges in the 5-truss community, for each vertex $x_i \in V_5(q, x_1)$, we "reverse" the edge (q, x_i) to (x_i, q), then further expand the community in x_i's neighborhood. Take vertex x_2 as an example. We reverse (q, x_2) to (x_2, q) and then query x_2's index $\mathcal{T}_{x_2}$ to get the vertex set $V_5(x_2, q) = \{q, x_1, x_3, x_4\}$, as x_1, x_3, x_4 are connected with q in $\mathcal{T}_{x_2}$. Then we can obtain the edges between x_2 and every vertex in $V_5(x_2, q)$. After this, the community is shown in Figure 3.21b. Similarly, we perform the reverse operation for each vertex x_1, x_3, x_4 and get the complete 5-truss community in Figure 3.21c. We can observe that in this search process, each edge in a community is accessed exactly twice, for example, accessing (q, x_2) from $\mathcal{T}_q$ and (x_2, q) from $\mathcal{T}_{x_2}$.

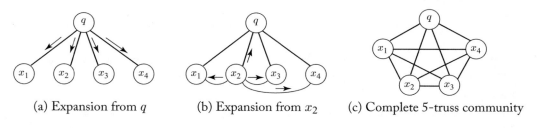

(a) Expansion from q (b) Expansion from x_2 (c) Complete 5-truss community

Figure 3.21: 5-truss community query on q using TCP-Index.

Algorithm 3.13 outlines the procedure of query processing using the TCP-Index. Similar to Algorithm 3.11, Algorithm 3.13 computes the k-truss communities for a query vertex v_q by expanding from each incident edge on v_q in a BFS manner. If there exists an unvisited edge (v_q, u) with $\tau((v_q, u)) \geq k$, (v_q, u) is the seed edge to form a new community C_l (lines 2-4). Then the algorithm performs a BFS traversal using a queue L in lines 5-13. For an unvisited edge (x, y), it searches the vertex set $V_k(x, y)$ from $\mathcal{T}_x$. The procedure for computing $V_k(x, y)$ is listed in lines 15-16. For each $z \in V_k(x, y)$, the edge (x, z) is added into C_l. Then we perform the reverse operation, i.e., if (z, x) is not visited yet, it is pushed into L for z-centered community expansion using $\mathcal{T}_z$. Note that (z, x) and (x, z) are considered different here. When L becomes empty, all edges in C_l have been found. The process iterates until all incident edges of v_q have been processed. Finally, a set of k-truss communities containing v_q are returned.

We show the correctness of Algorithm 3.13 in the following.

Lemma 3.3.1 *Given a query vertex $x \in V$ and an integer k, Algorithm 3.13 correctly computes all k-truss communities containing x.*

Algorithm 3.13 Query Processing Using TCP-Index

Input: $G = (V, E)$, an integer k, query vertex v_q
Output: k-truss communities containing v_q

1:   $visited \leftarrow \emptyset; l \leftarrow 0;$
2:   **for** $u \in N(v_q)$ **do**
3:     **if** $\tau((v_q, u)) \geq k$ **and** $(v_q, u) \notin visited$
4:       $l \leftarrow l + 1; C_l \leftarrow \emptyset; L \leftarrow \emptyset;$
5:       $L.push((v_q, u));$
6:       **while** $L \neq \emptyset$
7:         $(x, y) \leftarrow L.pop();$
8:         **if** $(x, y) \notin visited$
9:           compute $V_k(x, y);$
10:          **for** $z \in V_k(x, y)$ **do**
11:            $visited \leftarrow visited \cup \{(x, z)\}; C_l \leftarrow C_l \cup \{(x, z)\};$
12:            **if** the reversed edge $(z, x) \notin visited$
13:              $L.push((z, x));$
14: **return** $\{C_1, \cdots, C_l\};$
15: **Procedure** compute $V_k(x, y)$
16: **return** $\{z | z$ is connected with y in $\mathcal{T}_x$ through edges of weight $\geq k\};$

Proof. First, for an edge (y, z) in $\mathcal{T}_x$, by definition, $w(y, z) = \min\{\tau((x, y)), \tau((x, z)), \tau((y, z))\}$, so if $w(y, z) \geq k$, then $\triangle_{xyz}$ is included in a k-truss community of x.

Second, for two adjacent edges $(y, z_1), (y, z_2)$ in $\mathcal{T}_x$, we can conclude that $\triangle_{xyz_1}, \triangle_{xyz_2}$ are adjacent via edge (x, y).

Third, $V_k(x, y)$ contains the set of vertices which are connected with y through edges of weight $\geq k$ in $\mathcal{T}_x$. Based on the above two points, it leads to the discovery of all the triangles with weight $\geq k$ that can reach edge (x, y) in x's neighborhood. These connected triangles appear in the same k-truss community containing x.

Last, for an edge (x, z) where $z \in V_k(x, y)$, the same operation on its reverse edge (z, x) will further expand the k-truss community in z's neighborhood via $\mathcal{T}_z$. Thus, the k-truss community is expanded via adjacent triangles in a BFS manner.

The correctness of Algorithm 3.13 follows from the above points. $\square$

Theorem 3.3.3 *The time complexity of Algorithm 3.13 is $O(|Ans|)$, where $Ans = C_1 \cup \ldots \cup C_l$ is the union of the produced k-truss communities and $|Ans|$ is the number of edges in Ans.*

Proof. Each edge (x, y) in the generated communities is accessed exactly twice: accessing (x, y) from $\mathcal{T}_x$ and (y, x) from $\mathcal{T}_y$. Thus, the time complexity of Algorithm 3.13 is $O(|Ans|)$. $\square$

Complexity Comparison. By using the TCP-Index and the simple k-truss index, each edge in a k-truss community is accessed *exactly twice vs. at least* $2(k - 2)$ *times*. In addition, the TCP-Index successfully avoids the unnecessary access of disqualified edges whose trussness is less than k. These are the key reasons that explain the difference in the query time between Algorithms 3.13 and 3.11, i.e., $O(|Ans|)$ vs. $O(d_{Amax}|Ans|)$. It is worth noting that the TCP-Index construction has exactly the same time and space complexity as the simple k-truss index.

Case Study of k-truss and $(k-1,1)$-OCS Models on DBLP

We present a case study to compare the k-truss and $(k-1,1)$-OCS community models. A collaboration network is built from the DBLP data set[1] for this purpose. A vertex represents an author and an edge is added between two authors if they have co-authored three or more papers. The network contains 234,879 vertices and 541,814 edges.

We query the 5-truss community containing "Jiawei Han" which is shown in Figure 3.22. For comparison, we follow the case study in [54] which uses the $(k-1,1)$-OCS model to query "Jiawei Han" by setting $k = 5, \alpha = 4, \gamma = 1$, which produces communities at a similar scale as shown in Figure 3.23. Note that we duplicate some authors who participate in more than one community in Figure 3.23, e.g., "Jian Pei", "Jian Pei_1" and "Jian Pei_2", for a better visualization effect. We have the following observations:

- The k-truss model generates five communities containing "Jiawei Han" (see Figure 3.22), among which the four smaller ones are also found by the $(k-1,1)$-OCS model and depicted using the same color in Figure 3.23.

- The largest 5-truss community depicted in blue in Figure 3.22, however, is decomposed into seven smaller communities by the $(k-1,1)$-OCS model in Figure 3.23. This phenomenon can be explained by the different mechanisms of the two community models. The $(k-1,1)$-OCS model tends to find the small, clique-based "*paper communities*," in which all the involved scholars appear in the same paper. For example, a paper community is formed by "Jiawei Han", "Philip S. Yu", "Chen Chen", "Xifeng Yan", and "Feida Zhu". In contrast, such small paper communities can be merged into a larger dense one by the condition of triangle connectivity in the k-truss model. For example, two small paper communities can be merged if they share a common edge as ("Jiawei Han", "Philip S. Yu") and form a 5-truss graph after being merged.

- A less restrictive community criterion can be realized by tuning α and γ in [54]. But in the experiment, if we set $\alpha < k - 1$ or $\gamma < 1$, it cannot output all communities within the time limit of 60 seconds set in the executable code of [54], owing to the expensive quasi-clique enumeration.

- Finally, we observe a community containing "Guozhu Dong" and five other authors (depicted in purple) in Figure 3.23 is completely subsumed by another bigger community (depicted in black) in the same figure. Such duplicate output, which is not desired, may

[1]http://dblp.uni-trier.de/xml/

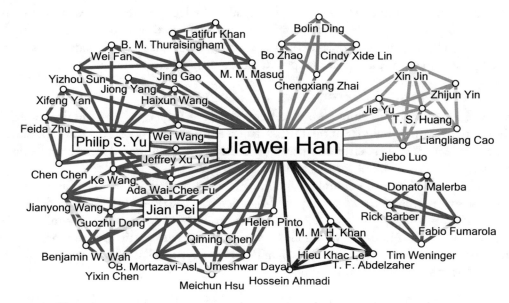

Figure 3.22: Five 5-truss communities containing Jiawei Han.

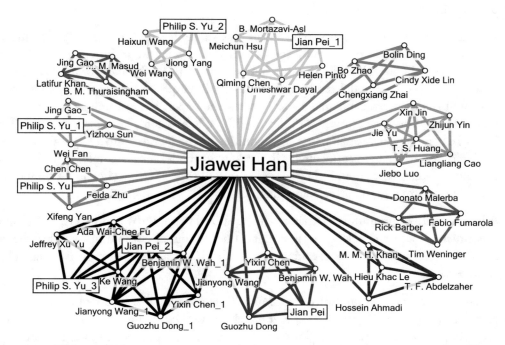

Figure 3.23: Eleven 4-adjacency-1.0-quasi-5-clique communities containing Jiawei Han.

be explained by the approximate heuristics for clique enumeration and expansion used in [54].

3.3.2   CLOSEST TRUSS COMMUNITY SEARCH

Motivation. In the k-truss community model discussed above, given one query node q and a parameter k, a k-truss community containing q is a maximal k-truss containing q, in which each edge is "triangle connected" with other edges. Triangle connectivity is strictly stronger than classical edge connectivity. The k-truss community model works well to find all overlapping communities containing a single query node q. It is natural to search for communities containing a set of query nodes in real applications, but the above community model, extended for multiple query nodes, has the following limitations. Due to the strict requirement of triangle connectivity constraint, the model may fail to discover any community for query nodes. For example, for the graph of Figure 3.24a and query nodes $Q = \{v_4, q_3, p_1\}$, the above k-truss community model cannot find a qualified community for any k, since the edges (v_4, q_3) and (q_3, p_1) are not triangle connected in any k-truss.

In this section, we present the problem of closest community search [96], i.e., given a set of query nodes, find a dense connected subgraph that contains the query nodes, in which nodes are close to each other. Based on graph diameter, we find the closest truss community containing query nodes with the smallest diameter.

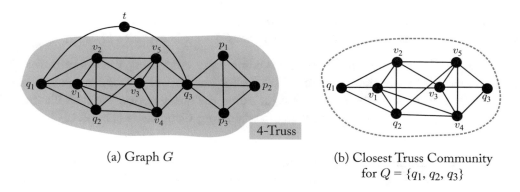

(a) Graph G

(b) Closest Truss Community
for $Q = \{q_1, q_2, q_3\}$

Figure 3.24: An example of closest truss communit.

Notions and Notations

For a pair of nodes $u, v \in G$, we denote by $\mathsf{dist}_G(u, v)$ the length of the shortest path between u and v in G, where $\mathsf{dist}_G(u, v) = +\infty$ if u and v are not connected. We make use of the notions of graph query distance and graph diameter.

Definition 3.3.6 (Query Distance) *Given a graph G and a set of query nodes $Q \subset V$, for each vertex $v \in G$, the vertex query distance of v is the maximum length of a shortest path from v to a query node $q \in Q$, i.e., $\mathsf{dist}_G(v, Q) = \max_{q \in Q} \mathsf{dist}_G(v, q)$. For a subgraph $H \subseteq G$, the graph query distance of H is defined as $\mathsf{dist}_G(H, Q) = \max_{u \in H} \mathsf{dist}_G(u, Q) = \max_{u \in H, q \in Q} \mathsf{dist}_G(u, q)$.*

Definition 3.3.7 (Graph Diameter) *The diameter of a graph G is defined as the maximum length of a shortest path in G, i.e., $\mathsf{diam}(G) = \max_{u,v \in G} \{\mathsf{dist}_G(u, v)\}$.*

For the graph G in Figure 3.24a and $Q = \{q_2, q_3\}$, the vertex query distance of v_2 is $\mathsf{dist}_G(v_2, Q) = \max_{q \in Q} \{\mathsf{dist}_G(v_2, q)\} = 2$, since $\mathsf{dist}_G(v_2, q_3) = 2$ and $\mathsf{dist}_G(v_2, q_2) = 1$. Let H be the subgraph of Figure 3.24a shaded in gray. Then the query distance of H is $\mathsf{dist}_G(H, Q) = 3$. The diameter of H is $\mathsf{diam}(H) = 4$.

Problem Formulation

On the basis of the definitions of k-truss and graph diameter, the *closest truss community* is defined as follows.

Definition 3.3.8 (Closest Truss Community) *Given a graph G and a set of query nodes Q, G' is a closest truss community (CTC), if G' satisfies the following two conditions.*

(1) Connected k-truss. *G' is a connected k-truss containing Q with the largest k, i.e., $Q \subseteq G' \subseteq G$ and $\forall e \in E(G')$, $sup(e) \geq k - 2$.*

(2) Smallest Diameter. *G' is a subgraph of smallest diameter satisfying condition (1). That is, $\nexists G'' \subseteq G$, such that $diam(G'') < diam(G')$, and G'' satisfies condition (1).*

Condition (1) requires that the closest community containing the query nodes Q be densely connected. In addition, Condition (2) makes sure that each node is as close as possible to every other node in the community, including the query nodes. We next illustrate the notion of CTC as well as the consequence of considering Conditions (1) and (2) in different orders.

Example 3.3.5 In Definition 3.3.8, we first consider the connected k-truss of G containing query nodes with the largest trussness, and then among such subgraphs, regard the one with the smallest diameter as the closest truss community. Consider the graph G in Figure 3.24a, and $Q = \{q_1, q_2, q_3\}$; the subgraph in the region shaded grey is a 4-truss containing Q, and is a subgraph with the largest trussness that contains Q, and has diameter 4. Notice that in Figure 3.24a, although the nodes p_1, p_2, p_3 belong to the 4-truss and are strongly connected with q_3, they are far away from the query node q_1. Figure 3.24b shows another 4-truss containing Q but not p_1, p_2, p_3, and its diameter is 3. It can be verified that this is the 4-truss containing the query nodes Q, that has the smallest diameter. Thus, by Condition (2) of Definition 3.3.8, the 4-truss graph in Figure 3.24a will not be regarded the closest truss community, whereas the one in Figure 3.24b is indeed the CTC.

Example 3.3.6 Suppose we apply the conditions in Definition 3.3.8 in the opposite order. That is, we first minimize the diameter among connected subgraphs of G containing Q and look for the k-truss subgraph with the largest k in that subgraph. First, we find that the cycle of $\{(q_1, t), (t, q_3), (q_3, v_4), (v_4, q_2), (q_2, q_1)\}$ is a connected subgraph containing Q with the smallest diameter 2. Then, we find that this cycle is also the k-truss subgraph with the largest k containing itself. However, it is only a 2-truss, which has a loosely connected structure compared to Figure 3.24b. It is left as a simple exercise to the reader to verify that other subgraphs with the same smallest diameter 2 that contain $Q = \{q_1, q_2, q_3\}$ do not admit k-trusses with $k > 2$. This justifies the choice of the order in which Conditions (1) and (2) should be applied.

The problem of CTC search is stated as follows.

Problem 3.3.1 (CTC-Problem) *Given a graph $G(V, E)$ and a set of query vertices $Q = \{v_1, \ldots, v_r\} \subseteq V$, find a closest truss community containing Q.*

Problem Analysis

Since the closest truss community model is based on the concept of k-truss, the communities capture good structural properties of k-truss, such as *k-edge-connected* and *hierarchical structure*. In addition, since CTC is required to have minimum diameter, it also has *bounded diameter*.

Small diameter, k-edge-connected, hierarchical structure. First, it has been shown that the diameter of a connected k-truss with n vertices is no more than $\lfloor \frac{2n-2}{k} \rfloor$ [50]. Moreover, a k-truss community is $(k-1)$-edge-connected [50], as it remains connected whenever fewer than $k-1$ edges are removed [72]. In addition, k-truss-based community has *hierarchical structure* that represents the essence of a community at different levels of granularity [89], that is, k-truss is always contained in the $(k-1)$-truss for any $k \geq 3$.

Largest k. There is a trivial upper bound on the maximum possible trussness of a connected k-truss containing the query nodes.

Lemma 3.3.2 *For a connected k-truss H satisfying definition of CTC for Q, we have $k \leq \min \{\tau(q_1), \ldots, \tau(q_r)\}$ holds.*

Proof. First, we have $Q \subseteq H$. For each node $q \in Q$, q cannot be contained in a k-truss in G, whenever $k > \tau(q)$. Thus, the fact that H is a k-truss subgraph containing Q implies that $k \leq \min\{\tau(q_1), \ldots, \tau(q_r)\}$. □

Lower and upper bounds on diameter. Since the distance function satisfies the triangle inequality, i.e., for all nodes u, v, w, $\text{dist}_G(u, v) \leq \text{dist}_G(u, w) + \text{dist}_G(w, v)$, we can express the lower and upper bounds on the graph diameter in terms of the query distance as follows.

Lemma 3.3.3 *For a graph $G(V, E)$ and a set of nodes $Q \subseteq G$, we have $\text{dist}_G(G, Q) \leq \text{diam}(G) \leq 2\text{dist}_G(G, Q)$.*

Proof. First, the diameter $\mathsf{diam}(G) = \max_{v,u \in G} \mathsf{dist}_G(v,u)$, which is clearly no less than $\mathsf{dist}_G(G,Q) = \max_{v \in G, q \in Q} \mathsf{dist}_G(v,q)$ for $Q \subseteq G$. Thus, $\mathsf{dist}_G(G,Q) \le \mathsf{diam}(G)$. Second, suppose that the longest shortest path in G is between v and u. Then $\forall q \in Q$, we have $\mathsf{diam}(G) = \mathsf{dist}(v,u) \le \mathsf{dist}(v,q) + \mathsf{dist}(q,u) \le 2\mathsf{dist}_G(G,Q)$. The lemma follows. □

Hardness and Approximation

Hardness. In the following, we show the CTC-Problem is NP-hard. Thereto, we define the decision version of the CTC-Problem.

Problem 3.3.2 (CTCk-Problem) *Given a graph $G(V,E)$, a set of query nodes $Q = \{v_1, \ldots, v_r\} \subseteq V$ and parameters k and d, test whether G contains a connected k-truss subgraph with diameter at most d, that contains Q.*

Theorem 3.3.4 *The CTCk-Problem is **NP-hard**.*

Proof. We reduce the well-known NP-hard problem of Maximum Clique (decision version) to the CTCk-Problem. Given a graph $G(V,E)$ and a number k, the Maximum Clique Decision problem is to check whether G contains a clique of size k. Thus, we can construct an instance of the CTCk-Problem, consisting of graph G, $d = 1$, and $Q = \emptyset$.

We show that the instance of the Maximum Clique Decision problem is a YES-instance iff the corresponding instance of the CTCk-Problem is a YES-instance. Clearly, any clique with at least k nodes is a connected k-truss with diameter 1. On the other hand, given a solution H for the CTCk-Problem, H must contain at least k nodes since H is a k-truss, and $diam(H) = d = 1$, which implies H is a clique. □

The hardness of the CTC-Problem follows from this. The next natural question is whether the CTC-Problem can be approximated.

Approximation. For $\alpha \ge 1$, we say that an algorithm achieves an α-approximation to the CTC search problem if it outputs a connected k-truss subgraph $H \subseteq G$ such that $Q \subseteq H$, $\tau(H) = \tau(H^*)$ and $\mathsf{diam}(H) \le \alpha \cdot \mathsf{diam}(H^*)$, where H^* is the optimal CTC. That is, H^* is a connected k-truss with the largest k s.t. $Q \subseteq H^*$, and $diam(H^*)$ is the minimum among all such CTCs containing Q. Notice that the trussness of the output subgraph H matches that of the optimal solution H^* and that the approximation is only w.r.t. the diameter: the diameter of H is required to be no more than $\alpha \cdot diam(H^*)$.

Non-Approximability. We next show that the CTC-Problem cannot be approximated within a factor better than 2. This result is established through a reduction, again from the Maximum Clique Decision problem to the problem of approximating the CTC-Problem, given k. In the next section, we describe a 2-approximation algorithm for the CTC-Problem, thus essentially matching this lower bound. Note that the CTC-Problem with given parameter k is essentially the CTCk-Problem.

Theorem 3.3.5 *Unless* P = NP, *for any* $\varepsilon > 0$, *the* CTC-Problem *with given parameter k cannot be approximated in polynomial time within a factor* $(2 - \varepsilon)$ *of the optimal.*

Proof Sketch: It can be shown that a $(2 - \varepsilon)$-approximation algorithm for the CTC-Problem with given parameter k can be used to distinguish between the YES and NO instances of the Maximum Clique Decision problem.

CTC Search Algorithm

In this section, we present a greedy algorithm called Basic for the CTC search problem. Then, we show that this algorithm achieves a 2-approximation to the optimal result.

Basic Algorithmic Framework. Here is an overview of our algorithm Basic. First, given a graph G and query nodes Q, we find a maximal connected k-truss, denoted G_0, containing Q and having the largest trussness. As G_0 may have a large diameter, we iteratively remove nodes far away from the query nodes, while maintaining the trussness of the remainder subgraph at k.

Algorithm. Algorithm 3.14 outlines the procedure of finding a closest truss community based on a greedy strategy. For query nodes Q, we first find a maximal connected k-truss G_0 that contains Q, such that $k = \tau(G_0)$ is the largest (line 1). Then, we set $l = 0$. For all $u \in G_l$ and $q \in Q$, we compute the shortest distance between u and q (line 4), and obtain the vertex query distance $\mathsf{dist}_{G_l}(u, Q)$. Among all vertices, we pick up a vertex u^* with the maximum $\mathsf{dist}_{G_l}(u^*, Q)$, which is also the graph query distance $\mathsf{dist}_{G_l}(G_l, Q)$ (lines 5–6). Next, we remove the vertex u^* and its incident edges from G_l, and delete any nodes and edges needed to restore the k-truss property of G_l (lines 7–8). We assign the updated graph as a new G_l. Then, we repeat the above steps until G_l does not have a connected subgraph containing Q (lines 3–9). Finally, we terminate by output graph R as the closest truss community, where R is any graph $G' \in \{G_0, \ldots, G_{l-1}\}$ with the smallest graph query distance $\mathsf{dist}_{G'}(G', Q)$ (line 10). Note that each intermediate graph $G' \in \{G_0, \ldots, G_{l-1}\}$ is a k-truss with the maximum trussness as required.

Example 3.3.7 *We apply Algorithm 3.14 on G in Figure 3.24 for $Q = \{q_1, q_2, q_3\}$. First, we obtain the 4-truss subgraph G_0 shaded in gray, using a procedure we will shortly explain. Then, we compute all shortest distances, and get the maximum vertex query distance as $\mathsf{dist}_{G_0}(p_1, Q) = 4$, and $u^* = p_1$. We delete node p_1 and its incident edges from G_0; we also delete p_2 and p_3, in order to restore the 4-truss property. The resulting subgraph is G_1. Any further deletion of a node in the next iteration of the while loop will induce a series of deletions in line 8, eventually making the graph disconnected or containing just a part of query nodes. As a result, the output graph R, shown in Figure 3.24b, is just G_1. Also $\mathsf{dist}_R(R, Q) = 3$, and R happens to be the exact CTC with diameter 3, which in this example is optimal.*

Approximation Analysis

Algorithm 3.14 can achieve a 2-approximation to the optimal solution, that is, the obtained connected k-truss community R satisfies $Q \subseteq R$, $\tau(R) = \tau(H^*)$ and $\mathsf{diam}(R) \leq 2\mathsf{diam}(H^*)$,

---

Algorithm 3.14 Basic (G, Q)

Input: A graph $G = (V, E)$, a set of query nodes $Q = \{q_1, \ldots, q_r\}$.
Output: A connected k-truss R with a small diameter.

1: Find a maximal connected k-truss containing Q with the largest k as G_0;
2: $l \leftarrow 0$;
3: **while** $\text{connect}_{G_l}(Q) = \textbf{true do}$
4:      Compute $\text{dist}_{G_l}(q, u)$, $\forall q \in Q$ and $\forall u \in G_l$;
5:      $u^* \leftarrow \arg\max_{u \in G_l} \text{dist}_{G_l}(u, Q)$;
6:      $\text{dist}_{G_l}(G_l, Q) \leftarrow \text{dist}_{G_l}(u^*, Q)$;
7:      Delete u^* and its incident edges from G_l;
8:      Maintain k-truss property of G_l;
9:      $G_{l+1} \leftarrow G_l$; $l \leftarrow l + 1$;
10: $R \leftarrow \arg\min_{G' \in \{G_0, \ldots, G_{l-1}\}} \text{dist}_{G'}(G', Q)$;

---

for any optimal solution H^*. Since any graph in $\{G_0, \ldots, G_{l-1}\}$ is a connceted k-truss with the largest k containing Q by Algorithm 3.14, and $R \in \{G_0, \ldots, G_{l-1}\}$, we have $Q \subseteq R$ and $\tau(R) = \tau(H^*)$. In the following, we show that $\text{diam}(R) \leq 2\text{diam}(H^*)$. We start with a few key results. For graphs G_1, G_2, we say $G_1 \subseteq G_2$ to mean $V(G_1) \subseteq V(G_2)$ and $E(G_1) \subseteq E(G_2)$.

Lemma 3.3.4 *Given two graphs G_1 and G_2 with $G_1 \subseteq G_2$, for $u, v \in V(G_1)$, $\text{dist}_{G_2}(u, v) \leq \text{dist}_{G_1}(u, v)$ holds. Moreover, if $Q \subseteq V(G_1)$, then $\text{dist}_{G_2}(G_1, Q) \leq \text{dist}_{G_1}(G_1, Q)$ also holds.*

Proof. It trivially follows from the fact that G_2 preserves the paths between the nodes in G_1. □

Recall that in Algorithm 3.14, in each iteration i, a node u^* with the maximum $\text{dist}(u^*, Q)$ is deleted from G_i, but $\text{dist}_{G_i}(G_i, Q)$ is *not* monotonously nonincreasing during the process, hence $\text{dist}_{G_{l-1}}(G_{l-1}, Q)$ is not necessarily the minimum. Note that in Algorithm 3.14, G_l is not the last feasible graph (i.e., connected k-truss containing Q), but G_{l-1} is. The observation is shown in the following lemma.

Lemma 3.3.5 *In Algorithm 3.14, it is possible that for some $0 \leq i < j < l$, we have $G_j \subset G_i$, and $\text{dist}_{G_i}(G_i, Q) < \text{dist}_{G_j}(G_j, Q)$ holds.*

Proof. It is easy to see that, because for a vertex $v \in G$, $\text{dist}_G(v, Q)$ is non-decreasing monotone w.r.t. subgraphs of G. More precisely, for $v \in G_i \cap G_j$, $\text{dist}_{G_i}(v, Q) \leq \text{dist}_{G_j}(v, Q)$ holds. □

An important observation is that if an intermediate graph G_i obtained by Algorithm 3.14 contains an optimal solution H^*, i.e., $H^* \subset G_i$ and $\text{dist}_{G_i}(G_i, Q) > \text{dist}_{G_i}(H^*, Q)$, then the algorithm will not terminate at G_{i+1}.

Lemma 3.3.6 *In Algorithm 3.14, for any intermediate graph G_i, we have $H^* \subseteq G_i$ and $\text{dist}_{G_i}(G_i, Q) > \text{dist}_{G_i}(H^*, Q)$, then G_{i+1} is a connected k-truss containing Q and $H^* \subseteq G_{i+1}$.*

Proof. Suppose $H^* \subseteq G_i$ and $\text{dist}_{G_i}(G_i, Q) > \text{dist}_{G_i}(H^*, Q)$. Then there exists a node $u \in G_i \setminus H^*$ s.t. $\text{dist}_{G_i}(u, Q) = \text{dist}_{G_i}(G_i, Q) > \text{dist}_{G_i}(H^*, Q)$. Clearly, $u \notin Q$. In the next iteration, Algorithm 3.14 will delete u from G_i (Step 7), and perform Step 8. The graph resulting from restoring the k-truss property is G_{i+1}. Since H^* is a connected k-truss containing Q, the restoration step (line 8) must find a subgraph G_{i+1} s.t. $H^* \subseteq G_{i+1}$, and G_{i+1} is a connected k-truss containing Q. Thus, the algorithm will not terminate in iteration $(i + 1)$. □

The polynomial Algorithm 3.14 can find a connected k-truss community R having the minimum query distance to Q, which is optimal.

Lemma 3.3.7 *For any connected k-truss H with the highest k containing Q, $\text{dist}_R(R, Q) \leq \text{dist}_H(H, Q)$.*

Proof. The following cases may occur for G_{l-1}, which is the last feasible graph obtained by Algorithm 3.14.

Case (a): $H \subseteq G_{l-1}$. We have $\text{dist}_{G_{l-1}}(G_{l-1}, Q) \leq \text{dist}_{G_{l-1}}(H, Q)$; otherwise, if $\text{dist}_{G_{l-1}}(G_{l-1}, Q) > \text{dist}_{G_{l-1}}(H, Q)$, we can deduce from Lemma 3.3.6 that G_{l-1} is not the last feasible graph obtained by Algorithm 3.14, a contradiction. Thus, by Step 10 in Algorithm 3.14 and the fact that $\text{dist}_{G_{l-1}}(G_{l-1}, Q) \leq \text{dist}_{G_{l-1}}(H, Q)$, we have $\text{dist}_R(R, Q) \leq \text{dist}_{G_{l-1}}(G_{l-1}, Q) \leq \text{dist}_{G_{l-1}}(H, Q) \leq \text{dist}_H(H, Q)$.

Case (b): $H \nsubseteq G_{l-1}$. There exists a vertex $v \in H$ deleted from one of the subgraphs $\{G_0, \ldots, G_{l-2}\}$. Suppose the first deleted vertex $v^* \in H$ is in graph G_i, where $0 \leq i \leq l - 2$, then v^* must be deleted in Step 7, but not in Step 8. This is because each vertex/edge of H satisfies the condition of k-truss, and will not be removed before any vertex is removed from G_i. Then, we have $\text{dist}_{G_i}(G_i, Q) = \text{dist}_{G_i}(v^*, Q) = \text{dist}_{G_i}(H, Q)$, and $\text{dist}_{G_i}(G_i, Q) \geq \text{dist}_R(R, Q)$ by Step 10. As a result, $\text{dist}_R(R, Q) \leq \text{dist}_{G_i}(H, Q) \leq \text{dist}_H(H, Q)$. □

Based on the preceding lemmas, we have the following.

Theorem 3.3.6 *Algorithm 3.14 provides a 2-approximation to the* CTC-Problem *as $diam(R) \leq 2diam(H^*)$.*

Proof. Since $\text{dist}_R(R, Q) \leq \text{dist}_{H^*}(H^*, Q)$ by Lemma 3.3.7, we get $diam(R) \leq 2\text{dist}_R(R, Q) \leq 2\text{dist}_{H^*}(H^*, Q) \leq 2diam(H^*)$ by Lemma 3.3.3. The theorem follows from this. □

Complexity Analysis

In the implementation of Algorithm 3.14, we do not need to keep all intermediate graphs, but just record the removal of vertices/edges at each iteration. Let G_0 be the maximal connected k-truss found in line 1 of Algorithm 3.14. Let $n' = |V(G_0)|$ and $m' = |E(G_0)|$, and let d'_{max} be the maximum degree of a vertex in G_0.

At each iteration i of Algorithm 3.14, we delete at least one node and its incident edges from G_i. Clearly, the number of removed edges is no less than $k - 1$, thus the total number of iterations is $t \leq \min\{n' - k, m'/(k - 1)\}$, i.e., t is $O(\min\{n', m'/k\})$. We have the following.

Theorem 3.3.7 *Algorithm 3.14 takes $O((|Q|t + \rho)m')$ time and $O(m')$ space, where $t \in O(\min\{n', m'/k\})$, and ρ is the arboricity of graph G_0. Furthermore, we have $\rho \leq \min\{d'_{max}, \sqrt{m'}\}$.*

Proof Sketch: First, listing all triangles of G_0 and creating a series of k-truss graphs $\{G_0, \ldots, G_{l-1}\}$ take $O(\rho m')$ time in all, where ρ is the arboricity of graph G_0. Second, the computation of shortest distances by a BFS traversal starting from each query node $q \in Q$ takes $O(t|Q|m')$ time for t iterations. Third, for the space consumption, we only record the sequence of removed edges from G_0 for attaching a corresponding label to graph G_i at each iteration i, which takes $O(m')$ space in all. We refer the reader to [97] for complete details of the proof.

Case Study

Figure 3.25b shows a **closest truss community** [96] detected on DBLP network using the query $Q = \{$"Alon Y. Halevy," "Michael J. Franklin," "Jeffrey D. Ullman," "Jennifer Widom."$\}$ It has 14 authors, 81 edges, and an edge density of 0.89. Figure 3.25a shows a larger connected 9-truss containing the same query nodes, which includes the graph of Figure 3.25b as a subgraph. It is clear that this larger 9-truss includes several authors who are far away from and loosely connected with queried authors, and has an edge density of 0.18. This illustrates the superiority of **closest truss community**.

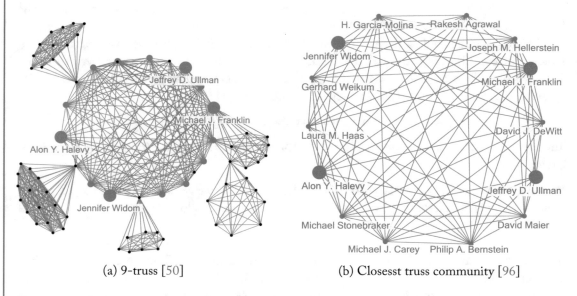

(a) 9-truss [50]   (b) Closesst truss community [96]

Figure 3.25: Community search on DBLP network using query $Q =\{$"Alon Y. Halevy," "Michael J. Franklin," "Jeffrey D. Ullman," "Jennifer Widom."$\}$

3.4   QUERY-BIASED DENSEST COMMUNITY MODEL

Motivation. Most community models find communities that contain a set of query nodes and also maximizes (or minimizes) a goodness metric. However, most models using goodness metrics tend to include irrelevant subgraphs in the detected communities. Such irrelevant subgraphs are referred as "free riders" in the literature. Wu et al. [180] introduce a query-biased node weighting scheme to reduce the free rider effect. The core idea of the proposed solutions is to give large node weights to such free riders far from query nodes, leading to a low density of a community involving these free riders. Finally, the communities with the largest density are returned as answers.

In this section, we discuss the community model based on the densest subgraphs developed by Wu et al. [180]. Given a graph G, the densest subgraph of G achieves the largest average degree among all possible subgraphs of G. Given a set of query nodes, the discovered communities should be densely connected in the local neighborhood of query nodes. In the following, we first use random walk-based proximity values to weight the nodes, with regard to the query nodes. The nodes farther away from the query nodes will have larger weights, which intuitively means that they are less important and thus will be levied more penalty in the calculation of density. After node weighting, we then introduce a new goodness metric of the query-biased density, and show that the query-biased densest subgraph is a target community in the neighborhood of the query node.

3.4.1   NOTIONS AND NOTATIONS

We first define the terms proximity, query-biased node weight, and query-biased density.

Proximity and Query-Biased Node Weight. To measure proximity, we use a variant of the degree normalized penalized hitting probability, which is referred to simply as the penalized hitting probability [180]. Let $w(u, v)$ be the edge weight between u and v, $w(u)$ be the degree of node u, and $w_{\max}$ be the maximum node degree. The transition probability from u to v is $\frac{w(u,v)}{w_{\max}}$, which is normalized by the maximum degree.[2] The penalized hitting probability penalizes the random walk for each additional step. The probability of hitting the query nodes for the first time is used as the proximity value. The penalized hitting probability can be defined as follows.

Definition 3.4.1 (Penalized Hitting Probability) *Given a graph $G(V, E)$ and a set of query nodes Q, the proximity value of $u \in V$ with regard to the query nodes Q is defined as*

$$r(u) = \begin{cases} 1, & \text{if } u \in Q; \\ c \sum_{v \in N_u} \frac{w(u,v)}{w_{\max}} \cdot r(v), & \text{if } u \in V - Q; \end{cases}$$

where c, $(0 < c < 1)$ is a decay factor.

Note that the power iteration method [148] can be used to solve the above linear system in $O(\kappa m)$ time, where κ is the number of iterations.

---

[2]It follows that the weight of an edge can never exceed the maximum node degree in the graph.

Then, the query-biased node weight can be defined as follows.

Definition 3.4.2 (Query-Biased Node Weight) *The query-biased node weight $\pi(u)$ of node u is defined as the reciprocal of the penalized hitting probability $r(u)$, i.e., $\pi(u) = 1/r(u)$.*

From Definitions 3.4.1 and 3.4.2, we always have $0 \leq r(u) \leq 1$ and $\pi(u) \geq 1$. Consider the example of graph and query nodes in Figure 3.26a. The nodes in community A are densely connected to the query node through multiple short paths. Thus, the random walker will have a high probability of hitting the query node starting from any node in A. On the other hand, there are only a few long paths connecting the query node to the nodes not in A. Starting from these nodes, a random walker will have low probabilities to hit the query node, since the probabilities are penalized by the path lengths. Thus, the nodes in A will have higher proximity values than the nodes not in A. The distribution of the node weights, i.e., the reciprocal of the proximity values (i.e., the penalized hitting probabilities), is shown in Figure 3.26b, where a lighter color indicates a higher proximity value.

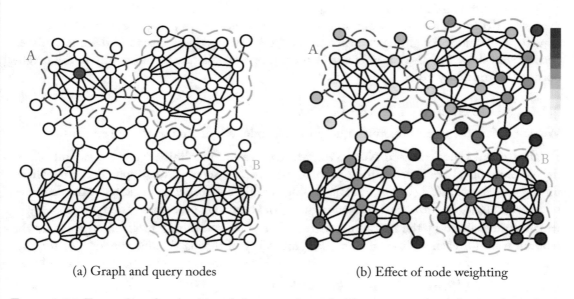

(a) Graph and query nodes   (b) Effect of node weighting

Figure 3.26: Examples of query-biased densest subgraph. The query node is the purple node in Figure 3.26a; There exist three communities A, B, and C. Effect of node weighting with $c = 0.9$ in Figure 3.26b. Darker color represents higher node weight; Subgraph A is the query-biased densest subgraph. Figures are borrowed from [180]. Used with Permission.

Query-Biased Density. Based on the query-biased node weights, the query-biased density is defined as follows.

Definition 3.4.3 (Query-Biased Density) *Given a graph $G(V, E)$ and a set of query nodes Q, the query-biased density of a subgraph G_S of G induced by a set of nodes S is defined as*

$$\rho(S) = \frac{|E(S)|}{\pi(S)},$$

where $|E(S)|$ is the number of edges in the induced subgraph G_S, and $\pi(S) = \sum_{u \in S} \pi(u)$ is the sum of the query-biased weights of nodes in S.

    If the node weights $\pi(u) = 1$, the query-biased density degenerates to the classic density $\frac{e(S)}{|S|}$. In the following, we use the query-biased density and density interchangeably if there is no ambiguity. After node weighting, the densest subgraph is "shifted" to, i.e., is biased toward, the neighborhood of the query nodes. For example, in the graph shown in Figure 3.26a, before node weighting, the densest subgraph is B. Figure 3.26b shows the node weights after applying the node weighting scheme. A darker (lighter) color represents a larger node weight (proximity). After node weighting, subgraph A becomes the query-biased densest subgraph, which is as desired.

3.4.2   PROBLEM FORMULATION

To make sure the discovered communities will be densely connected and close to the neighborhood of the query nodes, we require the query-biased densest subgraph to always (1) contain the query nodes and (2) be connected. As a result, the problem of query-biased densest community search (QDC) can be formulated as follows.

Problem 3.4.1 (Query-Biased Densest Community Search (QDC)) *Given a graph $G(V, E)$ and a set of query nodes Q, find an induced subgraph G_S such that*

(1) $Q \subseteq S$;

(2) $\rho(S)$ *is maximized; and*

(3) G_S *is connected.*

3.4.3   ALGORITHMS

Wu et al. [180] propose an efficient algorithm to solve the QDC problem. Because the problem of QDC is NP-hard [180], it is challenging to develop efficient algorithms for find optimal communities. Wu et al. [180] instead relax the constraint of connectivity and define a variant QDC' of QDC, without the connectivity requirement. The intuition of this relaxation is as follows. If there exists an optimal answer to the QDC' problem and the discovered community is connected, then this community is also an optimal solution to the QDC problem.

Problem 3.4.2 (QDC') *Given a graph $G(V, E)$ and a set of query nodes Q, find an induced subgraph G_S such that*

Algorithm 3.15 The algorithmic framework for the QDC problem

Input: A graph $G = (V, E)$, a set of query nodes Q, a decay factor c.
Output: A query-biased densest subgraph G_S containing Q.

1: Compute the node weights for every node by Definition 3.4.2;
2: Compute the optimal solution G_S of the QDC$'$ problem by Algorithm 3.16;
3: **if** G_S is connected **then**
4:     **return** G_S;
5: **if** G_S contains a connected component G_T containing query nodes Q and at least one non-query node **then**
6:     **return** G_T;
7: Apply the Maximum Adjacency Search in Algorithm 3.17 to find a heuristic solution G_S to QDC;
8: **return** G_S;

---

(1) $Q \subseteq S$ and

(2) $\rho(S)$ is maximized.

Algorithmic Framework. The overall algorithm for the QDC problem is outlined in Algorithm 3.15. It first computes the optimal solution G_S to QDC$'$ using Algorithm 3.16 (line 2). If G_S is connected, G_S is also the optimal solution to QDC (lines 3–4) and is returned as the output. However, if G_S is disconnected but there exists a connected subgraph G_T of G_S such that G_T contains all query nodes of Q and at least one non-query node, this connected subgraph G_T is returned as an approximate solution to QDC (lines 5–6). Otherwise, we apply another heuristic algorithm to find a solution G_S to QDC using Algorithm 3.17 (lines 7–8). In the following, we present the details of Algorithms 3.16 and 3.17.

Algorithm for the QDC$'$ problem. Wu et al. [180] develop an exact polynomial time algorithm for the QDC$'$ problem, outlined in Algorithm 3.16. This algorithm uses a new graph operation called *subgraph contraction*, defined as follows.

Definition 3.4.4 (Subgraph Contraction) *Given a graph $G(V, E)$ and a set of nodes Q, the operation of contracting a subgraph G_Q of G into a supernode q results in a new graph $G'(V', E')$, where the node set $V' = (V - Q) \cup \{q\}$ and the weight of supernode q as $r(q) = \sum_{v \in Q} r(v)$. The edge set E' is constructed as follows.*

(1) Keep edge (u, v) and its weight $w(u, v)$ if $(u, v) \in E$ and $u \notin Q, v \notin Q$.

(2) Add an edge (u, q) with weight $w(u, q) = \sum_{v \in Q} w(u, v)$, if $u \notin Q$.

(3) Add a self-loop edge (q, q) with weight $w(q, q) = \sum_{v,u \in Q} w(u, v)$, if $w(q, q) > 0$.

The operation of subgraph contraction preserves the density of graph G and G'. That is, for any $S \subset V - Q$, subgraphs $G_{Q \cup S}$ and $G'_{\{q\} \cup S}$ have the same density, so do subgraphs G_S and G'_S. Note that $G_{Q \cup S}$ is the induced subgraph of G by vertex set $S \cup Q$. $G'_{q \cup S}$ is the induced

Algorithm 3.16 The algorithm for the QDC′ problem

Input: A graph $G = (V, E)$, a set of query nodes Q, node weights π.
Output: A query-biased densest subgraph G_S containing Q.

1: $i \leftarrow 0$; $Q_0 \leftarrow Q$; $S \leftarrow \varnothing$;
2: $G_0 \leftarrow$ contract G_{Q_0} into a supernode q_0;
3: **while true do**
4:     Compute the densest subgraph G_{i_S} using the parametric maximum flow algorithm [149];
5:     **if** $q_i \in S$ **then**
6:         $S^* \leftarrow S - \{q_i\} \cup Q_i$;
7:         **break**;
8:     $Q_{i+1} \leftarrow S \cup Q_i$;
9:     $G_{i+1} \leftarrow$ contract $G_{Q_{i+1}}$ into q_{i+1};
10:    $i \leftarrow i + 1$;
11: **return** G_{S^*};

---

subgraph of contraction graph G' by vertex set $q \cup S$, which also corresponds to the subgraph $G_{Q \cup S}$ in G.

Example 3.4.1 *Figure 3.27 shows an example of subgraph contraction [180]. In Figure 3.27a, each node and edge have the same unit weight in graph G. Note that the purple node in G is a query node. The densest subgraph of G is a 6-clique enclosed by the green curve, which has a density of 2.5. However, the densest subgraph does not include the query node, indicating it cannot be the answer of the QDC problem. We contract the densest subgraph along with the purple node into a supernode in the new graph G′ in Figure 3.27b. The densest subgraph of G′, enclosed by the purple curve, has a density of 2.38. This densest subgraph contains the supernode, indicating that it also contains the query node. Therefore, this densest subgraph is the optimal answer, which is also highlighted using the purple curve in Figure 3.27a.*

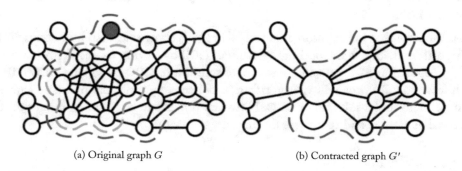

(a) Original graph G (b) Contracted graph G'

Figure 3.27: An example of subgraph contraction [180]. Used with Permission.

The procedure is outlined in Algorithm 3.16. Initially, the subgraph induced by the query nodes is contracted into a supernode (lines 1–2). In each iteration in lines 3–5, we find the densest subgraph G_{iS} in G_i using the classical parametric maximum flow algorithm [149]. If the subgraph G_{i_S} contains the supernode q_i, G_{S^*} where the vertex set $S^* \leftarrow S - \{q_i\} \cup Q_i$, it is an optimal solution of the QDC' problem and returned. Otherwise, it adds the set S into Q_i, which increases the density of the current subgraph G_{Q_i}. And then, it contracts $G_{S \cup Q_i}$ into a supernode and repeats this process until the densest subgraph G_{i_S} contains the supernode q_i.

Complexity Analysis of Algorithm 3.16. Algorithm 3.16 runs in $O(\tau t)$ time, where τ is the number of iterations and t is the running time of solving the densest subgraph problem using maximum parametric flow [149]. Since at least one node is newly contracted into a supernode in each iteration, we have $\tau \leq n$ [180].

In the following, we describe the heuristic algorithm developed by Wu et al. [180] for the QDC problem. This is used when solving QDC' does not give the desired solution.

Maximum Adjacency Search. Algorithm 3.17 presents the algorithm of maximum adjacent search, that is, to find a heuristic solution G_S to QDC. First, the algorithm uses Mehlhorn's algorithm [131] to compute the Steiner tree connecting all the given query vertices (line 1). As a result, the query vertices become connected together and this tree is used as the initial subgraph. When computing the Steiner tree, the edge weight is set to the reciprocal of the original edge weight. Next, the algorithm starts a local search process (lines 2–5). In each iteration, it finds a vertex u with the maximum adjacency value, i.e., $u \leftarrow \arg\max_{v \in V - S_i} w(\{v\}, S_i)/\pi(v)$. Finally, the intermediate subgraph with the maximum density during the local search process is returned as the query-biased densest subgraph. A parameter L is set to control the search space. When the vertex size of S_i is larger than L, the algorithm will terminate.

Complexity Analysis of Algorithm 3.17. The algorithm runs for at most L iterations. Let d_{avg} be the average degree of nodes. Then, for each iteration, it takes $O(i \cdot d_{avg})$ time to find a node with the maximum adjacency value (line 4 of Algorithm 3.17). As a result, the time complexity of the local search process is $O(\sum_{i=0}^{L}(i \cdot d_{avg})) \subseteq O(L^2 d_{avg})$. Finding the Steiner tree takes $O(m + n \log n)$ time [131].

Remarks. We note that the experimental results in [180] show that with more than 90% probability, Algorithm 3.15 gets the optimal solution of QDC by solving QDC'. With more than 5% probability, Algorithm 3.15 gets an approximate solution of QDC by solving QDC'. Therefore, only with less than 5% probability, Algorithm 3.15 needs to apply the heuristic algorithm in Algorithm 3.17 to find a solution of QDC. However, it needs to be borne in mind that this has no theoretical guarantee and that these findings are empirical.

3.5   SUMMARY

In this section, we summarize the various community models over simple graphs $G(V, E)$ that were discussed in this chapter. These community models are based on different dense subgraph definitions, such as clique [139], quasi-clique [54], densest subgraph [180], k-core [18, 55, 122, 157], and k-truss [89, 96]. In the following, we compare these models using metrics w.r.t. the

Algorithm 3.17 Maximum Adjacency Search Algorithm

Input: A graph $G = (V, E)$, a set of query nodes Q, node weights π, a parameter L.
Output: A query-biased densest subgraph G_S containing Q.

1: Compute the Steiner tree T connecting Q using the Mehlhorn's algorithm [131];
2: $S_0 \leftarrow$ the vertex set $V(T)$; $i \leftarrow 0$;
3: **while** $|S_i| \leq L$ **do**
4:     $u \leftarrow \arg\max_{v \in V - S_i} w(\{v\}, S_i)/\pi(v)$;
5:     $S_{i+1} \leftarrow S_i \cup \{u\}$;
6:     $i \leftarrow i + 1$;
7: $x \leftarrow \arg\max_i \rho(S_i)$; $S^* \leftarrow S_i$;
8: **return** G_{S^*};

following aspects: (i) consideration of query vertices, (ii) cohesive structure, (iii) index structure, (iv) query processing efficiency, and (v) quality of approximation. Table 3.2 shows a comparison of representative works on densely connected community search.

Query Vertices. Cui et al. [54] study the problem of online search of overlapping communities given a single query vertex, and design the α-adjacency γ-quasi-k-clique model. Huang et

Table 3.2: A comparison of representative works on cohesive community search. Here, "-" means that there exists no index for community search. Heuristic algorithms have non-approximate answers.

Method	Query Nodes	Cohesive Subgraph	Index Structure	Query Processing Efficiency	Quality Approximation
(α, γ)-OCS [54]	Single	α-adjacency-γ-quasi-k-clique	-	NP-hard	Exact
Global-Core [157]	Multiple	k-core	-	$O(n + m)$	Exact
Constrained-Core [157]	Multiple	k-core	-	NP-hard	Non-approximate
Local-Core [55]	Single	k-core	-	$O(n + m)$	Exact
Minimum-Core [18]	Multiple	k-core	Shell-Index	NP-hard	Non-approximate
k-Influential [122]	Multiple	k-core	ICP-Index	$O(|Ans|)$	Exact
Triangle-Connected-Truss [89]	Single	k-truss	TCP-Index	$O(|Ans|)$	Exact
Closest-Truss [96]	Multiple	k-truss	Truss-Index	NP-hard	2-approximation
QDC [180]	Multiple	Densest-subgraph	-	NP-hard	Non-guarantee-approximate

al. [89] propose a k-truss community model based on triangle connectivity to find all overlapping communities of a given query vertex. They ignore the diameter of the resulting community. Cui et al. [55] find a k-core community for a query vertex using local search. In addition, the influential community model [122] finds top-r communities with the highest influence scores over the entire graph; no query vertices are considered. Extending any of the above models from one (or zero) query vertex to multiple query vertices raises interesting challenges. The works [157], [18], [96], and [180] support community search with multiple query vertices.

Cohesive Structure. (α, γ)-OCS [54] is developed based on the α-adjacency-γ-quasi-k-clique. There exist several different models based on k-core subgraph, e.g., [157], [55], [18], and [122]. Sozio et al. [157] propose a k-core-based community model, called the Cocktail Party model, with distance and size constraints. The Triangle-Connected-Truss community model [89] and Closest-Truss community model [96] are based on the connected k-truss. Conceptually, k-truss is a more cohesive definition than k-core, as k-truss is based on triangles, where each "friendship" is endorsed by multiple common "friends," whereas k-core simply considers the vertex degree [165]. Most recently, Wu et al. [180] study the query-biased densest connected subgraph (QDC) problem for avoiding subgraphs irrelevant to query vertices in the community found. While QDC [180] is also defined based on a connected graph containing the query vertices similarly to Closest-Truss, it optimizes a fundamentally different function called query-biased edge density, which is calculated as the overall edge weight averaged over the weight of vertices in a community.

Index Structure and Query Processing Efficiency. Several studies [18, 89, 96, 122] propose indexes to speed up the query processing for their community search models. Barbieri et al. [18] design Shell-Index to quickly find a maximal connected k-core, and then solve the NP-hard problem of finding the minimum-sized community containing query nodes. Similarly, [122] proposes ICP-Index to find k-Influential communities in the optimal time cost of $O(|Ans|)$, where $|Ans|$ is the size of the answer community. Both Shell-Index and ICP-Index are designed for core-based community models. On the other hand, Huang et al. [89] design an elegant tree structure of TCP-Index to find the truss-based communities in the optimal time complexity of $O(|Ans|)$. The simple index of Truss-Index is used in [96] for finding a maximal connected k-truss containing all query nodes with the largest number of k, aiming at speeding up the query processing of approximation algorithms, due to NP-hardness of the problem. Other community models are not equipped with indexes, including (α, γ)-OCS [54], Global-Core [157], Constrained-Core [157], Local-Core [55], and QDC [180]. Among these methods without using indexes, Global-Core [157] and Local-Core [55] can find the optimal solution in time complexity of $O(n + m)$, whereas the other methods consider the NP-hard problems without proposing polynomial-time algorithms achieving some approximation guarantee.

Quality of Approximation. The problems proposed in (α, γ)-OCS [54], Constrained-Core [157], Minimum-Core [18], and QDC [180] are NP-hard to compute, and do not admit approximations without further assumptions. [180] gives an approximation solution to QDC by relaxing the problem. Unfortunately, as shown in [180], this could fail in real applications, for two reasons. First, the algorithm may find a solution consisting of several connected components with query vertices split between them. Second, the approximation factor can be large, which can deteriorate further with a larger number of query vertices. In contrast, for Closest-Truss, there is an efficient 2-approximation algorithm for finding the closest truss community containing any set of query vertices.

CHAPTER 4

Attributed Community Search

In Chapter 3, we give an overview of community search in simple graphs, which only capture the structural characteristics of networks. Community search on a simple graph aims to find densely connected communities containing all query nodes. In applications such as analysis of protein protein interaction (PPI) networks, citation graphs, and collaboration networks, nodes tend to have attributes. Most simple structural community search algorithms ignore these attributes and cannot find communities with good cohesion w.r.t. their node attributes.

This chapter focuses on attributed community search in attributed networks, where nodes are associated with attributes or predicates. Many real networks contain attributes in nodes, e.g., in social networks, a person has attributes including name, interests, skills, etc. We consider an undirected, unweighted simple graph $G = (V, E)$ with $n = |V(G)|$ nodes and $m = |E(G)|$ edges. W.l.o.g. we assume that the graphs we consider are connected. Note that this implies that $m \geq n - 1$. We consider attributed graphs and denote the set of all attributes in a graph by $\mathcal{A}$. Each node $v \in V$ contains a set of zero or more attributes, denoted $\mathsf{attr}(v) \subseteq \mathcal{A}$. The multiset union of attributes of all nodes in G is denoted $\mathsf{attr}(V)$. Note that $|\mathsf{attr}(V)| = \sum_{v \in V} |\mathsf{attr}(v)|$. For an attribute $w \in \mathcal{A}$, we use $V_w \subseteq V$ to denote the set of nodes having attribute w, i.e., $V_w = \{v \in V \mid w \in \mathsf{attr}(v)\}$. The problem of attributed community search is generally defined as follows. Given a set of query nodes and query attributes, the attributed community search is to find the communities containing the query nodes with a cohesive structure and sharing homogeneous query attributes. We introduce two models for attributed community search, based on two major models for dense subgraphs—k-core [65] and k-truss [93].

4.1 INTRODUCTION

In this section, we first introduce attributed networks and attributed communities and illustrate them with examples. Then, we review the approaches for cohesive community search discussed in Chapter 3 and point out their limitations for attributed community search. Finally, we identify the commonly accepted desiderata of a good attributed community.

4.1.1 ATTRIBUTED NETWORKS

In real-life applications, graphs are used to represent different types of entities. These entities often have properties which are important for making sense of communities over the graphs. For example, authors in collaboration networks have areas of expertise; sensors in sensor networks have the parameters they measure (e.g., temperature, pressure, etc.); proteins in protein

protein interaction (PPI) networks have molecular functions, biological processes, and cellular components as properties. Such networks can be modeled using *attributed graphs* [198] where attributes associated with nodes capture their properties. Figure 4.1 shows an example of a collaboration network. The nodes $q_i, v_j, \ldots$ represent authors. Node attributes (e.g., e.g., "DB," "DM," "ML," "IR") represent authors' topics of expertise (e.g., "Database," "Data Mining," "Machine Learning," "Information Retrieval"). In finding communities (with or without query nodes) over attributed graphs, we might want to ensure that the nodes in the discovered communities have homogeneous attributes. For instance, in the application of PPI networks, it has been found that communities with homogeneous attributes among nodes more accurately predict protein complexes [85]. Furthermore, we might wish to query, not just using query nodes, but also using query attributes. To illustrate, consider searching for communities in the network of Figure 4.1 with query nodes $\{q_1, q_2\}$. Based on structure alone, the subgraph H shown in Figure 4.1 is a good candidate answer for this search, as it is densely connected. However, attributes of the authors in this community are not homogeneous: the community is a mix of authors working in different topics—"DB," "DM," "IR," and "ML."

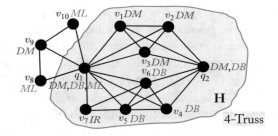

Figure 4.1: An example attributed graph G.

Real-world Examples. We use three real-world examples for illustrating the applications of attributed community search.

1. As discussed above, in collaboration networks, authors typically have areas of expertise or keywords describing research interests. Attributed community search aims at finding a densely-connected collaboration community in which attributes of the authors are homogeneous. A detailed case study of "Jiawei Han" on DBLP collaboration network using different sets of query attributes (e.g., {analysis, mine, data, information, network} and {mine, data, pattern, database}) for community search can be found in Section 4.4.1.

2. In the application of PPI networks, proteins have molecular functions, biological processes, and cellular components as properties. It has been found that communities with homogeneous attributes among nodes more accurately predict protein complexes [85]. The task of attributed community search has been successfully applied to identify protein complexes

in the yeast Saccharomyces cerevisiae, from the BioGRID database [85]. A detailed case study of "transcription factor TFIIIC complex" discovery can be found in Section 4.4.2.

3. Attributed community search can also be applied to social circle discovery in online social networks (e.g., Facebook [93]), where users have various kinds of attributes, e.g., education, location(s), hobbies, etc.

4.1.2 LIMITATIONS OF COHESIVE COMMUNITY SEARCH WITHOUT QUERY ATTRIBUTES

Initial community search methods, developed mainly with graph structure in mind, include those based on k-core [55, 122, 157], k-truss [96], and α-adjacency-γ-quasi-k-clique community model [54] (see Chapter 3 for a comprehensive treatment). Recall that a k-core [122] is a subgraph in which each node has at least k neighbors within the subgraph. A k-truss [96] is a subgraph in which each edge is contained in at least $(k - 2)$ triangles within the subgraph. The α-adjacency-γ-quasi-k-clique community model [54] allows two γ-quasi-k-cliques overlapping in α nodes to be merged into one community. In Figure 4.1, for $k = 4$, $\gamma = 1.0$, and $\alpha = 3$, and query nodes $Q = \{q_1, q_2\}$, all these community models will report H as the top answer and are thus unsatisfactory.

The subgraph H_1 obtained from H by removing node v_7 with unique attribute {"IR"}, is a more homogeneous community than H and also densely connected (see Figure 4.2a). Clearly, it is a better answer than H. In general, communities found by most previous community search methods can be hard to interpret owing to the heterogeneity of node attributes. Furthermore, the communities reported could contain smaller dense subgraphs with more homogeneity in attributes, which are missed by most previous methods. Consider now querying the graph of Figure 4.1 with query nodes $\{q_1, q_2\}$ *and* attributes (i.e., keywords) {"DB," "DM"}. We would expect this search to return subgraph H_1 (Figure 4.2a), since all community nodes have the related attributes either "DB" or "DM" in H_1. On the other hand, for the same query nodes, if we search with attribute {"DB"} (resp., {"DM"}), we expect the subgraph H_2 (resp., H_3) to be returned as the answer (Figure 4.2b and c). Both H_2 and H_3 are dense subgraphs where all authors share a common topic ("DB" or "DM"). This shows that using query attributes can help with community search, by distinguishing between communities that are homogeneous w.r.t. different (sets of) attributes.

Given a query consisting of nodes and attributes (keywords), a natural question is whether we can filter out nodes not having those attributes and then run a conventional community search method on the filtered graph. To see how well this may work, consider querying the graph in Figure 4.1 with query node q_1 and query attribute {"ML"}. Filtering out nodes without attribute {"ML"} and applying community search yields the chain consisting of v_{10}, q_1, v_8, which is not densely connected. On the other hand, the subgraph induced by $\{q_1, v_8, v_9, v_{10}\}$ is a 3-truss (see Figure 4.2d). Even though it includes one node without {"ML"}, it is more densely connected than the chain above and is a better answer than the chain as it brings out denser collaboration

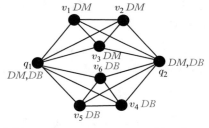

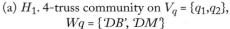

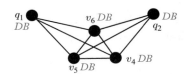

(a) H_1. 4-truss community on $V_q = \{q_1, q_2\}$, $Wq = \{\text{'}DB\text{'}, \text{'}DM\text{'}\}$

(b) H_2. 4-truss community on $V_q = \{q_1, q_2\}$, $Wq = \{\text{'}DB\text{'}\}$

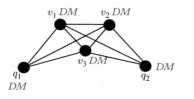

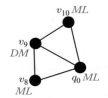

(c) H_3. 4-truss community on $V_q = \{q_1, q_2\}$, $Wq = \{\text{'}DM\text{'}\}$

(d) H_4. 3-truss community on $V_q = \{q_1\}$, $Wq = \{\text{'}ML\text{'}\}$

Figure 4.2: Attribute Communities for queries on different query nodes V_q and query attributes W_q.

structure among the authors in the community. Thus, a simple filtering-based approach will not work: as some denser subgraphs may be less homogeneous in their node attributes than some sparser ones and a careful balance has to be struck between density and attribute homogeneity.

4.1.3   DESIDERATA OF GOOD ATTRIBUTED COMMUNITIES

Given a query $Q = (V_q, W_q)$ with a set of query nodes $V_q \subseteq V$ and a set of query attributes W_q, the attributed community search (ACS) problem is to find a subgraph $H \subseteq G$ containing all query nodes V_q, where the nodes are densely connected, cover as many query attributes in W_q as possible, and share many attributes. Before formalizing the problem, we first identify the commonly accepted desiderata of a good attributed community.

Criteria of a good attributed community: Given a graph $G(V, E)$ and an ACS query $Q = (V_q, W_q)$, an attributed community is a connected subgraph $H = (V(H), E(H)) \subseteq G$ that satisfies the following.

1. (Participation) H contains all query nodes as $V_q \subseteq V(H)$.

2. (Cohesiveness) The cohesiveness measure of H, as measured by a cohesiveness function $\text{den}(H)$, is high.

3. (Attribute Coverage and Correlation) The coverage and correlation of query attributes W_q among the nodes of H, as measured by an attribute score function $f(H, W_q)$, is high.

4. (Communication Cost) The aggregate distance between nodes of H, as measured by a communication cost function $com(H)$, is low.

The participation condition is straightforward. The cohesiveness condition is also straightforward since communities are supposed to be densely connected subgraphs. One can use any notion of dense subgraph previously studied, such as k-core and k-truss. The third condition captures the intuition that the more query attributes covered by H, the higher $f(H, W_q)$; also, the more attributes shared by the nodes of H, the higher $f(H, W_q)$. This motivates the need for designing functions $f(\cdot, \cdot)$ satisfying this property. Finally, keeping the communication cost low helps avoid irrelevant nodes in a community. This is related to the so-called free rider effect, studied in [96, 180] (also see Chapter 3). Intuitively, the closer the community nodes to query nodes, subject to all other conditions, the more relevant they are likely to be to the query. Note that sometimes a node that does not contain query attributes may still act as a "bridge" between other nodes that do, and help improve the density. A general remark is that other than the first condition, for conditions 2–4, we may either optimize a suitable metric or constrain the metric to be above a threshold (below a threshold for Condition 4).

4.2   K-CORE-BASED ATTRIBUTE COMMUNITY MODEL

In this section, we introduce a k-core-based attributed community model proposed by Fang et al. [65]. This model addresses the problem of finding a densely connected community with strictly homogeneous attributes, by focusing the discussion on conditions 2 and 3 of a good attributed community.

4.2.1   PROBLEM FORMULATION

We begin with the notion of connected k-cores.

Connected K-Cores. Recall that k-core is a subgraph defined on the minimum degree, which is one of the most common structure-cohesiveness metrics [18, 55, 122, 157]. The definition of a connected k-core (Definition 2.4.3) requires that every vertex in this connected subgraph has a degree of k or more.

Common Attributes. The shared attributes naturally reveal the common features among vertices, e.g., the common interests of users in a social network. These shared attributes can be used to explain how a community is formed.

Definition 4.2.1 (Common Attributes) *Given a set of vertices S, the set of common attributes is defined as a set of attributes shared by every vertex in S, i.e., $CA(S) = \cap_{v \in S} attr(v)$.*

Based on the definitions of connected k-cores and common attributes, the problem of k-core-based attributed community search can be formulated as follows.

Problem 4.2.1 (ACC) *Given a graph $G(V, E)$, a number k, a query vertex q, and a set of query attributes $W_q \subseteq$ attr(q), the problem of attributed core community (ACC) search is to find a set $\mathcal{H}$ of subgraphs, such that $\forall H \in \mathcal{H}$, H satisfies the following conditions.*

1. *(Structural Cohesiveness) H is a connected k-core containing q.*

2. *(Attributed Cohesiveness) The size of common query attributes CQA(H, W_q) is the largest, where* $CQA(H, W_q) = CA(V(H)) \cap W_q = \cap_{v \in V(H)}(\text{attr}(v) \cap W_q)$.

$H \in \mathcal{H}$ is called the attributed core community (ACC for short) of query vertex q, and CQA(H, W_q) the ACC-label of H. The two conditions in the ACC model are analyzed as follows. First, the condition of structural cohesiveness enforces the discovery of communities containing the given vertex q. Moreover, the second condition of attributed cohesiveness enables the retrieval of communities in which vertices have common query attributes of W_q. The model uses W_q to impose the semantics on the generated community. By default, if $W_q = \text{attr}(q)$, it means that the discovered communities $\mathcal{H}$ should have attributes common to those associated with q. If $W_q \subset \text{attr}(q)$, it means that the user is interested in communities $\mathcal{H}$ that are related to some (but not all) of the attributes of q.

Example 4.2.1 *Consider the graph G in Figure 4.3, if the query vertex $q = v_7$, query attributes $W_q = \{\text{"DM," "DB"}\}$, and number $k = 3$, the answer of ACC is shown in Figure 4.4a with the ACC-label $\{\text{"DB"}\}$, indicating that all vertices share the attribute "DB."*

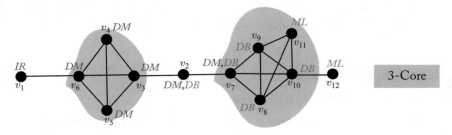

Figure 4.3: An example graph G for the attributed core community model.

Therefore, the objective function of maximizing CQA(H, W_q) would return the community containing the most related vertices, in terms of the number of common query attributes. Let us use Figure 4.4b to explain why this objective function is important. Consider the same query ($q = v_7$, $W_q = \{\text{"DM," "DB"}\}$, and $k = 3$) for graph G in Figure 4.3, *without* the condition of attribute coverage and correlation. Then, the community can be obtained shown in Figure 4.4b, in which vertices share no attributes.

Remarks. Note that, if there exists no ACC whose vertices share at least one common query attribute, it can instead return the subgraphs satisfying just the first condition of Structural

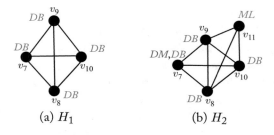

(a) H_1 (b) H_2

Figure 4.4: Attributed core community H_1 for the query vertex $q = v_7$ and query attributes $W_q = \{\text{"DM," "DB"}\}$.

Cohesiveness, as answers. In addition, there are other candidates for structural cohesiveness (e.g., k-truss, k-clique) and attributed coverage and correlation (e.g., Jaccard similarity, string edit distance, proximity, etc.). The model can be extended to support these criteria. In addition, the current formulation of the ACC model supports a single query node. A natural extension of ACC model can support multiple query nodes Q by requiring the input query attributes $W_q \subseteq \{\cap_{q \in Q} \text{attr}(q)\}$, due to the strict constraint of homogeneous attributes in the ACC model.

4.2.2 BASIC QUERY PROCESSING ALGORITHM

Given a query vertex q, a straightforward method for processing ACC queries consists of three steps. First, the algorithm enumerates all non-empty subsets of the query attributes W_q, say $S_0, S_1, S_2, \ldots, S_{2^l-1}$, where l is the number of query attributes ($l = |W_q|$). Then, for each subset S_i, it checks the existence of a k-core H where each vertex has attributes S_i. Finally, the algorithm generates all subgraphs having the most shared attributes among all such possible H. An obvious drawback of this straightforward method is the need to enumerate $2^l - 1$ possible subsets of query attributes. For large values of l, this method can be impractical. To realize efficient processing of ACC queries, Fang et al. [65] make use of a novel index-based method, which will be discussed next.

4.2.3 CLTREE-INDEX-BASED QUERY PROCESSING ALGORITHMS

The major limitation of the basic algorithm is that it needs to repeat two key steps—search the connected k-core and perform attribute filtering. This makes community search using the basic algorithm inefficient. To speed up query processing, Fang et al. [65] propose a novel index that organizes both k-cores and attributes into a tree structure, called CLTree-Index (Core Label Tree). Based on CLTree-Index, efficient algorithms are developed for answering ACC queries. We first introduce the index and then present a method for constructing the index.

CLTree-Index

Index Structure. At a high level, CLTree-Index is built upon the Shell-Index, discussed previously (see Section 3.2.2). Notice that the ACC model needs to find a connected k-core, thus CLTree-Index also makes use of the key property of k-cores, that a connected $(k + 1)$-core is contained in a k-core. This renders the structure of CLTree-Index very similar to the Shell-Index, except for the index of vertex attribute list. Specifically, the CLTree-Index of an attributed graph G is a tree-shaped data structure where each node S_i^k contains a set of vertices of G with core number k such that the subtree of T rooted at S_i^k is a maximal connected k-core of G, just as in a Shell-Index. In the following, we describe the structure (four elements) of each tree node in CLTree-Index.

1. Vertex-Set S_i^k: a set of graph vertices whose core numbers are k, i.e., $S_i^k \subseteq \Psi(k)$.

2. Level-Num k: the level number of a tree node of T, showing the core number of graph vertices in S_i^k.

3. Child-List: each tree node is associated with a list of child nodes at level k' where $k' > k$.

4. Inverted-List: a list of $< key, value >$ pairs, where the key is an attribute associated with vertices of G and the value is the list of vertices of G containing the key.

Example 4.2.2 *Figure 4.5 shows the* CLTree-Index *for graph G in Figure 4.3 (compare with the* Shell-Index *for the same graph in Figure 3.11). The index consists of four tree nodes at three levels. At level 2, there exists one tree node S_1^2 consisting of one vertex set $\{v_2\}$, indicating v_2 belongs to the 2-core. The corresponding attribute inverted-list shows that v_2 has two attributes of "DB" and "DM." In addition, S_1^2 has two child nodes S_1^3 and S_2^3 at level 3. The subtree of T rooted at S_1^2 represents a connected 2-core, which is an induced subgraph of G formed by $S_1^2 \cup S_1^3 \cup S_2^3$ $= \{v_2, v_3, v_4, v_5, v_6, v_7, v_8, v_9, v_{10}, v_{11}\}$, shown in Figure 4.3.*

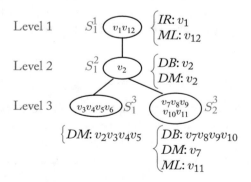

Figure 4.5: The CLTree-Index for graph G in Figure 4.3.

Algorithm 4.18 CLTree-Index Construction

Input: An attributed graph $G = (V, E)$.
Output: CLTree-Index of G.

1: Apply the Shell-Index construction on G using Algorithm 2.1;
2: Let T be Shell-Index of G;
3: **for** each tree node S in T **do**
4:    Generate attribute inverted-lists for S using $\{attr(v) : v \in S\}$;
5: **return** T as CLTree-Index of G;

CLTree-Index **Construction**

An algorithm for CLTree-Index construction is outlined in Algorithm 4.18. The algorithm applies Shell-Index construction (see Algorithm 2.1) on G to build the CLTree-Index, level by level in a bottom–up manner (lines 1–2). Specifically, tree nodes corresponding to larger core numbers are created prior to those with smaller core numbers. Based on the obtained Shell-Index T, the algorithm generates attribute inverted-lists for each tree node S in T, making use of the attribute sets of all vertices, i.e., $\{attr(v) : v \in S\}$. Finally, the algorithm returns the Shell-Index T.

Complexity analysis. The time complexity of Shell-Index construction is $O(\alpha(m) \times m)$, where m is the number of edges and $\alpha(m)$ is the inverse Ackermann function. It is well known that $\alpha(m)$ grows extremely slowly in m. Indeed, at most $\alpha^{-1}(4)$ should suffice for any conceivably large application. In addition, the time complexity of generating all attribute inverted-lists is $O(\sum_{v \in V} attr(v)) \subseteq O(attr(V))$, since the attributes of each vertex are scanned just once. Overall, the time complexity of Algorithm 4.18 can be regarded as $O(m + |attr(V)|)$. The space cost of CLTree-Index is $O(m + |attr(V)|)$, which has the same complexity as the size of the attributed graph G.

ACC-dec **Algorithm**

In this section, we present the algorithm for querying ACC based on the CLTreeindex, called ACC-dec. The general idea of ACC-dec is to enumerate the candidate attribute sets S from the largest size to the smallest, as the name of the algorithm suggests. The algorithm terminates once it finds a qualified connected k-core where each vertex has the same set of attributes S. There exist other incremental algorithms which proceed by successively examining candidate attribute sets of increasing size. Experiments show that the decremental algorithm discussed above is the most efficient in practice [65]. In this subsection, we sometimes use "candidate sets" to mean "candidate attribute sets."

The ACC-dec algorithm is outlined in Algorithm 4.19. It mainly consists of two phrases: (1) generation of candidate attribute sets and (2) verification of candidate attribute sets.

Generation of candidate attribute sets. ACC-dec exploits the following key observation. For an attribute set $S \subseteq W_q$ to be qualified, there must be at least k neighbors of q, say $X \subseteq N(q)$, $|X| = k$, that have attributes S, i.e., $\forall v \in X$, $S \subseteq$ attr(v). This is because for ACC H where $S = $ CQA(H, W_q), every vertex in H has degree at least k. This observation indicates that all candidate attribute sets can be directly generated based on the query attributes W_q and the attributes of vertices $N(q)$, without considering other vertices.

Specifically, given query attributes W_q and q's neighbors $N(q)$, it has an attribute database $\mathcal{D} = \{$attr$(v) \cap W_q : v \in N(q)\}$ (line 1 of Algorithm 4.19). The support of an attribute set $S \subseteq W_q$ is defined as the number of vertices whose attribute sets contain S in D, i.e., support$_D(S) = |\{v \in N(q) : S \subseteq attr(v)\}|$. The problem of generating all candidate attribute sets reduces to finding all subsets $S \subseteq W_q$ with support no less than k. For each such attribute set S, there exist at least k vertices containing the attributes S. A well-known frequent pattern mining algorithms (e.g., Apriori [77] and FP-Growth [78]) can be applied to find the frequent attribute sets with support no less than k. Suppose the largest cardinality of candidate sets is h. Categorizing the candidate sets by their cardinality, the algorithm can enumerate them as $\{\mathcal{S}_1, \ldots, \mathcal{S}_h\}$, where $\mathcal{S}_i = \{S : $ support$_D(S) \geq k, |S| = i\}$ and $1 \leq i \leq h$ (line 2 of Algorithm 4.19).

Example 4.2.3 *Consider an example query vertex q and its neighbors $N(q) = \{u_1, u_2, u_3, u_4, u_5, u_6\}$ in Figure 4.6a. The attributes of each vertex are also listed. Let the query attributes be $W_q = \{$"IR," "DM," "DB," "ML"$\}$, which is the same as the attribute set of q: attr $= \{$"IR," "DM," "DB," "ML"$\}$. Assume that the parameter $k = 3$; it needs to generate candidate attribute sets that are shared by at least 3 vertices of $N(q)$. Vertices u_1, u_4, and u_5 share three attributes, specifically $\mathcal{S}_3 = \{\{$"DM," "DB," "ML"$\}\}$, thus, this attribute set in $\mathcal{S}_3$ is a qualified candidate set with support 3, as shown in Figure 4.6b. Similarly, it can verify the qualified candidate sets in $\mathcal{S}_1$ and $\mathcal{S}_2$.*

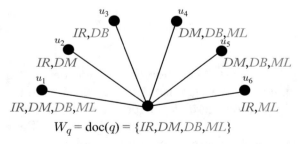

	$k = 3$
$\mathcal{S}_1$	$\{IR\}, \{DM\}, \{DB\}, \{ML\},$
$\mathcal{S}_2$	$\{DM,DB\}, \{DM,ML\}, \{DB,ML\},$
$\mathcal{S}_3$	$\{DM,DB,ML\},$

(a) Query vertex q and q's neighbors $N(q)$ (b) Candidate attributes sets

Figure 4.6: An example of candidate attribute sets generation. Here, query attributes $W_q = \{$"IR," "DM," "DB," "ML"$\}$ and parameter $k = 3$.

Algorithm 4.19 ACC-dec
___
Input: Graph $G = (V, E)$, query vertex q, query attributes W_q, number k.
Output: $\mathcal{H}$.

1: Create an attribute database $\mathcal{D} = \{\text{attr}(v) \cap W_q : v \in N(q)\}$ using W_q and $N(q)$.
2: Generate all candidate attribute sets from D as $\{\mathcal{S}_1, \ldots, \mathcal{S}_h\}$, where $\mathcal{S}_i = \{S : \text{support}_{\mathcal{D}}(S) \geq k, |S| = i\}$.
3: Find a subtree root node r_k in CLTree-Index.
4: Let H denotes the connected k-core, which is represented by the subtree rooted by r_k.
5: Create $V_1, V_2, \ldots, V_{h'}$ in the subtree rooted by r_k.
6: $l \leftarrow h; \mathcal{H} \leftarrow \emptyset$.
7: Let $\hat{V} \leftarrow V_h \cup \ldots \cup V_{h'}$.
8: **while** $l \geq 1$ **do**
9:     **for** $S \in \mathcal{S}_l$ **do**
10:         Find ACC H_S with common attributes S in H.
11:         **if** H_S exists **then**
12:             $\mathcal{H} \leftarrow \mathcal{H} \cup \{H_S\}$.
13:     **if** $\mathcal{H} \neq \emptyset$ **then**
14:         **return** $\mathcal{H}$.
15:     $l \leftarrow l - 1; \hat{V} \leftarrow \hat{V} \cup V_l$.
16: **return** $\mathcal{H}$.
___

Verification of candidate attribute sets. It is well known that the support satisfies the property of *anti-monotonicity*: given attribute sets $S_1 \subseteq S_2$, the number of vertices having attributes S_2 is no more than that of S_1. This implies S_2 can be verified faster than S_1. It motivates the rationale of Algorithm ACC-dec for examining larger candidate attribute sets before smaller ones (lines 3–15).

To find a maximal connected k-core containing q, the algorithm first identifies the root r_k at level k of CLTree-Index (line 3). Then, it traverses the subtree rooted at r_k to find vertices sharing common attributes of W_q. Let V_i be the set of *vertices* sharing exactly i attributes of W_q, i.e., $V_i = \{v \in V(H) : |W_q \cap \text{attr}(v)| = i\}$ (line 5). Then, the algorithm initializes the iteration number l as h (line 6), since it verifies the candidate sets with the largest size h first. The algorithm also dynamically maintains a set of vertices $\hat{V}$ that have at least l attributes of W_q (line 7). In the while loop, the algorithm examines the candidate attribute sets in decreasing order of cardinality. For each candidate set $S \subseteq \mathcal{S}_l$, the algorithm tries to find a connected subgraph H as ACC, in which every vertex has attributes S and at least k neighbors (lines 9–12). Finally, the algorithm terminates if at least one qualified ACC is found; otherwise, it examines smaller candidate sets in the next iteration to decrease l by 1 (lines 13–15).

4.3   K-TRUSS-BASED ATTRIBUTE COMMUNITY MODEL

In this section, we present a k-truss-based model for attributed community search proposed by Huang et al. [93]. We start by formalizing the intuitions behind the desiderata discussed in Section 4.1.3. We focus our discussion on conditions 2–4 of a good attributed community.

4.3.1 (k, d)-TRUSS

This section introduces a novel notion of dense and tight substructure called (k, d)-truss by paying attention to cohesiveness and communication cost.

Cohesiveness
Recall the notions of k-core and k-truss (see Definitions 2.4.1 and 2.4.4): a subgraph $H \subseteq G$ is a k-core, if every vertex of H has degree at least k in H and H is the largest w.r.t. this property; a subgraph $H \subseteq G$ is a k-truss, if every edge $(u, v) \in E(H)$ is contained in at least $k - 2$ triangles in H and H is the largest w.r.t. this property. A k-truss may be disconnected; a connected k-truss of a graph G is denoted as a connected subgraph $H \subseteq G$ where each edge is contained in at least $k - 2$ triangles in H (see Definition 2.4.5).

Intuitively, a connected k-truss is a connected subgraph in which each connection (edge) (u, v) is "endorsed" by $k - 2$ common neighbors of u and v [50]. A connected k-truss with a large value of k signifies strong inner-connections between members of the subgraph. In a k-truss, each node has degree at least $k - 1$, i.e., it is a $(k - 1)$-core, and a connected k-truss is also $(k - 1)$-edge-connected, i.e., it remains connected as long as fewer than $(k - 1)$ edges are removed [19].

Example 4.3.1 *Consider the graph G (Figure 4.1). The edge $e(v_1, v_2)$ is contained in three triangles $\triangle_{q_1v_1v_2}$, $\triangle_{q_2v_1v_2}$ and $\triangle_{v_3v_1v_2}$, thus its support is $\sup_G(e) = 3$. Consider the subgraph H_3 of G (Figure 4.2c). Every edge of H_3 has support ≥ 2, thus H_3 is a 4-truss. Note that even though the edge $e(v_1, v_2)$ has support 3, there exists no 5-truss in the graph G in Figure 4.1.*

Communication Cost
For a pair of nodes $u, v \in G$, let $\mathsf{dist}_G(u, v)$ denote the length of the shortest path between u and v in G, where $\mathsf{dist}_G(u, v) = +\infty$ if u and v are not connected. The diameter of a graph G is the maximum length of a shortest path in G, i.e., $\mathsf{diam}(G) = \max_{u,v \in G}\{\mathsf{dist}_G(u, v)\}$. The notion of graph query distance is defined in the following.

Definition 4.3.1 *[Query Distance [96]] Given a graph G and query vertices $V_q \subseteq V$, the vertex query distance of vertex $v \in V$ is the maximum length of a shortest path from v to a query vertex $q \in V_q$ in G, i.e., $\mathsf{dist}_G(v, V_q) = \max_{q \in V_q} \mathsf{dist}_G(v, q)$. Given a subgraph $H \subseteq G$ and $V_q \subseteq V(H)$, the graph query distance of H is defined as $\mathsf{dist}_H(H, V_q) = \max_{u \in H} \mathsf{dist}_H(u, V_q)$ $= \max_{u \in H, q \in V_q} \mathsf{dist}_H(u, q)$.*

Given a subgraph $H \subseteq G$, the query distance $\text{dist}_H(H, V_q)$ measures the communication cost between the vertices of H and the query vertices. A good community should have a low communication cost, i.e., small $\text{dist}_H(H, V_q)$.

For the graph G in Figure 4.1 and query vertices $V_q = \{q_1, q_2\}$, the vertex query distance of v_7 is $\text{dist}_G(v_7, V_q) = \max_{q \in V_q}\{\text{dist}_G(v_7, q)\} = 2$. Consider the subgraph H_2 in Figure 4.2b. The graph query distance of H_2 is $\text{dist}_{H_2}(H_2, V_q) = \text{dist}_{H_2}(q_1, q_2) = 2$. The diameter of H_2 is $\text{diam}(H_2) = 2$.

(k, d)-Truss

Based on the notions of k-truss and query distance, a new notion of (k, d)-truss capturing dense cohesiveness and low communication cost is defined as follows.

Definition 4.3.2 ((k, d)-truss) *Given a subgraph $H \subseteq G$, query vertices V_q, and numbers k and d, H is a (k, d)-truss iff H is a connected k-truss containing V_q and $\text{dist}_H(H, V_q) \leq d$.*

By definition, the cohesiveness of a (k, d)-truss increases with k, and its proximity to query nodes increases with decreasing d. For instance, the community H_2 in Figure 4.2b for $V_q = \{q_1, q_2\}$ is a (k, d)-truss with $k = 4$ and $d = 2$.

4.3.2 ATTRIBUTE SCORE FUNCTION

We introduce an attribute score function for gauging the goodness of an attributed community w.r.t. attribute coverage. We first present the key properties that should be obeyed by a good attribute score function for a community. Let $f(H, W_q)$ denote the attribute score of community H w.r.t. query attributes W_q. We say that a node v of H covers an attribute $w \in W_q$, if $w \in \text{attr}(v)$. We say that a node of H is irrelevant to the query if it does not cover any of the query attributes.
Principle 1: The more query attributes that are covered by some node(s) of H, the higher should be the score $f(H, W_q)$. The rationale is obvious.
Principle 2: The more nodes that contain an attribute $w \in W_q$, the higher the contribution of w should be toward the overall score $f(H, W_q)$. The intuition is that attributes that are covered by more nodes of H signify homogeneity within the community w.r.t. shared query attributes.
Principle 3: The more nodes of H that are irrelevant to the query, the lower the score $f(H, W_q)$.

We next discuss a few choices for defining $f(H, W_q)$ and show their pros and cons, before presenting an example function that satisfies all three principles. Note that the scores $f(H, W_q)$ are always compared between subgraphs H that meet the same structural constraint of (k, d)-truss. An obvious choice is to define $f(H, W_q) := \sum_{w \in W_q} \text{score}(H, w)$, where $\text{score}(H, w)$, the contribution of attribute w to the overall score, can be viewed as the relevance of H w.r.t. w. This embodies Principle 1 above. Inspired by Principle 2, another definition can be made as $\text{score}(H, w) := |V(H) \cap V_w|$, i.e., the number of nodes of H that cover w. Unfortunately, this choice suffers from some limitations by virtue of treating all query attributes alike. Some attributes may not be shared by many community nodes while others are and this distinction is ignored by the above definition of $f(H, W_q)$. To illustrate, consider the community H_2 in Figure 4.2b and the query $Q = (\{q_1\}, \{\text{"DB"}\})$; H_2 has five vertices associated with the attribute "DB" and achieves a score of 5. The subgraph H of the graph G shown in Figure 4.1 also has the same score of 5. However, while the community in Figure 4.2b is clearly a good community, as all nodes carry attribute "DB," the subgraph H in Figure 4.1 includes several irrelevant nodes without attribute "DB." Notice that both H_2 and H are 4-trusses so there has no way of discriminating between them, which is undesirable.

An alternative is to define $\text{score}(H, w)$ as $\frac{|V_w \cap V(H)|}{|V(H)|}$ as this captures the popularity of attribute w. Unfortunately, this fails to reward larger communities. For instance, consider the query $Q = (\{q_1, v_4\}, \{\text{"DB"}\})$ over the graph G in Figure 4.1. The subgraph H_2 in Figure 4.2b as well as its subgraph obtained by removing q_2 is a 4-truss and both will be assigned a score of 1.

In view of these considerations, $f(H, W_q)$ is defined as a weighted sum of the score contribution of each query attribute, where the weight reflects the popularity of the attribute.

Definition 4.3.3 (Attribute Score) *Given a subgraph $H \subseteq G$ and an attribute w, the weight of an attribute w is $\theta(H, w) = \frac{|V_w \cap V(H)|}{|V(H)|}$, i.e., the fraction of nodes of H covering w. For a query $Q = (V_q, W_q)$ and a community H, the attribute score of H is defined as $f(H, W_q) = \sum_{w \in W_q} \theta(H, w) \times \text{score}(H, w)$, where $\text{score}(H, w) = |V_w \cap V(H)|$ is the number of nodes covering w.*

The contribution of an attribute w to the overall score is $\theta(H, w) \times \text{score}(H, w) = \frac{|V_w \cap V(H)|^2}{|V(H)|}$. This depends not only on the number of vertices covering w but also on w's popularity in the community H. This choice discourages vertices unrelated to the query attributes W_q which decrease the relevance score, without necessarily increasing the cohesion (e.g., trussness). At the same time, it permits the inclusion of essential nodes, which are added to a community to reduce the cost of connecting query nodes. They act as an important link between nodes that are related to the query, leading to a higher relevance score. Such additional nodes are referred as *Steiner nodes*. For example, consider the query $Q = (\{q_1\}, \{\text{"ML"}\})$ on the graph G in Figure 4.1. As discussed in Section 4.1.2, the community H_4 in Figure 4.2d is preferable to the chain of nodes v_8, q_1, v_{10}. Notice that it includes v_9 with attribute "DM" (but not "ML"); v_9 is thus a Steiner node. It can be verified that $f(H_4, W_q) = \frac{9}{4}$ which is smaller than the attribute score of the chain, which is 3. However, H_4 is a 3-truss whereas the chain is a 2-truss. It is easy to see that any supergraph of H_4 in Figure 4.1 is at most a 3-truss and has a strictly smaller attribute score.

The more query attributes a community has that are shared by more of its nodes, the higher its attribute score. For example, consider the query $Q = (\{q_1\}, \{\text{"DB," "DM"}\})$ on the running example graph of Figure 4.1. The communities H_1, H_2, H_3 in Figure 4.2 are all potential answers for this query. $f(H_2, W_q) = 5 \cdot 1 + 2 \cdot \frac{2}{5} = 5.8$; by symmetry, $f(H_3, W_q) = 5.8$; on the other hand, $f(H_1, W_q) = 5 \cdot \frac{5}{8} + 5 \cdot \frac{5}{8} = 6.25$. Intuitively, we can see that H_2 and H_3 are mainly focused on one area ("DB" or "DM") whereas H_1 has 5 nodes covering "DB" and "DM" each and also has the highest attribute score.

Remark 4.1   We stress that the main message of this subsection is the identification of key principles that an attribute score function must satisfy in order to be effective in measuring the goodness of an attributed community. Specifically, these principles capture the important properties of high attribute coverage and high attribute correlation within a community and minimal number of nodes irrelevant to given query. Any score function can be employed as long as it satisfies these principles. The algorithmic framework presented in Section 4.3.4 is flexible enough to handle an ATC community model equipped with any such score function.

4.3.3   ATTRIBUTED TRUSS COMMUNITY MODEL

Combining the structure constraint of (k, d)-truss and the attribute score function $f(H, W_q)$, an *attributed truss community* (ATC) is defined as follows.

Definition 4.3.4 (Attributed Truss Community)   *Given a graph G, a query $Q = (V_q, W_q)$, and two numbers k and d, H is an attributed truss community (ATC), if H satisfies the following conditions.*

1.   *H is a (k, d)-truss containing V_q.*

2.   *H has the maximum attribute score $f(H, W_q)$ among all subgraphs satisfying condition (1).*

In terms of structure and communication cost, condition (1) not only requires that the community containing the query nodes V_q be densely connected, but also that each node be close to the query nodes. In terms of query attribute coverage and correlation, condition (2) ensures that a maximum number of query attributes are covered by as many nodes as possible.

Example 4.3.2   *For the graph G in Figure 4.1, and query $Q = (\{q_1, q_2\}, \{\text{"DB," "DM"}\})$ with $k = 4$ and $d = 2$, H_1 in Figure 4.2a is the corresponding ATC, since H_1 is a $(4, 2)$-truss with the largest score $f(H, W_q) = 6.25$ among all subgraphs of G, as seen before.*

The ATC-Problem can now be formally formulated as follows.

Problem Statement
Given a graph $G(V, E)$, query $Q = (V_q, W_q)$, and two parameters k and d, find an ATC H, such that H is a (k, d)-truss with the maximum attribute score $f(H, W_q)$.

We remark that if there exists more than one (k, d)-truss with the same highest attribute score, any such (k, d)-truss can be regraded as an answer.

It was shown in [93] that ATC-Problem is NP-hard. Furthermore, the attribute score function $f(H, W_q)$ is non-monotone and is neither submodular nor supermodular w.r.t. sets of vertices.[1] This intuitively implies that the prospects of an efficient approximation algorithm for the ATC-Problem are not promising.

4.3.4 ATINDEX-BASED GREEDY ALGORITHM

In this section, we present a greedy algorithmic framework for finding an ATC. It leverages the notions of attribute marginal gain (to be defined later in this section). The algorithm first finds a (k, d)-truss, and then iteratively removes the vertices with the smallest attribute score contribution. To further improve the algorithm efficiency while ensuring high quality, we also introduce a novel index called attributed-truss index (ATindex). It maintains known graph structure and attribute information.

ATindex

The ATindex consists of three components: *structural trussness, attribute trussness,* and *inverted attribute index.*

Structural Trussness. Recall that trusses have a hierarchical structure, i.e., for $k \geq 3$, a k-truss is always contained in some $(k - 1)$-truss [89]. For any vertex as well as for any edge, there exists a k-truss with the largest k containing it. We echo for convenience the definition of trussness of vertex, edge, and subgraph, originally defined in Section 2.4.2.

Definition 4.3.5 (Trussness) *Given a subgraph $H \subseteq G$, the trussness of H is the minimum support of an edge in H plus 2, i.e., $\tau(H) = 2 + \min_{e \in E(H)}\{\sup_H(e)\}$. The trussness of an edge $e \in E(G)$ is $\tau_G(e) = \max_{H \subseteq G \wedge e \in E(H)}\{\tau(H)\}$. The trussness of a vertex $v \in V(G)$ is $\tau_G(v) = \max_{H \subseteq G \wedge v \in V(H)}\{\tau(H)\}$.*

Consider the graph G in Figure 4.1, the trussness of the edge $e(q_1, v_1)$ is 4, because there exists a 4-truss containing $e(q_1, v_1)$ in Figure 4.2c, and any subgraph H containing $e(q_1, v_1)$ has $\tau(H) \leq 4$, i.e., $\tau_G(e(q_1, v_1)) = \max_{H \subseteq G \wedge e \in E(H)}\{\tau(H)\} = 4$.

Based on the trussness of a vertex (edge), it can infers in constant time whether there exists a k-truss containing it. We describe the construction of the structural trussness index as follows. For each vertex $v \in V$, it keeps the vertex trussness of v, and also maintains the edge trussness of its incident edges in decreasing order of trussness. This supports efficient checking of whether vertex v or its incident edge is present in a k-truss, avoiding expensive k-truss search. Also, one can efficiently retrieve v's incident edges with a given trussness value. In addition, it uses a hashtable to maintain all the edges and their trussness. Notice that for a graph G, $\tau(\emptyset)$ denotes the maximum structural trussness of G.

Attributed Trussness. Structural trussness index is not sufficient for ATC queries. Given a vertex v in G with structural trussness $\tau_G(v) \geq k$, there is no guarantee that v will be present in a

---

[1]A set function $g : 2^U \to \mathbb{R}^{\geq 0}$ is submodular if for all sets $S \subset T \subset U$ and an element $x \in U \setminus T$, $g(T \cup \{x\}) - g(T) \leq g(S \cup \{x\}) - g(S)$, i.e., the marginal gain of g has the "diminishing returns" property. The function $g(.)$ is supermodular if $-g(.)$ is submodular.

(k, d)-truss with large attribute score w.r.t. query attributes. For example, consider the graph G and vertex v_1 with $\tau_G(v_1) = 4$ in Figure 4.1. Here, v_1 will not be present in an ATC for query attributes $W_q =\{$"ML"$\}$ since it does not have attribute "ML." On the other hand, v_1 is in an ATC w.r.t. $W_q =\{$'DM'$\}$. By contrast, v_9 is *not* present in a 4-truss w.r.t. attribute "DM" even though it has that attribute. To make such searches efficient, for each attribute $w \in \mathcal{A}$, we consider an attribute projected graph, which only contains the vertices associated with attribute w, formally defined below.

Definition 4.3.6 *(Attribute Projected Graph and Attributed Trussness).* *Given a graph G and an attribute $w \in \mathcal{A}$, the projected graph of G on attribute w is the subgraph of G induced by V_w, i.e., $G_w = (V_w, E_{V_w}) \subseteq G$, where V_w is the set of vertices of G which contain attribute w. For each vertex v and edge e in G_w, the attributed trussnesses of v and e w.r.t. w in G_w are, respectively, defined as $\tau_{G_w}(v) = \max_{H \subseteq G_w \wedge v \in V(H)} \{\tau(H)\}$ and $\tau_{G_w}(e) = \max_{H \subseteq G_w \wedge e \in E(H)}\{\tau(H)\}$.*

For instance, for the graph G in Figure 4.1, the projected graph G_w of G on $w =$"DB" is the graph H_2 in Figure 4.2b. For vertices v_1 and v_4, even though both have the same structural trussness $\tau_G(v_1) = \tau_G(v_4) = 4$, in graph H_2, vertex v_4 has attribute trussness $\tau_{H_2}(v_4) = 4$ w.r.t. $w =$"DB," whereas vertex v_1 is not even present in H_2, indicating that vertex v_4 is more relevant w.r.t. "DB" than v_1. Suppose v_1 has attribute "DB" in addition to "DM." Even then the attribute trussness of v_1 is still less than that of v_4 w.r.t. the attribute "DB," because vertex v_1 still cannot be present in 4-truss of H_2 w.r.t. $w =$"DB."

Inverted Attribute Index. We describe an inverted index for each attribute $w \in \mathcal{A}$, denoted invA$_w$. It maintains an inverted list of the vertices in V_w, i.e., the vertices containing attribute w, in decreasing order of the vertex structural trussness. Thus, invA$_w$ is in the format $\{(v_1, \tau_G(v_1)), \ldots, (v_l, \tau_G(v_l))\}$, $\tau_G(v_j) \geq \tau_G(v_{j+1})$, $j \in [l-1]$. The inverted attribute index and structural trussness index can both be used to speed up query processing.

ATindex Construction

Algorithm 4.20 outlines the procedure for ATindex construction. It first constructs the index of structural trussness using the structural decomposition algorithm of [165], then constructs the index of attribute trussness and finally the inverted attribute index. The algorithm is self-explanatory. Now, we show the time and space complexity of the algorithm and the space requirement of ATindex. It takes $O(m\rho)$ time and $O(m)$ space for applying the truss decomposition algorithm on a graph G with m edges [89]; here, ρ is the arboricity of G, and it is known that $\rho \leq \min\{d_{\max}, \sqrt{m}\}$. Then, for each keyword $w \in \mathcal{A}$, Algorithm 4.20 invokes the truss decomposition algorithm on the projected graph $G_w \subseteq G$, which takes $O(|E(G_w)|\rho)$ time and $O(m)$ space. In implementing this algorithm, each G_w can be dealt with separately, and its memory can be released after the completion of truss decomposition and write attribute trussness index to disk. Overall, ATindex construction takes $O(\rho(m + \sum_{w \in \mathcal{A}} |E(G_w)|))$ time and $O(m)$ space, and the index occupies $O(m + \sum_{w \in \mathcal{A}} |E(G_w)|)$ space.

Algorithm 4.20 ATindex Construction(G)

Input: A graph $G = (V, E)$.
Output: ATindex of G.

1: Apply the truss decomposition algorithm [165] on G.
2: **for** $v \in G$ **do**
3:    Keep the structural trussness of v and its incident edges in record.
4: **for** $w \in A$ **do**
5:    Project G on attribute w as G_w.
6:    Apply the truss decomposition algorithm [165] on G_w.
7:    Construct an inverted node list invA$_w$.
8: **for** $e = (u, v) \in G$ **do**
9:    Build a hashtable to preserve its structural trussness value $\tau_G(e)$ and attribute trussness value $\tau_{G_w}(e)$, where $w \in A(v) \cap A(u)$.

Next, we present a search framework of greedy algorithm called BULK, which is outlined in Algorithm 4.21.

Algorithm Overview

BULK has three steps. First, it finds the maximal (k, d)-truss of G as a candidate. Second, it iteratively removes vertices with the smallest "attribute marginal gains" from the candidate graph, and maintains the remaining graph as a (k, d)-truss, until no longer possible. Finally, it returns a (k, d)-truss with the maximum attribute score among all generated candidate graphs as the answer. If there exists more than one (k, d)-truss with the maximum attribute scores, BULK just outputs one answer.

The details of the algorithm follow. First, it finds the maximal (k, d)-truss of G as G_0. As the vertices are removed in increasing order of their attribute marginal gains, we need to maintain the (k, d)-truss property.

(k, d)-truss **maintenance**: repeat until no longer possible:
   (i) *k-truss*: remove the edges contained in $< (k - 2)$ triangles; and
   (ii) *query distance*: remove the vertices with query distance $> d$ and their incident edges;
   Note that the two steps above can trigger each other: removing edges can increase query distance and removing vertices can reduce edge support.

Attribute Marginal Gain. Before we proceed further, we introduce a useful definition for node removal, called node attribute score as follows.

Definition 4.3.7 (Node Attribute Score) *Given a graph H and query attributes W_q, the node attribute score of $v \in V(H)$ is defined as* $f_H(v, W_q) = \sum_{w \in W_q \cap attr(v)} 2|V_w \cap V(H)| - 1$.

In the following, it starts from the maximal (k, d)-truss G_l where $l = 0$, and find a (k, d)-truss with a large attribute score by successively deleting the vertices with the smallest attribute marginal gains, defined below.

Definition 4.3.8 (Attribute Marginal Gain) *Given a graph H, a set of query attributes W_q, and a vertex $v \in V(H)$, the* attribute marginal gain *is defined as* $\mathsf{gain}_H(v, W_q) = \mathsf{f}(H, W_q) - \mathsf{f}(H - S_H(v), W_q)$, *where $S_H(v) \subset V(H)$ is v together with the set of vertices that violate the (k, d)-truss property after the removal of v from H.*

Notice that by definition, $v \in S_H(v)$. For example, consider the graph G in Figure 4.1 and the query $Q = (\{q_1\}, \{\text{"ML"}\})$, with $k = 3$ and $d = 2$. The vertex v_9 does not contain the attribute "ML," and the attribute score contribution is $\mathsf{f}_G(v_9, W_q) = 0$ by Definition 4.3.7, indicating no attribute score contribution by vertex v_9. However, the fact is that v_9 is an important bridge for connections among the vertices q_1, v_8, and v_{10} with attribute "ML." The deletion of v_9 will thus lead to the deletion of v_8 and v_{10}, due to the 3-truss constraint. Thus, $S_G(v_9) = \{v_8, v_9, v_{10}\}$. The marginal gain of v_9 is $\mathsf{gain}_G(v_9, W_q) = \mathsf{f}(G, W_q) - \mathsf{f}(G - S_G(v_9), W_q) = \frac{3}{4} - \frac{1}{9} > 0$. This shows that the deletion of v_9 from G decreases the attribute score. It illustrates that attribute marginal gain can more accurately estimate the effectiveness of vertex deletion than attribute score contribution, by naturally incorporating look-ahead.

One concern is that $\mathsf{gain}_H(v, W_q)$ needs the exact computation of $S_H(v)$, which has to simulate the deletion of v from H by invoking (k, d)-truss maintenance, which is expensive. An important observation is that if vertex v is to be deleted, its neighbors $u \in N(v)$ with degree $k - 1$ will also be deleted, to maintain k-truss. Let $P_H(v)$ be the set of 1-hop neighbors of v that have degree $k - 1$ in H, i.e., $P_H(v) = \{u \in N(v) : \deg_H(u) = k - 1\}$. We introduce a local attribute marginal gain, viz., $\widehat{\mathsf{gain}}_H(v, W_q) = \mathsf{f}(H, W_q) - \mathsf{f}(H - P_H(v), W_q)$, to approximate $\mathsf{gain}_H(v, W_q)$. Continuing with the above example, in graph G, for deleting vertex v_9, note that $\deg(v_8) = \deg(v_{10}) = 2 = k - 1$, so we have $P_G(v_9) = \{v_8, v_9, v_{10}\}$, which coincides with $S_G(v_9)$. In general, $\widehat{\mathsf{gain}}_H(v, W_q)$ serves as a good approximation to $\mathsf{gain}_H(v, W_q)$ and has the advantage that it can be computed more efficiently.

Bulk Deletion. The second idea incorporated in BULK is bulk deletion. The idea is that instead of removing one vertex with the smallest attribute marginal gain, BULK removes a small percentage of vertices from the current candidate graph that have the smallest attribute marginal gain. More precisely, let G_i be the current candidate graph and let $\epsilon > 0$. It identifies the set of vertices S such that $|S| = \frac{\epsilon}{1+\epsilon}|V(G_i)|$ and the vertices in S have the smallest attribute marginal gain, and remove S from G_i, instead of removing a vertex at a time. Notice that the resulting ATC G_{i+1} has size $|V(G_{i+1})| \le \frac{1}{1+\epsilon}|V(G_i)|$ after the deletion of S. BULK can safely terminate the algorithm once the size of G_i drops below k vertices and return the best ATC obtained so far, in view of the k-truss constraint. Thus, it follows that the number of iterations t drops from $O(\min\{n, m/k\})$ to $O(\log_{1+\epsilon} \frac{n}{k})$.

Algorithm 4.21 BULK (G, Q)

Input: A graph $G = (V, E)$, a query $Q = (V_q, W_q)$, numbers k and d, parameter ε.
Output: A (k, d)-truss H with the maximum $f(H, W_q)$.

1: Find the maximal (k, d)-truss G_0.
2: Let $l \leftarrow 0$;
3: **while** connect$_{G_l}(Q) =$ **true do**
4:     Find a set of vertices S of the smallest $\hat{gain}_{G_l}(v, W_q)$ with the size of $|S| = \frac{\varepsilon}{1+\varepsilon}|V(G_i)|$;
5:     Delete S and their incident edges from G_l;
6:     Maintain the (k, d)-truss of G_l;
7:     $G_{l+1} \leftarrow G_l; l \leftarrow l + 1$;
8: $H \leftarrow \arg\max_{G' \in \{G_0, ..., G_{l-1}\}} f(G', W_q)$;

Finally, the candidate answer with the maximum attribute score generated during this process is returned as the final answer, i.e., $\arg\max_{G' \in \{G_0, ..., G_{l-1}\}} f(G', W_q)$. The detailed description is presented in Algorithm 4.21.

To help efficient processing of ATC queries, another technique is to develop a local exploration algorithm (called LocATC in [93]). The idea is to first efficiently detect a small neighborhood subgraph around query vertices, which tends to be densely and closely connected with the query attributes. Then, Algorithm 4.21 is applied to shrink the candidate graph into a (k, d)-truss with large attribute score. The details can be found in [93], which also contains a comprehensive performance evaluation of various algorithms for attributed community search.

4.4   SUMMARY

In this section, we present two case studies of the ACC and ATC models using real-world networks. Specifically, we show ACC communities on the DBLP network and ATC communities on the protein-protein interaction (PPI) network and discuss their significance.

4.4.1   CASE STUDY ON THE DBLP NETWORK

The DBLP network contains 977,288 nodes and 3,432,273 edges, where each node represents an author and each edge corresponds to co-authorship between two authors. For each author, the 20 most frequent keywords from his/her publication titles are chosen as the associated attributes. For the input query for the ACC model, we consider a single query node q corresponding to a renowned researcher in database and data mining, namely $q =$ "Jiawei Han," and set the parameter $k = 4$. Figure 4.7 shows two attributed core communities of "Jiawei Han," where the query attribute sets W_q are {analysis, data, information, network} and {mine, data, pattern, database}, respectively. Both communities are dense subgraphs that are 4-cores. Figure 4.7a shows the group of Jiawei Han's collaborators involved in graph analysis where each author's top keywords from their publications are {analysis, mine, data, information, network}. Figure 4.7b shows an-

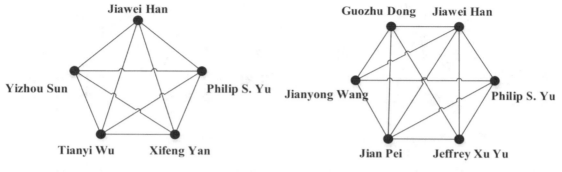

(a) W_q = {analysis, data, information, network}   (b) W_q = {mine, data, pattern, database}

Figure 4.7: Two attributed core communities for a query author q ="Jiawei Han" with different query attributes W_q. Here, $k = 4$.

other group of Jiawei Han's collaborators working on pattern mining [65] where each author's top publication keywords are {mine, data, pattern, database}.

4.4.2 CASE STUDY ON THE PPI NETWORK WITH GROUND-TRUTH COMMUNITIES

In this section, we show the effectiveness of the ATC model and algorithms on the protein-protein interaction (PPI) network Krogan. The dataset is from the BioGRID database, where the PPI data are related to the yeast saccharomyces cerevisiae [85]. Each protein has three kinds of attributes: biological processes, molecular functions, and cellular components. There are 255 known protein complexes for Sacchromyces cerevisiae in the MIPS/CYGD [85], which are regarded as ground-truth communities.

We examine the details of the discovered protein complexes to investigate biologically significant clues, which help us to better understand the protein complexes. Figure 4.8a shows one complex "transcription factor TFIIIC complex" in saccharomyces cerevisiae, which has been identified by biologists previously. The graph contains 6 nodes and 12 edges, with density 0.8 and diameter 2. We adopt the following procedure for checking whether a protein is present in a complex. Taking gene id "854277" as an example, we can go to the NCBI,[2] input "854277" in the search box, and select the category of "Gene," then we will obtain information related to this gene, from which we can check whether this gene is one of the proteins in the protein complex.[3] We randomly sample a query as $Q = (V_q, W_q)$ where V_q ={854277, 856100} and W_q ={"GO:0001009," "GO:0001041"}, and set the parameters $k = 3$ and $d = 3$.

[2]https://www.ncbi.nlm.nih.gov/
[3]http://wodaklab.org/cyc2008/resources/CYC2008_complex.tab

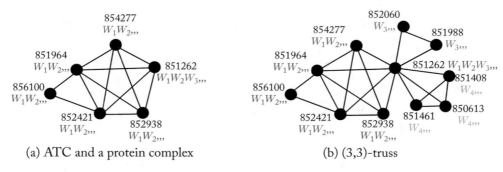

(a) ATC and a protein complex   (b) (3,3)-truss

Figure   4.8: $Q = (\{q_1, q_2\}, \{w_1, w_2\})$ where $q_1 = 854277$, $q_2 = 856100$ and $w_1 =$ "GO:0001009," $w_2 =$ "GO:0001041."

To illustrate the importance of the consideration of protein attributes in detecting protein complexes, we simply use the structure and find the $(3, 3)$-truss shown in Figure 4.8b. This community contains 11 proteins including 6 proteins of the ground-truth complex of Figure 4.8a. The other 5 proteins not present in the ground-truth complex are associated with no query attributes, but have other attributes w_3 and w_4, as shown in Figure 4.8b. When we look up the database of Gene Ontology,[4] we see that the attributes of "biological processes"— "GO:0001009" and "GO:0001041," respectively, represent "transcription from RNA polymerase III hybrid type promoter" and "transcription from RNA polymerase III type 2 promoter."

Except query attributes, we omitted details of other attributes from Figure 4.8 for simplicity. The ATC model is able to identify all proteins that preform the same biological process of transcription from RNA polymerase.[5] Overall, the ATC model successfully identifies all proteins that constitute the ground-truth complex in Figure 4.8a. Other than these two homogeneous attributes, interestingly, we also discover another two attributes shared by all proteins in terms of "molecular functions." Specifically, the attributes "GO:0001003" and "GO:0001005," respectively, perform DNA binding activity, viz., "RNA polymerase III type 2 promoter sequence-specific DNA binding" and " RNA polymerase III type 1 promoter sequence-specific DNA binding." Overall, this discovered complex actually exists in the cell nucleus, with the same attribute "cellular components" of "GO:0005634" in all proteins.

4.4.3   COMPARISON BETWEEN ACC AND ATC MODELS

The key distinctions between attributed k-core model (ACC) and attributed k-truss model (ATC) are as follows. (1) The k-truss community model is based on k-trusses, which have well-known

---

[4]http://geneontology.org/ontology/go-basic.obo
[5]Specifically, the local exploration algorithm LocATC, not discussed here but elaborated upon in [93], is able to identify all these proteins. LocATC is a more efficient version of the BULK algorithm discussed in the previous section.

advantages such as denser structure, over k-cores. A connected k-core has no guarantee to be 2-edge-connected, even with a large core value k. (2) The approach of ACC model may miss useful communities. For example, consider the example graph in Figure 4.1 with query node $\{q_2\}$ *and* attributes {"DB," "DM"}, and parameter $k = 3$. The ACC model will return the subgraphs H_2 (Figure 4.2b) and H_3 (Figure 4.2c) as answers. However, the subgraph H_1 (Figure 4.2a) will not be discovered, due to the strict homogeneity constraint imposed by the ACC model. (3) Furthermore, the ATC model minimizes the query distance of the community which has the benefit of avoiding the free rider effect, unlike the ACC model. (4) On the flip side, the computation of finding a connected maximal k-core is faster than the computation of finding a connected maximal k-truss, although this speed comes at a price as noted above.

4.4.4 COMPARISON WITH OTHER RELATED WORKS

We conclude this chapter by making a brief comparison of attributed community search with other work that is broadly relevant. Besides cohesive community search, this list includes keyword search, team formation, and community detection in attributed graphs. Table 4.1 shows a detailed comparison of representative works on these topics.

Keyword Search. Keyword search over relational databases has been extensively studied [5, 22, 58, 83, 84, 102]. Most of the works focus on finding minimal connected tuple trees from a relational database [5, 58, 83, 102]. There are two basic approaches: DBXplorer [5] DISCOVER-

Table 4.1: A comparison of representative works on keyword search (KS), team formation (TF), cohesive community search (CCS), and attributed community search (ACS)

Method	Topic	Participation Condition	Attribute Function	Cohesiveness Constraint	Communication Cost
[22]	KS	X	✓	X	✓
[58]	KS	X	✓	X	✓
[119]	KS	X	✓	X	✓
[112]	TF	X	✓	X	✓
[70]	TF	X	✓	✓	✓
[103]	TF	X	✓	X	✓
[157]	CCS	✓	X	✓	✓
[54]	CCS	✓	X	✓	X
[96]	CCS	✓	X	✓	✓
[65]	ACS	✓	✓	✓	X
Ours	ACS	✓	✓	✓	✓

I [84] and DISCOVER-II [83] fall in the first category and use SQL to find tuple-trees. The other approach materializes a relational database as a graph, and finds trees from the graph, e.g., see BANKS-I [22] and BANKS-II [102].

Keyword search over graphs looks for a substructure containing all or a subset of the input keywords. The works [119, 141] report subgraphs instead of trees as answers to a keyword search query. However, keyword search over graphs does not consider the cohesive structure involving the query nodes and keywords. A natural question is whether we can model the information suitably and leverage keyword search over graphs to find the right communities. For example, in addition to modeling authors as nodes, we could also model authors' attributes as nodes and directly connect them to the author nodes and query the resulting graph with the union of the author id's and the keywords. Figure 4.9 illustrates this for a small subgraph of Figure 4.1 and an example query $W_q = \{q_1, \text{"DB"}\}$, where q_1 represents an author id. A keyword search finds answers corresponding to trees or subgraphs with minimum communication cost that connect the input keywords/nodes, where the communication cost is based on diameter, query distance, weight of spanning tree or Steiner tree. On this example graph, if we search for the query node q_1 and attribute "DB," we will get the single edge connecting q_1 and "DB" as the answer as this is the subgraph with minimum communication cost connecting these two nodes. Clearly, this is unsatisfactory as a community. Overall, keyword search by itself cannot return the right communities over attributed graphs.

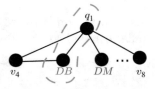

Figure 4.9: Keyword Search with query $W_q = \{q_1, \text{"DB"}\}$.

Team Formation. Lappas et al. [112] introduce the problem of discovering a team of experts from a social network, where node attributes represent user skills, such that the team satisfies all skills required for a given task and has a low communication cost. Kargar and An [103] study the team formation problem with a team leader who communicates with each team member to monitor and coordinate the project. Most of the team formation studies [9, 103, 112, 118, 129] focus on minimizing the communication cost, but ignore the constraint of densely connected subgraph required by community search. Gajewar and Sarma [70] extend the team formation problem to allow for potentially more than one member possessing each required skill, and use maximum density measure or minimum diameter as the objective. Compared with the problem of attributed community search, these studies do not consider both dense structure and distance constraint at the same time, and also have no constraint on query nodes.

Community Detection in Attributed Graphs. In contrast with (attributed) community search, the goal of community detection in attributed graphs is to find all densely connected components (communities) with homogeneous attributes [43, 90, 146, 198]. Zhou et al. [198] model the community detection problem as graph clustering, and combine structural and attribute similarities through a unified distance measure. When high-dimensional attributed communities are hard to interpret or discover, the papers [76, 90] consider subspace clustering on high-dimensional attributed graphs. A survey of clustering on attributed graphs can be found in [30]. It is practically hard and inefficient to adapt the above community detection approaches [90, 146, 198] for online attributed community search: community detection is inherently global and much of the work involved in finding all communities may be irrelevant to the particular community being searched, since the latter is query driven.

CHAPTER 5

Social Circle Analysis

In this chapter, we discuss a special kind of communities arising in social networks, called social circles. For a user, the subgraph of the entire network induced only by his or her friends is called an **ego-network**. Online social networks allow users to manually categorize their friends into different social circles within their **ego-networks** (e.g., "circles" on Google+) [117, 170]. The task of social circle discovery is to automatically identify all social circles for a given user. Social circles can be used for content filtering, for privacy management, and for sharing groups of users that other users may wish to follow. In the following, we first formally define an **ego-network** and then discuss two different research problems of social circle discovery.

5.1 EGO-NETWORKS

We start from the definition of **ego-network** as follows.

Definition 5.1.1 (Ego-Network) *Given a graph $G(V, E)$ and a vertex $u \in V$, the* **ego-network** *of u, denoted $G_{N(u)}$, is a subgraph of G induced by the vertex set $N(u)$, consisting of the neighbors of u. More precisely, $G_{N(u)}$ is the graph (V_u, E_u), where $V_u = N(u)$, and $E_u = \{(v, w) \in E : v, w \in N(u)\}$.*

In the literature, the term "neighborhood induced subgraph of u" [87, 88] has also been used to indicate the **ego-network** of u. The "center" node u of the **ego-network** (the "ego") is not included in $G_{N(u)}$, rather $G_{N(u)}$ includes only u's neighbors. Consider the graph in Figure 5.1a. For vertex f, the set of neighbors is $N(f) = \{a, e, g, i\}$. The **ego-network** of f is the neighborhood induced subgraph of f, namely $G_{N(f)} = (\{a, e, g, i\}, \{(a, g), (g, i)\})$, shown in Figure 5.1b.

Upon social **ego-networks**, we discuss two different problems of social circle analysis. The first problem is the so-called structural diversity search on structural graphs. Based on a large scale study on Facebook, Ugander et al. [163] found that social circles play a pivotal role in determining the process of information diffusion of social contagion. Their study shows that the number of connected components in an individual's neighborhood is a better determinant of contagion diffusion rather than the size of the individual's neighborhood. A social circle represents a distinct social context of a user, and the multiplicity of social contexts is termed structural diversity in [163]. Using their study of a social contagion process in Facebook, they show that a user is much more likely to join Facebook and become engaged if he or she has a larger structural diversity. The papers [87, 88] study the problem of finding k users with the highest structural di-

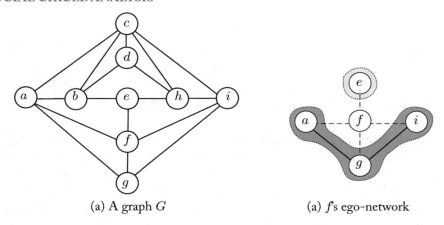

(a) A graph G (a) f's ego-network

Figure 5.1: A running example of structural diversity.

versity in graphs, which can be beneficial to political campaigns, promotion of health practices, marketing, and so on. Despite the apparent connection to social influence, note that the problem of structural diversity search is different from the problem of influence maximization. The task of influence maximization is to target a set of k seed vertices in order to maximize the expected spread of influence in the social network. Naturally different from influence maximization, our problem is to find the k vertices that most easily *get affected* instead of *affecting others*.

The second problem is social circle discovery on attributed graphs. McAuley and Leskovec [117] propose an unsupervised community model to automatically detect circles in ego-networks. Their techniques can discover circles that are disjoint, overlapping, or hierarchically nested.

5.2   STRUCTURAL DIVERSITY SEARCH

In this section, we focus on the problem of *structural diversity search* in social networks. We first introduce some background on social contagion and its relationship with social circles. Then, we give a formal definition of structural diversity w.r.t. the number of social circles. Finally, the problem formulation of structural diversity search is presented followed by efficient algorithms for the problem.

5.2.1   MOTIVATIONS

Social Contagion. Online social networks are becoming more and more important means for users to communicate with each other and to spread information in the real world [110]. In an online social network, the phenomenon of information diffusion, such as diffusion of fads, political opinions, and the adoption of new technologies, has been termed *social conta-*

gion [32, 105, 140, 163], which is a process similar to the propagation of epidemic or infection. Traditionally, the models of social contagion are based on analogies with biological contagion, where the probability that a user is influenced by the contagion grows monotonically with the number of his or her friends who have been affected already [14, 59, 175]. However, such models recently have been challenged [143, 163], as the social contagion process is typically more complex and the social decision can depend more subtly on the network structure.

Case Studies on the Facebook Social Network. Ugander et al. [163] study two social contagion processes in Facebook: the process that a user joins Facebook in response to an invitation email from an existing Facebook user, and the process that a user becomes an engaged user after joining. They find that the probability of contagion is tightly controlled by the number of social circles in a user's neighborhood, rather than by the number of friends in the neighborhood. A social circle represents a distinct social context of a user, and the multiplicity of social contexts is termed structural diversity [163]. A user is much more likely to join Facebook and become engaged if he or she has a larger structural diversity, i.e., a larger number of distinct social contexts, who are Facebook users themselves.

Applications. As discussed in [88, 163], the analysis of structural diversity in a social network can be beneficial to a wide range of applications such as political campaign, promotion of health practices, and marketing. For example, in a political campaign, to convince individuals to change their opinions, it is obviously more important that they receive messages from multiple directions than simply receiving many endorsements [163]. In the promotion of health practices, we can find such top users with the highest structural diversity, and inject vaccines for them for reducing the infection probability. For all of these applications, a fundamental problem is to find individuals in a social network with high structural diversity [163].

5.2.2   PROBLEM FORMULATION

The structural diversity of a vertex is defined as follows.

Definition 5.2.1 (Structural Diversity [163]) *Given a graph $G = (V, E)$ and an integer t where $1 \leq t \leq n$, the structural diversity of a vertex $v \in V$, denoted score(v), is the number of connected components in the* ego-network $G_{N(v)}$ *whose size, measured by the number of vertices, is larger than or equal to t. The parameter t is called the component size threshold for a social circle.*

For example, the ego-network $G_{N(f)}$ in Figure 5.1b contains a size-1 connected component $\{e\}$ and a size-3 connected component $\{a, g, i\}$. If $t = 1$, then *score*(f) = 2. Alternatively, if $t = 2$, *score*(f) = 1 as there is only one component $\{a, g, i\}$ whose size is no less than 2. We define the top-k structural diversity search problem as follows.

Problem 5.2.1 (Structural Diversity Search) *Given a graph G and two integers k and t where $1 \leq k, t \leq n$, the goal of top-k structural diversity search is to find a set of k vertices in G with the highest structural diversity w.r.t. the component size threshold t.*

Example 5.2.1 *Let us revisit the example in Figure 5.1. Suppose that $k = 1$ and $t = 1$. Then, $\{e\}$ is the answer to top-1 structural diversity search, as e is the vertex with the highest structural diversity, with $score(e) = 3$.*

As an alternative to top-k structural diversity search, it is interesting to consider the search for all vertices whose structural diversity exceeds a given number, called structural diversity threshold. Such a query is called an *iceberg query* [63]. In what follows, we shall focus on top-k structural diversity search. However, the techniques discussed can be easily extended to process iceberg queries. In addition, for convenience, we assume that $m \in \Omega(n)$, which does not affect the complexity analysis of the proposed algorithms [87, 88].

5.2.3   A SIMPLE DEGREE-BASED APPROACH

In this section, we present a simple degree-based algorithm for top-k structural diversity search. To compute the structural diversity $score(v)$ for a vertex v, we can perform a breadth-first search in $G_{N(v)}$ to find connected components and return the number of components whose sizes are no less than t. We call this procedure bfs-search, and omit the corresponding straightforward pseudocode.

Next we present a useful lemma which leads to a pruning strategy in the degree-based algorithm.

Lemma 5.2.1 *For any vertex v in G, $score(v) \leq \lfloor \frac{d(v)}{t} \rfloor$ holds.*

Proof. Suppose to the contrary that $score(v) > \lfloor \frac{d(v)}{t} \rfloor$. By the definition of structural diversity, $G_{N(v)}$ has $\lfloor \frac{d(v)}{t} \rfloor + 1$ or more components whose size is greater than or equal to t. Then, the total number of vertices in these components is $\geq (\lfloor \frac{d(v)}{t} \rfloor + 1) \cdot t > \frac{d(v)}{t} \cdot t = d(v)$, which contradicts to the fact that the number of vertices in $G_{N(v)}$ is $d(v)$. Hence, the lemma is established. □

We define $\overline{bound}(v) := \lfloor \frac{d(v)}{t} \rfloor$. Equipped with Lemma 5.2.1 and the bfs-search procedure, we present the degree-based approach in Algorithm 5.22, which computes the structural diversity of vertices in descending order of their degrees. After initialization (lines 1–2), Algorithm 5.22 sorts the vertices in descending order of their degrees (line 3). Then it iteratively finds the unvisited vertex v^* with the maximum degree, and calculates $\overline{bound}(v^*)$ (lines 5–6). If the answer set S has k vertices and $\overline{bound}(v^*) \leq \min_{v \in S} score(v)$, the algorithm terminates (lines 7–8). The rationale is as follows. By Lemma 5.2.1, we have $score(v^*) \leq \overline{bound}(v^*) \leq \min_{v \in S} score(v)$. For any vertex $w \in V$ with a smaller degree, we have $score(w) \leq \overline{bound}(w) \leq \overline{bound}(v^*) \leq \min_{v \in S} score(v)$. Therefore, we can safely prune the remaining vertices and terminate. On the other hand, if such conditions are not satisfied, then the algorithm computes $score(v^*)$ by invoking bfs-search, and checks whether v^* should be added into the answer set S (lines 10–13). Finally, the algorithm outputs S.

The following example illustrates Algorithm 5.22.

Algorithm 5.22 degree (G, k, t)

Input: $G = (V, E)$, integer k, component size threshold t.
Output: Top-k search result S.

1: $S \leftarrow \emptyset$;
2: **for** $v \in V$ **do** $score(v) \leftarrow -1$;
3: sort all vertices in descending order of their degrees;
4: **while** $\exists v \in V$ s.t. $score(v) = -1$
5:    $v^* \leftarrow \arg\max_{v \in V, \, score(v)=-1} d(v)$;
6:    $\overline{bound}(v^*) \leftarrow \lfloor \frac{d(v^*)}{t} \rfloor$;
7:    **if** $|S| = k$ and $\overline{bound}(v^*) \leq \min_{v \in S} score(v)$ **then**
8:       **break**;
9:    $score(v^*) \leftarrow$ bfs-search (G, t, v^*);
10:   **if** $|S| < k$ **then** $S \leftarrow S \cup \{v^*\}$;
11:   **else if** $score(v^*) > \min_{v \in S} score(v)$ **then**
12:     $u \leftarrow \arg\min_{v \in S} score(v)$;
13:     $S \leftarrow (S - \{u\}) \cup \{v^*\}$;
14: **return** S;

Example 5.2.2 *Consider the graph in Figure 5.1a. Suppose that $k = 1$ and $t = 1$. The top-k computation process is illustrated in Figure 5.2. The sorted vertex list is $c, a, b, f, h, i, d, e, g$ in descending order of degrees. The algorithm computes the structural diversity of these vertices in turn, and terminates before computing $score(g)$ (see Figure 5.2). This is because we have $\min_{v \in S} score(v) = score(e) = 3$ and $\overline{bound}(g) = 3 \leq \min_{v \in S} score(v)$. Therefore, Algorithm 5.22 can save one structural diversity computation. It is easy to verify from the table in Figure 5.2 that the algorithm cannot terminate earlier.*

v	c	a	b	f	h	i	d	e	g
bound	5	4	4	4	4	4	3	3	3
score	1	2	2	2	2	2	1	3	-
S	$\{c\}$			$\{a\}$				$\{e\}$	

Figure 5.2: Illustration of the **degree** algorithm.

Theorem 5.2.1 *For $1 \leq k \leq n$ and $1 \leq t \leq n$, Algorithm 5.22 performs top-k structural diversity search in $O(\sum_{v \in V} (d(v))^2)$ time and $O(m)$ space.*

Proof. The algorithm first sorts all vertices in $O(n)$ time using the bin-sort algorithm [53]. It has to calculate the structural diversity for every vertex to answer a top-k query in the worst case. Consider a vertex v. When the algorithm computes $score(u)$ for each neighbor $u \in N(v)$, it has to scan the adjacency list of v, taking $O(d(v))$ time. Since there are $|N(v)| = d(v)$ neighbors, the total cost for scanning v's adjacency list is $O((d(v))^2)$. Thus, it takes $O(\sum_{v \in V} (d(v))^2)$ time to calculate the structural diversities for all vertices. In addition, one can maintain the top-k results in $O(n)$ time and $O(n)$ space using a variant of bin-sort list. Thus, the time complexity of Algorithm 5.22 is $O(\sum_{v \in V} (d(v))^2)$.

In terms of the space consumption, the graph storage takes $O(n + m)$ space, and $\mathcal{S}$ takes $O(n)$ space. Thus, the space complexity of Algorithm 5.22 is $O(n + m) \subseteq O(m)$. □

Remark 5.1   The worst-case time complexity of Algorithm 5.22 is bounded by $O(\sum_{v \in V} d(v) \cdot d_{\max}) = O(m d_{\max}) \subseteq O(mn)$.

5.2.4   A NOVEL TOP-k SEARCH FRAMEWORK

The degree-based upper bound in Lemma 5.2.1 is loose. As a result, the degree-based algorithm is not very efficient for top-k search. To improve the efficiency, the key challenge is to develop a tighter upper bound. To this end, in this section, we discuss a novel framework with a tighter pruning bound and present a new algorithm called fast-bound-search to compute the structural diversity score. Before discussing the framework, we present two structural properties of graphs, which are very useful for developing the new bound.

Two Structural Properties

Property 5.2   For any vertex $v \in V$, if a vertex $u \in N(v)$ forms a size-1 component in $G_{N(v)}$, then v also forms a size-1 component in $G_{N(u)}$.

Proof. We prove by contradiction. Suppose that in $G_{N(u)}$, v is adjacent to another vertex w in a component. Then we can infer that $w \in N(u)$ and $w \in N(v)$. As u and w are adjacent and both are in $N(v)$, u and w, possibly with other vertices, form a component of size at least 2 in $G_{N(v)}$, which contradicts to the fact that u forms a size-1 component in $G_{N(v)}$. The property follows. □

As an example, in Figure 5.1b, vertex e forms a size-1 component in $G_{N(f)}$. Symmetrically, vertex f also forms a size-1 component in $G_{N(e)}$.

Property 5.3   If three vertices u, v, w form a triangle in G, then the sets $\{u, v\}$, $\{v, w\}$, and $\{u, w\}$ belong to the same component in $G_{N(w)}$, $G_{N(u)}$, and $G_{N(v)}$ respectively.

Proof. Immediately follows from the definition. □

For instance, in Figure 5.1a, vertices a, f, g form a triangle in G. We can observe that $\{a, g\}$ belong to a connected component in $G_{N(f)}$ in Figure 5.1b. Similarly, $\{a, f\}$ (resp., $\{f, g\}$) belong to a connected component in $G_{N(g)}$ (resp., $G_{N(a)}$).

Based on the two properties above, we can save considerable computational cost in computing the structural diversity scores. For example, if we find that vertex u forms a size-1 component in $G_{N(v)}$, then we know that v also forms a size-1 component in $G_{N(u)}$ by Property 5.2. Thus, when we compute $score(u)$, we do not need to perform a breadth-first search from v, because we already know v forms a size-1 component in $G_{N(u)}$. If we can efficiently record such *structural information* of v's neighbors when we compute $score(v)$, we can save on the associated computational cost. More importantly, such structural information can help us get a tighter upper bound on structural diversity scores. In the following subsection, we shall make use of a modified disjoint-set forest data structure to maintain such structural information efficiently.

Disjoint-Set Forest Data Structure

We adapt the classical disjoint-set forest data structure and the Union-Find algorithm [53] to maintain the structural information for each vertex efficiently. The modified structure consists of four operations: Make-Forest, Find-Set, Union, and Isolate. Compared to the classical disjoint-set forest data structure, the new structure includes an additional operation Isolate which is used to record the structural information described in Property 1, i.e., a vertex forms a size-1 component. The modified structure is thus called Union-Find-Isolate. Algorithm 5.23 describes the four operations.

Make-Forest: For each vertex $v \in V$, we create a disjoint-set forest structure, denoted as $g[v]$, for its neighbors $N(v)$ using the Make-Forest (v) procedure in Algorithm 5.23. Specifically, for each $u \in N(v)$, we build a single-node tree $T[u]$ with three fields: parent, rank, and count. The parent is initialized to be u itself, the rank is set to 0 and the count is set to 1, as there is only one vertex u in the tree. In addition, we also create a virtual node $T[0]$ which is used to collect all size-1 components in $G_{N(v)}$. The parent of $T[0]$ is set to 0 and the count is set to 0 because there is no size-1 component identified yet. For convenience, we refer to the operation of creating a single-node tree (line 4) or a virtual node (line 5) as a Make-Set operation.

Find-Set: Following classic techniques [53], the Find-Set (x) procedure is used to find the root of $T[x]$ using the *path compression* heuristic.

Union: Following [53], the Union(x, y) procedure applies the *union by rank* heuristic to union the two trees $T[fx]$ and $T[fy]$ which x and y belong to, respectively. Here, fx and fy are the roots of these two trees. If fx and fy have unequal rank, the one with a higher rank is set to be the parent of the other vertex with a lower rank. Otherwise, we arbitrarily choose one of them as the parent and increase its rank by 1. For both cases, we update the *count* of the root of the new tree.

Isolate: Procedure Isolate(x) unions a size-1 tree $T[x]$ into the virtual tree $T[0]$. It sets $T[x].parent$ to 0, and increases $T[0].count$ by 1. Isolate(x) essentially labels x as a size-1 component if we find x is not adjacent to any other node in a neighborhood induced subgraph.

We can apply the disjoint-set forest structure to maintain the connected components in $G_{N(v)}$. For any vertex $v \in V$, we create a rooted tree for every neighbor $u \in N(v)$ initially. If we find that u and w are adjacent in $G_{N(v)}$, then we process it by $g[v]$.Union(u, w). If we identify that u forms a size-1 component in $G_{N(v)}$, we process it by $g[v]$.Isolate(u). Take $G_{N(f)}$ in Figure 5.1b as an example again. First, we create $g[f]$ by Make-Forest (f) as shown in Figure 5.3a. Since vertices a and g are adjacent, we invoke $g[f]$.Union(a, g) and the resulting structure is shown in Figure 5.3b. The combined tree is rooted at g and has 2 vertices. Vertex e forms a size-1 component, thus we invoke $g[f]$.Isolate(e) and the result is shown in Figure 5.3c.

	Parent	Rank	Count		Parent	Rank	Count		Parent	Rank	Count
T[0] = {	0 ,	0 ,	0 }	T[0] = {	0 ,	0 ,	0 }	**T[0] = {**	**0 ,**	**0 ,**	**1 }**
T[a] = {	a ,	0 ,	1 }	**T[a] = {**	**g ,**	**0 ,**	**1 }**	T[a] = {	g ,	0 ,	1 }
T[e] = {	e ,	0 ,	1 }	T[e] = {	e ,	0 ,	1 }	**T[e] = {**	**0 ,**	**0 ,**	**1 }**
T[g] = {	g ,	0 ,	1 }	**T[g] = {**	**g ,**	**1 ,**	**2 }**	T[g] = {	g ,	1 ,	2 }
T[i] = {	i ,	0 ,	1 }	T[i] = {	i ,	0 ,	1 }	T[i] = {	i ,	0 ,	1 }
(a) Make-Forest(f)				(b) $g[f]$.Union(a,g)				(c) $g[f]$.Isolate(e)			

Figure 5.3: Disjoint-set forest data structure g[f].

The time complexity of the Union-Find-Isolate algorithm is analyzed next.

Lemma 5.2.2 *A sequence of M* Make–Set, Union, Find-Set, *and* Isolate *operations, N of which are* Make-Set *operations, can be performed on a disjoint-set forest with "union by rank" and "path compression" heuristics in worst-case time* $O(M\alpha(N))$, *where* $\alpha(N)$ *is the inverse Ackermann function.*

Proof. The proof is similar to that in [53], thus it is omitted. □

Note that for any reasonably large values of N, $\alpha(N)$ is at most 4. In the following, for simplicity, we treat $\alpha(N)$ as a constant in the complexity analysis. Thus, essentially, the time complexity of the Union-Find-Isolate algorithm can be regarded as $O(M)$.

A Tighter Upper Bound

With the disjoint-set forest data structure $g[v]$, we can keep track of the structural information of the connected components in $G_{N(v)}$ and derive a tighter upper bound of $score(v)$ than the degree-based bound in Lemma 5.2.1. Before presenting the upper bound, we give a definition of the *identified size-1 set*.

Definition 5.2.2 *In the disjoint-set forest structure $g[v]$, if $u \in N(v)$ and $T[u].parent = 0$, we define $S_u = \{u\}$ as an* identified size-1 set, *and $|S_u| = 1$. If $u \in N(v)$, $T[u].parent = u$, we define $S_u = \{w \in N(v) : \text{Find-Set}(w) = u\}$ as an* unidentified set, *and $|S_u| := T[u].count$.*

By Definition 5.2.2, we know that each identified size-1 set results from an Isolate operation, and that the total number of the identified size-1 sets is $T[0].count$. Whenever the Union operation is performed on a pair of sets, respectively, containing elements x and y, i.e., the sets

Algorithm 5.23 Union-Find-Isolate

1: **procedure** Make-Forest (v)
2: $g[v] = \{T[u] : u \in N(v)\} \cup \{T[0]\}$;
3: **for** $u \in N(v)$ **do**
4:     $T[u].(parent, rank, count) \leftarrow (u, 0, 1)$;
5: $T[0].(parent, rank, count) \leftarrow (0, 0, 0)$;
6: **procedure** Find-Set (x)
7: **if** $x \neq T[x].parent$ **then**
8:     $T[x].parent \leftarrow$ Find-Set $(T[x].parent)$;
9: **return** $T[x].parent$;
10: **procedure** Union (x, y)
11: $fx \leftarrow$ Find-Set (x); $fy \leftarrow$ Find-Set (y);
12: **if** $fx \neq fy$ **then**
13:     **if** $T[fx].rank > T[fy].rank$ **then**
14:         $T[fy].parent \leftarrow fx$;
15:         $T[fx].count \leftarrow T[fx].count + T[fy].count$;
16:     **else**
17:         $T[fx].parent \leftarrow fy$;
18:         $T[fy].count \leftarrow T[fx].count + T[fy].count$;
19:         **if** $T[fx].rank = T[fy].rank$ **then**
20:             $T[fy].rank \leftarrow T[fy].rank + 1$;
21: **procedure** Isolate (x)
22: $T[x].parent \leftarrow 0$;
23: $T[0].count \leftarrow T[0].count + 1$;

with roots fx and fy in the Union-Find-Isolate data structure, we say that the corresponding sets get *merged*. According to Property 5.2, all identified size-1 sets do not get merged with other sets. On the other hand, unidentified sets may either get merged further with other sets or become identified size-1 sets. Consider the example in Figure 5.3c. $S_e = \{e\}$ is an identified size-1 set and $T[0].count = 1$. Both $S_g = \{a, g\}$ and $S_i = \{i\}$ are unidentified sets.

Let $S = \{S_u : u \in N(v) \land T[u].\text{parent} = u \lor T[u].\text{parent} = 0\}$ denote all disjoint sets in $g[v]$, excluding the virtual set $T[0]$. After traversing all the vertices and edges in $G_{N(v)}$, the set S computed by the algorithm contains all actual sets corresponding to the connected components in $G_{N(v)}$, and additionally we have $score(v) = |\{S_u : S_u \in S, |S_u| \geq t\}|$. However, before traversing the neighborhood induced subgraph $G_{N(v)}$, S may not contain all the actual sets corresponding to the connected components, but may include some intermediate results. Even with such intermediate results maintained in S, we can still use them to derive an upper bound. Specifically, we have the following lemma.

Lemma 5.2.3 *Let $S = \{S_1, \ldots, S_l\}$ be the disjoint sets of $g[v]$, a be the number of identified size-1 sets, b be the number of sets whose sizes are larger than or equal to t, and c be the total size of these b sets. Then, we have an upper bound on $score(v)$ as follows. If $t = 1$, $\overline{bound}(v) = b$; if $t > 1$, $\overline{bound}(v) = b + \lfloor \frac{d(v)-c-a}{t} \rfloor$.*

Proof. First, it is important to note that the current disjoint sets in S are not final, if we have not traversed all vertices and edges of $G_{N(v)}$. That is, some of them may be further merged by the Union operation and the number of sets may be reduced. The current number of sets whose size is greater than or equal to t is b and this number can only be reduced with the Union operation. In addition, besides the a identified size-1 sets and the c vertices from the above b sets, there are still $d(v) - c - a$ vertices which may potentially form sets whose sizes are greater than or equal to t. The maximum number of such potential sets is $\lfloor \frac{d(v)-c-a}{t} \rfloor$. Thus, we have $\overline{bound}(v) = b + \lfloor \frac{d(v)-c-a}{t} \rfloor$. $\qquad\square$

For any vertex $v \in V$, at the initialization stage, each neighbor vertex $u \in N(v)$ forms a size-1 component. Thus, $\overline{bound}(v) = 0 + \lfloor \frac{d(v)-0-0}{t} \rfloor = \lfloor \frac{d(v)}{t} \rfloor$, the same as the bound in Lemma 5.2.1. As the disjoint sets are gradually merged, $\overline{bound}(v)$ is refined toward $score(v)$ and becomes tighter. For example, in Figure 5.3c, suppose $t = 2$, then we obtain $S = \{S_e, S_g, S_i\}$ and the three parameters in Lemma 5.2.3 are $a = 1$, $b = 1$ and $c = 2$. It follows that $\overline{bound}(f) = 1 + \lfloor \frac{4-2-1}{2} \rfloor = 1$, which is equal to $score(f) = 1$. This bound, based on the disjoint-set forest, is obviously tighter than the degree-based bound $\lfloor \frac{4}{2} \rfloor = 2$ derived in Lemma 5.2.1.

Top-K Search Framework

Based on the disjoint-set forest data structure and the tighter upper bound, Huang et al. [87, 88] propose an advanced search framework for top-k structural diversity search.

Advanced Top-k framework: As shown in Algorithm 5.24, for each vertex $v \in V$, the algorithm initializes the disjoint-set forest data structure $g[v]$ by invoking Make-Forest (line 4). It also pushes each vertex v with the initial bound $\lfloor \frac{d(v)}{t} \rfloor$ into $\mathcal{H}$ which is a variant of bin-sort list. Then the algorithm iteratively finds the top-k results (lines 6–19). It first pops the vertex with the largest upper bound value from $\mathcal{H}$. Such a vertex and its bound are denoted as v^* and *topbound*, respectively, (line 7). The algorithm re-evaluates $\overline{bound}(v^*)$ from $g[v^*]$ based on Lemma 5.2.3, as the component information in $g[v^*]$ may have been updated. And then, it compares the refined bound $\overline{bound}(v^*)$ with the old bound *topbound*.

In order to avoid frequently calculating the upper bounds and updating $\mathcal{H}$, a new parameter $\theta \geq 1$ is introduced to compare $\theta \cdot \overline{bound}(v^*)$ with *topbound*.

If $\theta \cdot \overline{bound}(v^*) < topbound$, it suggests that $\overline{bound}(v^*)$ is substantially smaller than *topbound*. That is, the old bound *topbound* is too loose. Under this condition, if $|\mathcal{S}| < k$ or $\overline{bound}(v^*) > \min_{v \in S} score(v)$, the algorithm pushes v^* back to $\mathcal{H}$ with the refined bound $\overline{bound}(v^*)$ (lines 10–11). Otherwise, the algorithm can safely prune v^*. In both cases, the algorithm continues to pop the next vertex from $\mathcal{H}$ (lines 9–12).

If $\theta \cdot \overline{bound}(v^*) \geq topbound$, it means that $\overline{bound}(v^*)$ is not substantially smaller than *topbound*. In other words, the old bound is a relatively tight estimation. Then the algorithm moves to lines 13–14 to check the termination condition. If $|\mathcal{S}| = k$ and *topbound* $\leq$

Algorithm 5.24 Top-k-search

Input: $G = (V, E)$, the top-k value k, the component size threshold t, gradient ratio $\theta \geq 1$.
Output: Top-k search result S.

1:   $\mathcal{H} \leftarrow \emptyset; S \leftarrow \emptyset$;
2:   **for** $v \in V$ **do**
3:      $score(v) \leftarrow -1$;
4:      Make-Forest (v);
5:      $\mathcal{H}.push((v, \lfloor \frac{d(v)}{t} \rfloor))$;
6:   **while** $\mathcal{H} \neq \emptyset$
7:      $(v^*, topbound) \leftarrow \mathcal{H}.pop()$;
8:      compute $\overline{bound}(v^*)$ according to Lemma 5.2.3;
9:      **if** $\theta \cdot \overline{bound}(v^*) < topbound$ **then**
10:        **if** $|S| < k$ or $\overline{bound}(v^*) > \min_{v \in S} score(v)$ **then**
11:          $\mathcal{H}.push((v^*, \overline{bound}(v^*)))$;
12:        **continue**;
13:      **if** $|S| = k$ and $topbound \leq \min_{v \in S} score(v)$ **then**
14:        **break**;
15:      $score(v^*) \leftarrow$ fast-bound-search (G, t, v^*);
16:      **if** $|S| < k$ **then** $S \leftarrow S \cup \{v^*\}$;
17:      **else if** $score(v^*) > \min_{v \in S} score(v)$ **then**
18:        $u \leftarrow \arg\min_{v \in S} score(v)$;
19:        $S \leftarrow (S - \{u\}) \cup \{v^*\}$;
20: **return** S;

$\min_{v \in S} score(v)$, the algorithm can safely prune all the remaining vertices in $\mathcal{H}$ and terminate, because the upper bound of those vertices is smaller than $topbound$.

     If the early termination condition is not satisfied, the algorithm invokes the fast-bound-search algorithm (line 15) to compute $score(v^*)$. The fast-bound-search algorithm is shown in Algorithm 5.25 and will be described later. After computing $score(v^*)$, the algorithm uses the same process to update the set S by v^* as the degree algorithm (Algorithm 5.22) does (lines 16–19).

Fast-Bound-Search: Algorithm 5.25 shows the fast-bound-search procedure to compute $score(v)$. Based on the disjoint-set forest $g[v]$, we know that any vertex $u \in N(v)$ with $T[u].parent = 0$ corresponds to an identified size-1 component resulting from an Isolate operation. So fast-bound-search does not need to search such vertices again. It only adds the vertices whose $parent \neq 0$ into an unvisited vertex hashtable R (lines 1–2). This is an improvement from bfs-search, as fast-bound-search avoids scanning the identified size-1 components. For each vertex $u \in R$, the algorithm invokes the procedure fast-bound-bfs (lines 5-20) to search u's neighborhood in a breadth-first search manner. The key step is in procedure fast-bound-bfs for traversing a connected component. When accessing the adjacency list of vertex u having $d(u) > d(v)$, we will access the adjacency list of v instead (lines 10–13), i.e., we always se-

---

Algorithm 5.25 fast-bound-search (G, t, v)

Input: $G = (V, E)$, the component size threshold t, vertex v.
Output: $score(v)$.

1: $R \leftarrow \emptyset$;
2: **for** $u \in N(v)$ and $T[u].parent \neq 0$ **do** $R \leftarrow R \cup \{u\}$;
3: **for** $u \in R$ **do** fast-bound-bfs (u);
4: **return** count-components $(g[v], t)$;
5: **procedure** fast-bound-bfs (u)
6: $Q \leftarrow \emptyset$; $UnionFlag \leftarrow$ false;
7: $Q.EnQueue(u)$; $R \leftarrow R - \{u\}$;
8: **while** $Q \neq \emptyset$
9:     $u \leftarrow Q.DeQueue()$;
10:     **if** $d(u) > d(v)$ **then** $MinAdjL \leftarrow N(v)$;
11:     **else** $MinAdjL \leftarrow N(u)$;
12:     **for** $w \in MinAdjL$ **do**
13:         **if** $(w, u) \in E$ and $w \in R$ **then**
14:             $Q.EnQueue(w)$; $R \leftarrow R - \{w\}$;
15:             $g[v]$.Union (u, w); $UnionFlag \leftarrow$ true;
16:             **if** $score(u) = -1$ **then** $g[u]$.Union (v, w);
17:             **if** $score(w) = -1$ **then** $g[w]$.Union (v, u);
18: **if** $UnionFlag =$ false **then**
19:     $g[v]$.Isolate (u);
20:     **if** $score(u) = -1$ **then** $g[u]$.Isolate (v);
21: **procedure** count-components $(g[v], t)$
22: $score \leftarrow 0$;
23: **for** $u \in N(v)$ **do**
24:     **if** $T[u].parent = u$ and $T[u].count \geq t$ **then**
25:         $score \leftarrow score + 1$;
26: **if** $t = 1$ **then** $score \leftarrow score + T[0].count$;
27: **return** $score$;

---

lect the vertex with a smaller degree to access. Checking whether $(w, u) \in E$ in line 13 can be done efficiently by keeping all edges in a hashtable. Moreover, R can also be implemented by a hashtable. Thus, line 13 can be done in expected constant time by hashing.

To show the effectiveness of this improvement, we consider an example $G_{N(r)}$ in Figure 5.4. Suppose that r has two neighbors p and q with degree 1 and 100, respectively. To compute $score(r)$, a naive degree-based search method (Algorithm 5.22) needs to access the adjacency lists of p and q, and check $|N(p)| + |N(q)| = 101$ vertices. In contrast, fast-bound-search accesses $N(r)$ instead of $N(q)$ because $d(q) > d(r)$, thus the number of visited vertices is reduced to $|N(p)| + |N(r)| = 3$.

After using the breadth-first search to traverse all connected components of $G_{N(v)}$, the algorithm can compute $score(v)$ using the procedure count-components (lines 19–25) to count the number of sets in $g[v]$ whose sizes are at least t.

$$(p) - - - - (r) - - - - (q)$$
$$d(p) = 1 \qquad d(q) = 100$$

Figure 5.4: $G_{N(r)}$ has two vertices p and q with degree 1 and 100.

The following example illustrates how the Top-k-search framework (Algorithm 5.24) works.

Example 5.2.3 *Consider the graph shown in Figure 5.1a. Suppose that $t = 1$ and $k = 1$. We apply the Top-k-search algorithm with $\theta = 1$ and the running steps are depicted in Figure 5.5. First, we push each vertex v with the upper bound $\lfloor \frac{d(v)}{t} \rfloor$ into $\mathcal{H}$, as shown in Figure 5.5a. Second, we pop vertex c from $\mathcal{H}$ with topbound = 5. We calculate $\overline{bound}(c) = 5$ according to Lemma 5.2.3. Then, we compute score(c) by fast-bound-search. In $G_{N(c)}$, there is a single path connecting all vertices a, b, d, h, i in $N(c)$, so score(c) = 1. When the algorithm traverses the edge (a, b), we perform the operations $g[a]$.Union (c, b) and $g[b]$.Union (c, a) in $g[a]$ and $g[b]$, respectively, according to Property 5.3. Third, we push vertex c into S, as shown in Figure 5.5b. In the next iteration, we pop vertex a from $\mathcal{H}$ with topbound = 4. Then, we update $\overline{bound}(a) = 3$ as we know that vertices b and c are in the same set in $g[a]$. Since $\theta \cdot \overline{bound}(a) <$ topbound and $\overline{bound}(a) > \min_{v \in S}$ score(v), we push $(a, 3)$ into $\mathcal{H}$ again, as shown in Figure 5.5c. When the algorithm proceeds to process vertex f,*

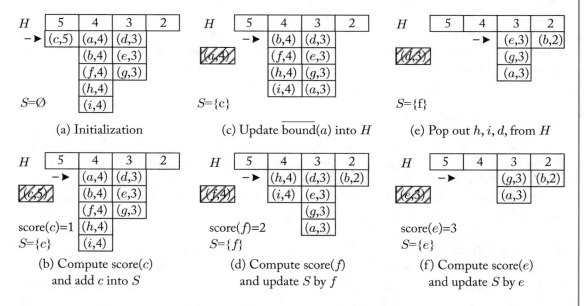

(a) Initialization

(b) Compute score(c) and add c into S

(c) Update $\overline{bound}(a)$ into H

(d) Compute score(f) and update S by f

(e) Pop out h, i, d, from H

(f) Compute score(e) and update S by e

Figure 5.5: Illustration of Top-k-search with fast-bound-search running on the graph in Figure 5.1a. $k = 1$, $t = 1$, and $\theta = 1$.

we have $\theta \cdot \overline{bound}(f) = topbound = 4$ and topbound $> \min_{v \in S} score(v)$. And then we compute score$(f) = 2$ and replace vertex c in S with f, as shown in Figure 5.5d. After that, we pop vertices h, i, d from $\mathcal{H}$ in turn. One can easily check that none of them satisfies the condition in line 10 of Algorithm 5.24. Thus, we do not push h, i, d back into $\mathcal{H}$ again, as shown in Figure 5.5e. Next we pop vertex e, compute score$(e) = 3$, and update S by e, as shown in Figure 5.5f. Since topbound in $\mathcal{H}$ is no greater than score$(e) = 3$, we can safely terminate. In this process, we only invoke fast-bound-search *three times to calculate the structural diversity scores, while the previous* degree*-based algorithm performs eight computations of structural diversity score, which is clearly more expensive.*

Complexity Analysis: Using fast-bound-search to compute structural diversity scores, Top-k-search achieves the following time complexity.

Theorem 5.2.2 *The* Top-k*-search framework using* fast-bound-search *takes* $O(\sum_{(u,v) \in E} \min\{d(u), d(v)\})$ *time and $O(m)$ space.*

According to [47], $O(\sum_{(u,v) \in E} \min\{d(u), d(v)\}) \subseteq O(\rho m)$ where ρ is the arboricity of a graph G and $\rho \leq \min \{\lceil \sqrt{m} \rceil, d_{\max}\}$ for any graph G. Thus, the worst-case time complexity of the Top-k-search framework using fast-bound-search is bounded by $O(\sum_{(u,v) \in E} \min\{d(u), d(v)\}) \subseteq O(\rho m) \subseteq O(m^{1.5})$.

Before closing this section, we note that the notion of structural diversity admits useful natural generalizations. Specifically, the notion we discussed thus far is based on the size of the connected components in the ego-network of a vertex, where all components are treated alike regardless of how densely connected or cohesive they are. One way of making our measurement of structural diversity scores more stringent is to count only those components which are cohesive, wherein one can use different definitions of cohesive subgraphs. In the next section, we conduct case studies based on one such extended notion of structural diversity.

5.2.5   CASE STUDIES

To gain more insight into the utility of the structural diversity search problem, in this section, we adopt a core-based notion of structural diversity. The idea is that rather than base structural diversity score on the number of components whose size is above a threshold, we base it on connected t-cores in the ego-network of the vertex in question. More precisely, the notion of *core-based structural diversity* measures diversity based on the number of components of the t-core of the neighborhood graph. The core-based structural diversity measure has been proven effective through case studies in [163], as the t-core notion can effectively exclude small and loosely connected components. In other words, in terms of graph structure, for a user with a small number of friends, a connected component is strong enough to represent a social circle; on the other hand, for a user with a large number of friends, since the structure of his/her neighborhood network becomes complex, a connected t-core as cohesive structure is a much better means to model the diversity of his/her social circle.

Compared with the component-based structural diversity which only imposes constraints of connectivity and size, the core-based structural diversity considers both the size and cohesiveness of each component. Thus, the core-based definition can help identify densely connected and more meaningful and distinct social contexts among a user's friends. On the other hand, the component-based structural diversity is more suitable for analyzing the social context diversity for nodes whose neighbors are not densely connected, since very few results can be discovered by the core-based structural diversity in this case.

In summary, component-based structural diversity is simpler. However, it does not consider the closeness of members in each component. Core-based structural diversity has more constraints by considering both cohesiveness and size. However, it is more difficult to compute and may lose the information of vertices that do not participate in a cohesive subgraph. Therefore, both definitions have advantages and disadvantages, and they can be jointly used to discover more social context diversity information in a large network. More comparisons and meaningful results for both component-based and core-based structural diversities using real-world networks can be found in the following case studies.

Identifying Ambiguous Names

Name ambiguity has long been viewed as a challenging problem in social network analysis. For example, when we for search a person named "Wei Wang" from the DBLP website, there are at least 173 distinct persons with the same name.[1] Our top-k structural diversity search method provides a novel approach for identifying ambiguous names in a social network, which is the first and important step for name disambiguation. In this case study, we build a collaboration network from the DBLP dataset.[2] A vertex represents an author name and an edge is added between two authors if they have co-authored three or more times. The network so constructed from DBLP contains 234,879 vertices and 541,814 edges [88].

We first apply the component-based structural diversity measure [87] on the DBLP network for finding top-5 authors with the highest number of connected components of size over 2. The result is shown in Table 5.1. As we can see, these five names are indeed popular but ambiguous, which can correspond to different distinct persons in the real world. For comparison, we select five famous authors who have a large degree, i.e., a large number of collaborators, and report their structural diversity score. Despite the large degree, their structural diversity score is far smaller than that of the ambiguous names. Intuitively, we can imagine that an ambiguous name corresponds to different distinct persons, each of who has his/her own research communities. This leads to a large number of non-overlapping research communities associated with an ambiguous name. In addition, we also observe that many of such communities are tiny and loosely connected. This is because the component-based structural diversity does not enforce a cohesive structure in the components.

---

[1]https://dblp.uni-trier.de/pers/hd/w/Wang:Wei
[2]http://dblp.uni-trier.de/xml/

Table 5.1: Ambiguous names (top-5 structural diversity result based on size-2 connected component) and selected famous authors in DBLP network. Ambiguous names obviously have much higher structural diversity scores than famous authors.

Ambiguous Name			Famous Authors		
Name	Degree	Score	Name	Degree	Score
Yang Liu	126	33	Christos Faloutsos	97	10
Xin Li	150	31	Philip S. Yu	140	5
Yan Zhang	157	29	Jiawei Han	132	4
Wei Wang	117	29	H. V. Jagadish	62	4
Wei Liu	151	28	Gerhard Weikum	103	2

We also apply the core-based structural diversity measure on the DBLP network for finding top-5 authors using 2-core subgraphs [88], and report the result in Table 5.2. By definition, the 2-core based measure discards all tree-shaped components, and counts the remaining cohesive components into the score. As a result, the obtained scores in Table 5.2 are smaller than the component-based scores in Table 5.1. Moreover, we observe that the core-based top-5 ambiguous names are different from the component-based top-5 names in Table 5.1. This suggests that these two diversity measures can complement each other.

This case study shows that our top-k structural diversity search provides an effective mechanism for finding ambiguous names in a social network.

Table 5.2: Ambiguous names (top-5 structural diversity result based on 2-core) and selected famous authors in DBLP network. Ambiguous names obviously have much higher structural diversity scores than famous authors.

Ambiguous Name			Famous Authors		
Name	Degree	Score	Name	Degree	Score
Yang Yang	107	15	Christos Faloutsos	97	6
Yu Zhang	105	15	Philip S. Yu	140	3
Ming Li	149	15	H. V. Jagadish	62	3
Peng Wang	80	14	Jiawei Han	132	2
Xin Li	150	13	Gerhard Weikum	103	2

Words with Diverse Meanings

In this case study, we apply the two structural diversity measures on a word association network.[3] The expected result is to find the words with the most diverse meanings, and to analyze and understand the different meanings of these words in different contexts. In this network, a vertex represents a word, and an edge between two words v and u represents an associative relationship of v and u, if word v comes to mind when word u is shown as a stimulus. The network contains 7,207 vertices and 31,784 edges.

We first query top-1 vertex in the word association network by counting the number of connected components of size over 2. The result is depicted in Figure 5.6. The word "black" has the highest structural diversity score of 9, indicating 9 distinct connected components in the neighborhood induced subgraph of "black," and each distinct component represents a certain meaning of "black." The largest connected component (depicted in red) contains 22 words, and most of those words can be roughly summarized by three words as "color," "race," and "dark." For example, "black" is a "color," and "black" is related to other colors such as "white," "red," "blue," "yellow," etc. For the other 8 connected components, each contains 2–3 words, and represents a distinct context of words associated with "black," such as {"penguin," "tuxedo" }, {"panther," "cat" }, {"death," "widow," "funeral" }, and so on.

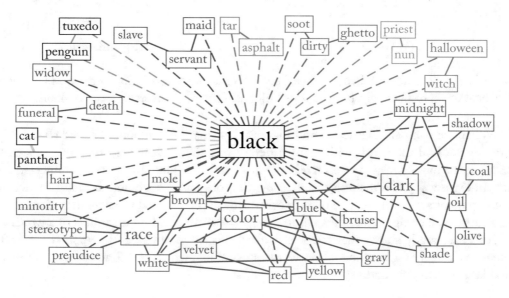

Figure 5.6: Top-1 structural diversity based on size-2 connected components in the word association network. The ego-network network of the center node "black," which has the highest structural diversity score of 9.

---

[3]http://www.netcom-analyzer.org/datasets/166

Next, we query top-2 vertices in the word association network using 2-core subgraphs. Two words, "word" and "Christmas", have the highest two structural diversity scores of 4 and 3, which are shown in Figure 5.7. As we can see, each vertex in the 2-core component in Figure 5.7 has at least two neighbor words. Specifically, the word "word" in Figure 5.7a has 4 distinct contexts of associated words with different meanings. For example, {"swear," "oath," "promise" } represent the synonym of "words" as "promise," and {"verb," "noun," "pronoun" } are different types of "word." The word "Christmas" has three distinct contexts of associated words, as shown in Figure 5.7b, {"reindeer," "sleigh," "Santa" } describe "Santa," {"present," "gift," "package" } represent "Christmas gifts" and {"tree," "ornament," "decoration" } are related to the "Christmas tree."

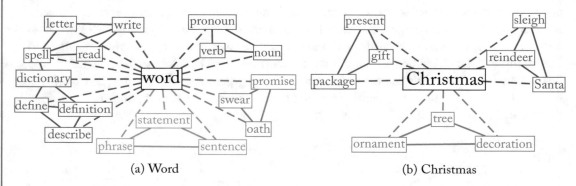

(a) Word   (b) Christmas

Figure 5.7: Top-2 structural diversity based on 2-core in word association network. Here "word" and "Christmas", respectively, has the top-2 highest structural diversity score as 4 and 3.

When we compare Figure 5.6 and Figure 5.7, using the component-based structural diversity, we can find the words with many different meanings. However, the terms in a certain context may be loosely related to each other (e.g., "hair" and "blue" in the same connected component in Figure 5.6). On the other hand, using the core-based structural diversity, the terms in each component are highly related to each other. But the core-based measure may discard some loosely connected components, thus fail to extract the corresponding meanings of a word.

This case study shows that top-k structural diversity search can be applied for finding different meanings of a word based on word associations, which is a fundamental problem in natural language understanding.

5.3   LEARNING TO DISCOVER SOCIAL CIRCLES

Given a user, the task of social circle discovery is finding all social circles in the ego-network of this user. In this section, we introduce a machine learning approach to address this problem. In principle, we could adopt a combinatorial perspective to social circle discovery. The reason we introduce the machine learning perspective here is two-fold. First, it offers a significant insight into query-dependent community detection using statistical/learning techniques, complementing the combinatorial perspective we have take for problems such as attributed community search. Second, the ego-network of this problem is usually small in size. The statistics of real-world datasets of ego-network can be found in Section 7.1.3. For example, the ego-network of Facebook has just 4,964 vertices. This indicates that the problem of social circle discovery can be addressed in an efficient way, although the learning model may be complex and time consuming to train. A detailed comparison of social circle discovery and attributed community search is provided next.

5.3.1 ATTRIBUTED COMMUNITY SEARCH AND SOCIAL CIRCLE DISCOVERY

Attributed community search [65, 93] aims to find all communities in a network that contain given query vertices, with homogeneous query attributes. Here, the network may have a large number of nodes and millions or even billions of edges. Moreover, community nodes may have a hop distance of more than 2. However, social circle discovery [117, 170], takes just one query vertex q as input and only focuses on q's ego-network to find all communities. In addition, the members of circles are required to be the neighbors of the query vertex q, and cannot be more than one hop away from q. In this sense, the problem of social circle discovery can be regarded as the task of community search in the ego-network of a given query vertex q with no input query attributes.[4]

Social circles. A model of circles should have the following properties. (1) Nodes within circles have common attributes, or "aspects." (2) Different circles should be formed by different aspects, e.g., a circle might be formed by a person's high school classmates, and another significantly different circle based on family members. (3) Circles can be overlapping, and "strong" circles are allowed to form within "weaker" ones. For example, a circle of friends from the same class may form within a circle from the same high school. One can make use of both attribute (profile) information and network structure to discover social circles. The attribute information can be used to provide an interpretable reason for a circle to form. This is similar to the task of attribute-driven community search. In the following, we discuss the difference between social circle discovery and attributed community search.

5.3.2 PROBLEM FORMULATION

The input of social circle model is an ego-network $G_{N(u)}$ where the vertex set is V_u and the edge set is E_u, along with attributed "profiles" attr(v) for each user $v \in N(u)$. The goal of social circle discovery is to predict a set of circles $\mathcal{C} = \{C_1, \ldots, C_K\}$, where $C_k \subseteq V_u$, and associated parameter vectors θ_k indicating how each circle is generated. Given two vertices x and y, we use pairwise features $\phi(x, y)$ to represent the common attributes shared by vertices x and y. In

---

[4]Recall that the ego-network of q does *not* contain q.

the next section, we present one method to construct the feature vectors $\phi(x, y)$ for one real application in Facebook.

5.3.3   A GENERATIVE MODEL FOR SOCIAL CIRCLE DISCOVERY

McAuley and Leskovec [117] present a generative model of social circles and devise an unsupervised algorithm to optimize the model. The model treats circle memberships as latent variables. Vertices in a social circle are regarded to have a chance to form an edge, which naturally results in the hierarchical and overlapping structure of circles. Thus, the probability that a pair of vertices $(x, y) \in V_u \times V_u$ form an edge can be modeled as

$$\Pr[(x, y) \in E_u] \propto \exp \left\{ \sum_{C_k \supseteq \{x,y\}} \langle \phi(x, y), \theta_k \rangle - \sum_{C_k \not\supseteq \{x,y\}} \alpha_k \langle \phi(x, y), \theta_k \rangle \right\}. \tag{5.1}$$

The first term

$$\sum_{C_k \supseteq \{x,y\}} \langle \phi(x, y), \theta_k \rangle$$

ranges over the circles containing both nodes x and y, and is a positive term. The second term

$$- \sum_{C_k \not\supseteq \{x,y\}} \alpha_k \langle \phi(x, y), \theta_k \rangle$$

ranges over all other circles that do not contain at least one of the nodes x and y, and thus is a penalty. The rationale is that $\langle \phi(x, y), \theta_k \rangle$ is high if both nodes belong to C_k and low if at least one of them does not belong to C_k, where α_k is a parameter to strike a balance between these two effects. In this way, vertices within a common circle are intuitively given an opportunity to form edges. This model also ensures the existence of hierarchical and overlapping circles naturally, which can explain the observed network data. Considering that each edge $e = (x, y) \in E_u$ is generated independently, we can write the probability of G as

$$P_\Theta(G_{N(u)}; \mathcal{C}) = \prod_{e \in E_u} Pr[e \in E_u] \times \prod_{e \notin E_u} Pr[e \notin E_u], \tag{5.2}$$

where $\Theta = \{(\theta_k, \alpha_k) : k = 1, \ldots, K\}$ is the set of our model parameters. To simply the equations, we define the following shorthand:

$$d_k(e) = \delta(e \in C_k) - \alpha_k \delta(e \notin C_k).$$

$$\Phi(e) = \sum_{C_k \in \mathcal{C}} d_k(e) \langle \phi(e), \theta_k \rangle.$$

Now, the model can be written into the log-likelihood of $G_{N(u)}$ based on Eq. (5.2):

$$l_\Theta(G_{N(u)}; \mathcal{C}) = \sum_{e \in E_u} \Phi(e) - \sum_{e \in V_u \times V_u} \log(1 + e^{\Phi(e)}). \tag{5.3}$$

Next, we describe how to maximize $l_\Theta(G_{N(u)}; C)$ by optimizing the circle memberships C and the user attribute similarity functions $\Theta = \{(\theta_k, \alpha_k) : k = 1, \ldots, K\}$.

Unsupervised Learning of Model Parameters

An unsupervised algorithm is presented to jointly optimize the latent variables and the attribute similarity parameters so as to best explain the observed ego-network data. Treating C as the latent variables, $\hat{\Theta} = \{\hat{\theta}, \hat{\alpha}\}$ is to maximize the regularized log-likelihood of Eq. (5.3), i.e.,

$$\hat{\Theta}, \hat{C} = \underset{\Theta, C}{\arg\max}\, l_\Theta(G_{N(u)}; C) - \lambda\Omega(\theta). \tag{5.4}$$

This problem can be solved using coordinate ascent on Θ and C [128]:

$$C^t = \underset{C}{\arg\max}\, l_{\Theta^t}(G_{N(u)}; C). \tag{5.5}$$

$$\Theta^{t+1} = \underset{\Theta}{\arg\max}\, l_\Theta(G_{N(u)}; C^t) - \lambda\Omega(\theta). \tag{5.6}$$

Note that since Eq. (5.3) is concave in θ, the gradient ascent is used to optimize Eq. (5.6). The partial derivatives are as follows:

$$\frac{\partial l}{\partial \theta_k} = \sum_{e \in V_u \times V_u} -d_k(e)\theta_k \frac{e^{\Phi(e)}}{1 + e^{\Phi(e)}} + \sum_{e \in E_u} d_e(k)\theta_k - \frac{\partial\Omega}{\partial\theta_k}$$

$$\frac{\partial l}{\partial \alpha_k} = \sum_{e \in V_u \times V_u} \delta(e \notin C_k)\langle\phi(e), \theta_k\rangle \frac{e^{\Phi(e)}}{1 + e^{\Phi(e)}} - \sum_{e \in E_u} \delta(e \notin C_k)\langle\phi(e), \theta_k\rangle.$$

For a fixed $C \setminus C_i$, the problem of solving $\arg\max_{C_i} l_\Theta(G_{N(u)}; C \setminus C_i)$ can be expressed as pseudo-boolean optimization in a pairwise graphical model [29]:

$$C_k = \underset{C}{\arg\max} \sum_{(x,y) \in V_u \times V_u} f_{(x,y)}(\delta(x \in C), \delta(y \in C)). \tag{5.7}$$

Specifically, it is hoped that the edges with high weight (under θ_k) to be included in circle C_k, and the edges with low weight to be excluded from C_k. Defining $o_k(e) = \sum_{C_k \in C \setminus C_i} d_k(e)\langle\phi(e), \theta_k\rangle$, the energy function f_e of Eq. (5.7) is defined as follows.
If $e \in E_u$, then the following holds:

$$f_e(0,0) = f_e(0,1) = f_e(1,0) = o_k(e) - \alpha_k\langle\phi(e), \theta_k\rangle - \log\left(1 + e^{o_k(e) - \alpha_k\langle\phi(e), \theta_k\rangle}\right)$$

$$f_e(1,1) = o_k(e) + \langle\phi(e), \theta_k\rangle - \log\left(1 + e^{o_k(e) + \langle\phi(e), \theta_k\rangle}\right);$$

Otherwise, if $e \notin E_u$, then the following holds:

$$f_e(0,0) = f_e(0,1) = f_e(1,0) = -\log\left(1 + e^{o_k(e) - \alpha_k\langle\phi(e),\theta_k\rangle}\right)$$
$$f_e(1,1) = -\log\left(1 + e^{o_k(e) + \langle\phi(e),\theta_k\rangle}\right).$$

In this problem formulation, the techniques of existing work on pseudo-boolean optimization can be adopted. McAuley and Leskovec [117] use the *QPBO* software [145] to solve Eq. (5.7) for each C_k in random order.

Equations (5.5) and (5.6) can be repeatedly computed until convergence, i.e., $C^{t+1} = C^t$. In addition, Eq. (5.4) is regularized using the l_1 norm as $\Omega(\theta) = \sum_{k=1}^{K} \sum_{i=1}^{|\theta_k|} |\theta_{ki}|$. This leads to sparse and readily interpretable parameters.

Finally, to identify the number of circles, the parameter K is computed for minimizing an approximation to the Bayesian Information Criterion (BIC) [7, 79],

$$\hat{K} = \arg\min_{K} BIC\left(K; \Theta^K\right),$$

where Θ^K is the set of parameters predicted for a specific K, and

$$BIC\left(K; \Theta^K\right) \simeq -2l_{\Theta^K}\left(G_{N(u)}; \mathcal{C}\right) + |\Theta^K|\log|E_u|.$$

CHAPTER 6

Geo-Social Group Search

The prosperity of smartphones and other smart devices and the popularity of social networking have led to the rapid growth of geo-social networks, which are also known as location-based social networks (LBSNs). A geo-social network may contain communities that are spatially proximate. Most structural community search algorithms discussed in the previous chapters do not consider the vertices' spatial information. In this chapter, we introduce the techniques of searching geo-social groups in geo-social networks by considering both the communities' structural cohesiveness and spatial proximity.

In the following discussions, we model a geo-social network as an undirected, unweighted simple graph $G = (V, E)$ with $n = |V(G)|$ vertices and $m = |E(G)|$ edges, where each vertex $v \in V$ contains its location information, denoted by p_v. Given a set of query vertices and a spatial constraint, a geo-social group search is to find the communities containing the query vertices with a cohesive structure as well as satisfying the given spatial constraint.

6.1 GEO-SOCIAL GROUP SEARCH

Popular geo-social networks include Facebook, Foursquare, Google+, Instagram, Places, etc. In these networks, a user is often associated with some location information (e.g., hometowns and check-in places). Figure 6.1 depicts a geo-social graph with ten users. The social layer shows the social relationship among the users and the spatial layer displays the location information of each user.

Definition 6.1.1 (Geo-Social Group Search) *Given a geo-social network $G = (V, E)$, a geo-social group search is represented as $Q_{gs} = (Q, \Lambda, \Theta)$, where Q is the query vertex set, Λ is a spatial condition denoting the spatial constraint, and Θ is the group's cohesiveness constraint. A geo-social group search finds a maximal (or minimal) subgraph $H \subseteq G$ which contains the query vertices in Q and satisfies the constraints of Λ and Θ.*

The geo-social group search has many real-life applications [64, 123]. Four representative applications are discussed in the following.

- *Spatial task outsourcing*: Given a set of spatial tasks, each associated with a spatial location, one needs to distribute them to a set of workers, each having a service region. To successfully accomplish the tasks, the service regions of the selected workers should cover the spatial tasks' locations, and the workers are expected to have good collaborative relationships so that the tasks can be efficiently completed. A geo-social group search directly

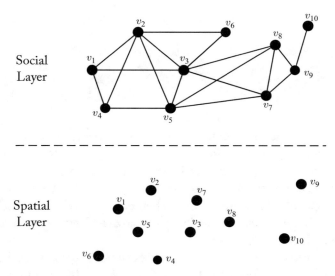

Figure 6.1: An example of geo-social network.

addresses this worker selection problem in spatial task outsourcing. In practice, the size of the group of selected workers should be minimum to minimize the employment cost.

• *Collaborative team organization*: Geo-social group searches are useful for marketing and promotion campaigns. For example, suppose each agent has several familiar market areas and several good collaborators. If a company wants to hire a marketing team to promote its products at some selected locations, a geo-social group search can help find a good team whose familiar market areas cover all promotion locations and that is cohesive while incurring the least cost for the company.

• *Event recommendation*: Many geo-social applications allow social network users to meet up physically. For example, *Meetup* suggests interesting events to users by tracking their locations and past events they have attended or expressed interest. Suppose that we want to recommend events to a user u. We can first find u's geo-social group, whose members are physically close to u. The events proposed by u's geo-social group members can then be recommended to u.

• *Social marketing*: People with close social relationships and with spatial proximity may shop in places that are also physically near. To promote sales, advertisements can be sent to the geo-social groups of users who purchased similar products before. For instance, if a user u has purchased some item, the system can advertise this item to u's geo-social group members.

By employing a different spatial constraint Λ and cohesive constraint Θ, many studies [64, 123, 124, 199] have been devoted to geo-social group query processing. In what follows, we present three representative query processing techniques according to the spatial constraint employed. It is worth noting that all of them employ the k-core as the structural cohesiveness constraint while their spatial constraints are different.

6.2   PROXIMITY-BASED GEO-SOCIAL GROUP SEARCH

This section introduces the geo-social group search based on spatial proximity proposed by Zhu et al. [199].

6.2.1   PROBLEM STATEMENT

Three proximity conditions are considered: spatial range, relaxed i-nearest-neighbors (riNN), and strict i-nearest-neighbors (iNN).[1] Accordingly, they correspond to three types of geo-social group search queries (GSGQ).

Definition 6.2.1 (Geo-Social Group Search with Range Constraint) *A $GSGQ_{range}$ is represented as $Q_{gs} = (\{v\}, range, k)$, where range is a rectangular spatial window, v's location $p_v \in$ range, and k is a positive integer. It aims at finding the maximal k-core subgraph containing v and located inside range.*

Take Figure 6.1 as an example, and let v_3 be the (only) query vertex, with $k = 3$. Figure 6.2 depicts an example of $GSGQ_{range}$. Six vertices, i.e., $\{v_1, v_2, v_3, v_5, v_7, v_8\}$, fall in the queried spatial range. Obviously, the community formed by vertices $\{v_3, v_5, v_7, v_8\}$ is the qualified k-core user group within the query range. Notice that even though v_1 and v_2 fall in the queried range, the output only includes v_3, v_5, v_7, v_8 as the latter vertices form a 3-core which does not include v_1 and v_2.

Definition 6.2.2 (Geo-Social Group Search with Relaxed i NN Constraint) *A $GSGQ_{riNN}$, represented as $Q_{gs} = (\{v\}, riNN, k)$, aims at finding the maximal k-core subgraph, $W \cup \{v\}$, of size no less than $i + 1$ and with the minimum value of maximum distance $d_{\max}(v, W)$, where $d_{\max}$ is defined as the maximum distance between v and any node in W. Here "relaxed" means the size of the resulting group is not exactly $i + 1$, and, instead, as a general requirement, the size should be the largest possible and should be at least $i + 1$.*

Definition 6.2.3 (Geo-Social Group Search with Strict i NN Constraint) *A $GSGQ_{iNN}$ is a strict form of $GSGQ_{riNN}$, which requires that the k-core subgraph on nodes $W \cup \{v\}$, have an exact size of $i + 1$.*

Let us revisit Figure 6.1 and assume that v_3 is the (only) query vertex, $i = 4$, and $k = 3$. Figure 6.3 shows the corresponding $GSGQ_{r4NN}$ and $GSGQ_{4NN}$. Specifically, the vertices bounded

---

[1]We are using iNN instead of the more conventional kNN to avoid conflict with other uses for "k" in this section.

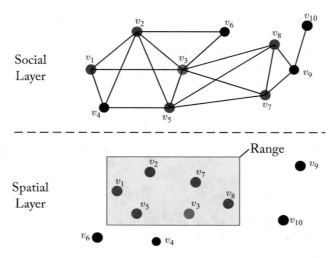

Figure 6.2: An example of $GSGQ_{range}$.

by the blue outline is the $GSGQ_{r4NN}$ and their minimum maximum distance to query vertex v_3 is shown in the spatial layer. In addition, $GSGQ_{4NN}$ is bounded by the red outline in Figure 6.3, which includes exactly five vertices.

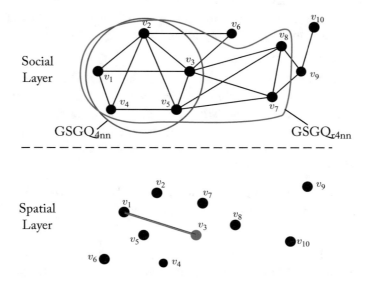

Figure 6.3: An example of $GSGQ_{riNN}$ and $GSGQ_{iNN}$.

Let $G[W]$ denote the subgraph induced by $W \subseteq V$. The maximum and minimum degrees of $G[W]$ are denoted $\Delta(G[W]) = \max_{v \in V} \deg_{G[W]}(v)$ and $\delta(G[W]) = \min_{v \in V} \deg_{G[W]}(v)$, respectively. The computational complexity of the above geo-social group searches is analyzed in the following theorems.

Theorem 6.2.1 *$GSGQ_{range}$ and $GSGQ_{riNN}$ can be obtained in polynomial time.*

Proof. Processing $GSGQ_{range}$ can be done by finding all the vertices located in the query range and running core decomposition once, while processing $GSGQ_{riNN}$ can be done by running core decomposition at most $|V|$ times (detailed in the next section). Since the time complexity of core decomposition is $O(|V| + |E|)$, both of the queries can be answered in polynomial time. □

Removing the relaxation makes the problem hard.

Theorem 6.2.2 *$GSGQ_{iNN}$ is NP-hard.*

Proof. We prove the NP-hardness by considering a more general problem without the requirement that the maximum distance to the query vertex should be minimum, from which the theorem follows. Given a graph G and two positive integers $\bar{k}$ and i, determining whether there exists a $\bar{k}$-plex of size $i + 1$, i.e., a set W such that $\delta(G[W]) \geq |W| - \bar{k}$ and $|W| = i + 1$, is NP-complete [17]. Since a k-core of size $i + 1$ is equivalent to a $(i + 1 - k)$-plex, we can find a $(i + 1 - k)$-plex of size $i + 1$ by iteratively applying $GSGQ_{iNN}$ for each user v in G. If a k-core of size $i + 1$ is found for a user v, then a $(i + 1 - k)$-plex of size $i + 1$ exists; otherwise such a $(i + 1 - k)$-plex does not exist. In this way, the $\bar{k}$-plex problem can be polynomially reduced to the generalized $GSGQ_{iNN}$. This proves that $GSGQ_{iNN}$ is NP-hard. □

6.2.2   R-TREE-BASED QUERY PROCESSING

Zhu et al. consider the GSGQ problems for large-scale LBSNs where the user information is stored on external disk storage [199]. A baseline approach of processing GSGQs on an R-tree index of user locations is as follows. For $GSGQ_{range}$ $Q_{gs} = (v, range, k)$, it first finds all users located inside *range* via R-tree, then computes the k-core W' of the subgraph formed by these users. If v exists in W', then $W = W' - \{v\}$ is the final result; otherwise, there is no result for Q_{gs}. Since the user filtering step can be done in $O(|V|)$ time and the core decomposition step can be done in $O(|V| + |E|)$ time, the complexity of this method is $O(|V| + |E|)$.

For $GSGQ_{riNN}$ $Q_{gs} = (v, riNN, k)$, according to its definition, the users are accessed in ascending order of their spatial distances to v. As such, $GSGQ_{riNN}$ can be processed similarly to iNN search on R-trees. Specifically, a priority queue H, whose priority score is spatial distance to v, and a candidate result set $\widetilde{W}$ are employed. At the beginning, $\widetilde{W}$ is initialized as $\{v\}$ and all the root entries of the R-tree are put into H. Each time the top entry e of H is popped up and processed. If e is a non-leaf entry, its child entries are accessed and put into H; otherwise, e is a leaf entry, i.e., a user, so e is added into $\widetilde{W}$. When the size of $\widetilde{W}$ exceeds i, the k-core W' of the subgraph formed by the users in $\widetilde{W}$ is computed. If $|W'| \geq i + 1$ and $v \in W'$, $W = W' - \{v\}$ is the result; otherwise, the above procedure is continued until the result is found. Since each round of k-core detection can be done in $O(|V| + |E|)$ time, the complexity of this method is $O(|V|(|V| + |E|))$.

For $GSGQ_{iNN}$ $Q_{gs} = (v, iNN, k)$, the processing is similar to $GSGQ_{riNN}$. The major difference is how to find the result from $\widetilde{W}$. Since the query asks for exactly i users, every possible user set of size $i + 1$ and containing v is checked to see if it is a k-core. If such a user set W' exists, then $W = W' - \{v\}$ is the result. There are $C_i^{|V-1|}$ possible user sets to be checked, where $C_i^{|V-1|}$ denotes the number of i-combinations from the user set $V - \{v\}$. Thus, the complexity of this method is $O(C_i^{|V-1|}(|V| + |E|))$.

Obviously, these methods are inefficient for GSGQs with a large k value, because a large k means tighter social constraints and thus result in users farther away from the query vertex, which increases the number of users to search and check. On the other hand, intuitively a large k means higher chances to prune the irrelevant users before finding the result users. As will be shown in the following sections, the efficiency can be significantly improved by filtering the irrelevant users and optimizing the processing order.

6.2.3 SOCIAL-AWARE R-TREE

Since a GSGQ query involves both spatial and social constraints, to expedite its processing, both spatial locations and social relations of the users should be indexed simultaneously. A novel Social-aware R-tree (SaR-tree) is designed in [199] to form the basis of GSGQ query processing solutions. In what follows, the concept of Core Bounding Rectangle (CBR) is introduced first and then the details of SaR-tree are presented, followed by a variant of of the SaR-tree, called SaR*-tree.

Definition 6.2.4 (Core Bounding Rectangle (CBR)) *Consider a user $v \in G$. Given a minimum degree constraint k, $CBR_{v,k}$ is a rectangle which contains v and inside which any user group with v (excluding the users on the bounding edges) cannot be a k-core. Formally, $CBR_{v,k}$ satisfies that $p_v \in CBR_{v,k}$ and $\forall W = \{v\} \cup \{u \mid u \in V, p_u \in CBR_{v,k}\}$, $\delta(G[W]) < k$ holds.*

Simply put, the CBR of a user v is a rectangle containing v, such that any user group in the CBR that includes v does not satisfy the minimum degree constraint. In other words, it is a localized social measure to a user. As a GSGQ query mainly requests the nearby users, the locality of CBR becomes very valuable for processing GSGQ queries. The definition above defines the concept of CBR. A user may have numerous CBRs and we choose the maximal CBR in the construction of the index. How to compute maximal CBR is explained below.

An example is shown in Figure 6.4. According to the acquaintance relations of user v_2, rectangular area r_1 is a $CBR_{v_2,2}$, because any user group inside r_1 that contains v_2 cannot be a 2-core. On the contrary, r_2 is not a $CBR_{v_2,2}$, because some user groups inside r_2 that contain v_2, e.g., $\{v_1, v_2, v_5\}, \{v_1, v_2, v_6\}, \{v_1, v_2, v_5, v_6\}$, are 2-cores. Note that $CBR_{v,k}$ is not unique

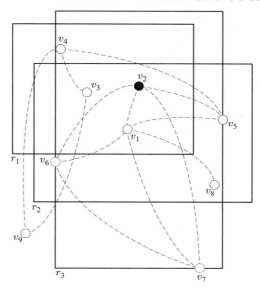

Figure 6.4: An example of CBR. The LBSN is shown on the spatial layer. The points represent the users as well as their positions, while the dashed lines denote the acquaintance relations among users.

for a given v and k. For example, r_3 is another $CBR_{v_2,2}$ for user v_2 because the users inside r_3, $\{v_1, v_2, v_3, v_4, v_8\}$, do not form 2-cores.

   From Definition 6.2.4, we can quickly exclude a user v from the result group by checking $CBR_{v,k}$ during query processing. For example, if the query range of $GSGQ_{range}$ is covered by $CBR_{v,k}$, then v can be safely pruned from the result. This property makes CBR a powerful pruning mechanism.

   Computing Maximal CBR of a User. A simple method to compute the maximal $CBR_{v,k}$ is to search neighboring users in ascending order of distance until there is a user u such that the core number of v in the subgraph formed by the users inside $\odot_{v,u}$ (i.e., the circle centered at v with radius $d(v, u)$) is no less than k, i.e., all user groups located within $\odot_{v,u}$ are not qualified as a k-core. $CBR_{v,k}$ can then be easily derived from $\odot_{v,u}$ as follows. We first compute the bounding box of the circle and move one bounding edge to go through u. Then we check the nodes inside the rectangle but outside the circle. For each of them, we move one bounding edge to go through it so that the node becomes outside of the new rectangle. An example is shown in Figure 6.5a, where a $CBR_{v_2,2}$ is constructed based on users v_5 and v_6. This generated CBR satisfies Definition 6.2.4 since the users inside it (i.e., v_1, v_2, v_3) do not form 2-cores. However, it is not a maximal one, thus limiting its pruning power in GSGQ processing. We improve this initial $CBR_{v,k}$ by recursively expanding it from each bounding edge until no edge can be further

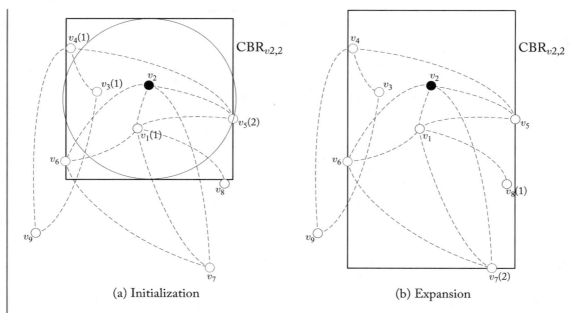

(a) Initialization   (b) Expansion

Figure 6.5: An example of computing $CBR_{v_2,2}$. The number after a user v_i denotes the core number of v_2 in the subgraph determined by v_i. For (a) the subgraph is formed by the users inside $\odot_{v_2,v_5}$; for (b) the subgraph is formed by the users inside $CBR_{v_2,2}$ when moving its bottom edge outward to go through v_7.

moved outward (see Figure 6.5b). During the expanding process, a greedy method is adopted in [199] to select the bounding edge which maximizes the area of the rectangle in each step of expansion.

To save storage cost, only a logarithmic number of CBRs, with respect to exponentially increased minimum degrees, are maintained for each user v—$CBR_{v,2^0}$, $CBR_{v,2^1}$, $CBR_{v,2^2}$, ..., $CBR_{v,2^{\lfloor \log_2 k_v \rfloor}}$—where k_v is the core number of v in G.

Based on CBR, we now present the basic SaR-tree. It is a variant of R-tree, in which each entry further maintains some aggregate social-relation information for the users covered by this entry. Figure 6.6 illustrates an SaR-tree. Similar to a conventional R-tree, the SaR-tree maintains a hierarchy of Minimum Bounding Rectangles (MBRs) that bound spatial objects. More specifically, the root node contains two MBRs A and B, which enclose sub-MBRs a, b and c, d, respectively. Besides, each entry of an SaR-tree maintains a set of CBRs, e.g., $CBR_{b,1}$, $CBR_{b,2}$ for entry b (detailed definitions given below in Definition 6.2.5). Considering that only one CBR of an entry is related to a GSGQ query, the storage is optimized by decoupling CBRs from MBR. As shown, the CBR page of a node can be directly accessed with a specified core number k. Perceptually, a CBR in the SaR-tree bounds a group of users from the social per-

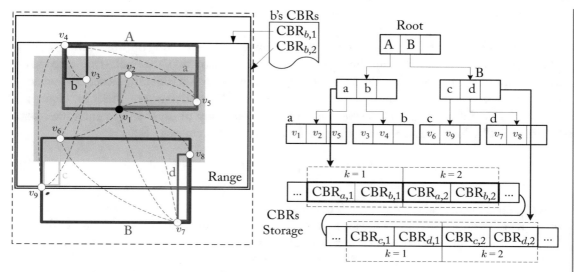

Figure 6.6: An example of SaR-tree.

spective while an MBR bounds the users from the spatial perspective. As such, the SaR-tree gains the power for both social-based and spatial-based pruning during GSGQ processing.

CBR of an Entry. To define the CBRs for each SaR-tree entry, the concept of CBR defined for each individual user is extended. Let MBR_e and V_e denote the MBR and the set of users covered by an entry e, respectively. A CBR of e is a rectangle which intersects MBR_e and inside which any user group containing any user from V_e cannot satisfy the minimum degree constraint. The formal definition of a CBR of entry e with respect to a minimum degree constraint k, denoted by $CBR_{e,k}$, is given as follows.

Definition 6.2.5 (CBR of an Entry) *Consider an entry e with MBR MBR_e and user set V_e. Given a minimum degree constraint k, $CBR_{e,k}$ is a rectangle which intersects MBR_e and inside which any user group containing any user from V_e (not including the users on the bounding edges) cannot be a k-core.*

Note that $CBR_{e,k}$ is required to intersect MBR_e to guarantee its locality. Figure 6.6 shows two examples of CBRs for entry b, where $V_b = \{v_3, v_4\}$. It can be seen that any user group inside $CBR_{b,2}$ and containing v_3 or v_4 (not including v_9 on the bounding edges) cannot be a 2-core. Thus, during GSGQ processing, we may safely prune entry b, for example, if the query range of a $GSGQ_{range}$ (with a minimum degree constraint of 2) is fully covered by $CBR_{b,2}$.

Based on the concept of CBRs, the SaR-tree can be directly built on top of the R-tree. That is, we can first construct a standard R-tree based on the locations of the users and then embed the CBRs into each entry. In this way, the SaR-tree indexes both spatial locations and social relations of the users. Note that the users in the SaR-tree are organized merely based on their locations—they are spatially close, but may not be well clustered in terms of their social relations.

SaR*-Tree. R*-tree [21] is a well-known variant of the R-tree that optimizes the grouping of spatial objects for minimizing the disk I/O cost. Inspired by this, the SaR*-tree is proposed as a variant of SaR-tree. It has the same node structure but uses a different closeness metric to group users into nodes. Specifically, instead of using only the spatial area of MBR for closeness, the SaR*-tree defines a new closeness metric $I(V)$ for a group of users V that integrates both CBRs and MBRs to measure the combined social and spatial closenesses:

$$I(V) = ||MBR_V|| \cdot \sum_k (|| \cup_{v \in V} CBR_{v,k} - CBR_{V,k}||), \tag{6.1}$$

where $|| \cdot ||$ is the area of an MBR or a CBR, and $\cup_{v \in V} CBR_{v,k} - CBR_{V,k}$ quantifies the similarity of CBRs of the users in V. Obviously, a small $I(V)$ indicates that the users of V have both close locations and similar CBRs, which increases the chance of being pruned together during query processing. This new closeness metric is used in the SaR*-tree construction.

Similar to the SaR-tree, the SaR*-tree is also constructed by iteratively inserting users. During this construction, CBRs and MBRs are generated at the same time and used for further user insertion. Moreover, if a node N of the SaR*-tree overflows, it will be split. The details about these two operations in the SaR*-tree construction, i.e., *user insertion* and *node split*, are described below.

- *User insertion.* When a user v is inserted into the SaR*-tree, for a node N with entries $e_1, e_2, \ldots, e_m$, we will select the entry e_i with the minimal $I(V_{e_i} \cup \{v\})$ to insert v.

- *Node split.* When a node N of the SaR*-tree overflows, we split N into two sets of entries N_1 and N_2 with the minimal $I(\cup_{e_i \in N_1} V_{e_i}) + I(\cup_{e_j \in N_2} V_{e_j})$. Then, the parent node of N uses two entries to point to N_1 and N_2, respectively. This splitting may propagate upward until the root.

6.2.4   SAR-TREE-BASED QUERY PROCESSING

This section presents the detailed algorithms based on SaR-tree for processing various GSGQ queries, namely, $GSGQ_{range}$, $GSGQ_{riNN}$, and $GSGQ_{iNN}$. Note that the CBRs of an SaR-tree can be used in different ways for processing these queries.

$GSGQ_{range}$ Processing

When processing a $GSGQ_{range}$ query, $Q_{gs} = (v, range, k)$, each entry of the SaR-tree that may cover result users will be visited and possibly further explored. Consider an example query GSGQ $Q_{gs} = (v_1, range, 2)$ in Figure 6.6, where the shaded area is the query range. When entry b (which covers users v_3 and v_4) is visited, b would need further exploration if only considering MBR_b like in regular R-tree. However, with $CBR_{b,2}$, it can easily decide that any user

Algorithm 6.26 Processing $GSGQ_{range}(G, Q_{gs})$

Input: LBSN $G = (V, E)$, $Q_{gs} = (v, range, k)$.
Output: Result of Q_{gs}.

1: Let $k' = 2^{\lfloor \log_2 k \rfloor}$;
2: **if** $k_v < k$ or $range \subset CBR_{v,k'}$ **then**
3:     **return** $\emptyset$;
4: Initialize H with the root entries of index tree;
5: **while** H has non-leaf entries **do**
6:     Pop the first non-leaf entry e from H;
7:     **for** each child entry e' of e **do**
8:         **if** $range \cap MBR_{e'} \neq \phi$ and $k_{e'} \geq k$ and $range \not\subset CBR_{e',k'}$ **then**
9:             Put e' into H;
10: Get the users $\widetilde{W}$ corresponding to the entries of H;
11: Compute the maximum k-core W' of $G[\widetilde{W}]$;
12: **if** $v \in W'$ **then**
13:     **return** $W = W' - \{v\}$;
14: **else**
15:     **return** $\emptyset$;

---

group inside the query range and containing any user in V_b (i.e., v_3 or v_4), cannot be a 2-core, because the query range is covered by $CBR_{b,2}$. Since V_b does not contain any result user, entry b can be simply pruned from further processing. Considering the SaR-tree only maintains the CBRs with respect to exponentially increased minimum degrees, given a minimum degree k, $CBR_{v,2^{\lfloor \log_2 k \rfloor}}$ is used to represent $CBR_{v,k}$ in $GSGQ_{range}$ processing. Similar ideas are also applied in $GSGQ_{riNN}$ and $GSGQ_{iNN}$ processing.

Algorithm 6.26 details the procedure of processing a $GSGQ_{range}$ query based on an SaR-tree. At the beginning, the algorithm accesses the CBR of user v. If $k_v < k$ or $range \subset CBR_{v,2^{\lfloor \log_2 k \rfloor}}$, it means the core number of v is smaller than k in the subgraph formed by the users inside $range$. Thus, the algorithm cannot find any k-core containing v inside $range$ and there is no answer to Q_{gs} (lines 2–3). Otherwise, the algorithm moves on to find all candidate users $\widetilde{W}$ via the proposed pruning schemes (lines 4–10). Then, it computes the maximum k-core W' of $G[\widetilde{W}]$ by applying the core decomposition algorithm (line 11). If $v \in W'$, $W = W' - \{v\}$ is the answer; otherwise, there is no answer to Q_{gs} (lines 12–15).

Back to the example in Figure 6.6, when applying the baseline algorithm based on R-tree, five users, i.e., v_2, v_3, v_5, v_6, and v_8, would need to be accessed. In contrast, in the proposed algorithm, by using both MBRs and CBRs, there is no need to access index node b (as well as its covered user v_3) and user v_8 since $range \subset CBR_{b,2}$ and $range \subset CBR_{v_8,2}$. As a result, only three users are accessed, achieving a great saving on in-memory computation and I/O cost.

GSGQ$_{riNN}$ **Processing**

To process a *GSGQ$_{riNN}$* query $Q_{gs} = (v, riNN, k)$ on an SaR-tree, a priority queue H is maintained, whose priority score is the spatial distance from v to both *MBR$_e$* and *CBR$_{e,k}$*. Let $L_{CBR_{e,k}}$ denote the set of bounding edges of *CBR$_{e,k}$* and $d(v, l)$ denote the distance from v to edge l. The distance from v to *CBR$_{e,k}$*, where v is located inside *CBR$_{e,k}$*, is defined as the minimum distance from v to reach any bounding edge of *CBR$_{e,k}$*. Formally,

$$d_{in}(v, CBR_{e,k}) = \begin{cases} \min_{l \in L_{CBR_{e,k}}} d(v, l), & v \in CBR_{e,k} \\ 0, & \text{otherwise.} \end{cases}$$

H uses $d_e = \max\{d(v, MBR_e), d_{in}(v, CBR_{e,k})\}$ of an entry e as the sorting key in the queue. The rationale for adopting this priority queue is as follows. By Definition 6.2.5 and the definition of d_{in}, any user group inside the area $\odot(v, d_{in}(v, CBR_{e,k}))$ and containing any user in V_e cannot be a k-core. In other words, if some users covered by entry e belong to a candidate group which satisfies the social acquaintance constraint, the maximum distance of the candidate group to v is expected to be at least d_e.

Algorithm 6.27 presents the details of processing a *GSGQ$_{riNN}$* query based on an SaR-tree. A set $\widetilde{W}$ is used to store the currently visited users and initialized as $\{v\}$. The entries in H are visited in ascending order of d_e. If a visited entry e is not a leaf entry, it will be further explored and its child entries with $k_{e'} \geq k$ are inserted into H (lines 7–10); otherwise, we get its corresponding user u (line 12) and the algorithm proceeds with the following steps. If $k_u < k$, it means u cannot be a result user. Thus, the algorithm continues checking the next entry of H. On the other hand, if $k_u \geq k$, u is added into the candidate set $\widetilde{W}$ (lines 13–14). Then, the algorithm computes the maximum k-core, denoted as W', in the subgraph formed by $\widetilde{W}$ (line 16). If $|W'| \geq i + 1$ and $v \in W'$, $W' - \{v\}$ is the result (lines 17–18); otherwise, the above procedure is continued until the result is found or shown to be non-existent.

GSGQ$_{iNN}$ **Processing**

For a *GSGQ$_{iNN}$* query $Q_{gs} = (v, iNN, k)$, the same processing framework as in Algorithm 6.27 is adopted. However, when a valid W' is found for *GSGQ$_{riNN}$* at line 16, more steps will be needed to obtain the result of *GSGQ$_{iNN}$*. Let W' be the maximum k-core formed by the set of currently visited users $\widetilde{W}$. Only if $|W'| \geq i + 1$ and $v \in W'$, it is possible to find a k-core of size $i + 1$ in $\widetilde{W}$ that contains v. Moreover, such a k-core must be a subgraph of W'. Thus, a function *FindExactiNN* is invoked to check all user sets of size $i + 1$ in W' that contain v. If such a user set W'' is found, $W'' - \{v\}$ is the result of Q_{gs}; otherwise, the above procedure is repeated and Algorithm 6.27 continues to find the next candidate W'.

Due to the NP-hardness of *GSGQ$_{iNN}$*, the in-memory processing function *FindExactiNN* has a great impact on the performance of the algorithm. A naive idea of checking all possible combinations of the user sets has an obviously exponential cost in i. Two in-memory opti-

Algorithm 6.27 Processing $GSGQ_{riNN}(G, Q_{gs})$

Input: LBSN $G = (V, E)$, $Q_{gs} = (v, riNN, k)$.
Output: Result of Q_{gs}.

```
 1: if k_v < k then
 2:     return ∅;
 3: W̃ = {v};
 4: Initialize H with the entries of the root node;
 5: while H ≠ φ do
 6:     Pop the first entry e from H;
 7:     if e is not a leaf entry then
 8:         for each child entry e' of e do
 9:             if k_e' ≥ k then
10:                 Compute d_e' and put e' into H;
11:     else
12:         Get the corresponding user u of e;
13:         if k_u ≥ k then
14:             W̃ = W̃ ∪ {u};
15:             if the first entry e' in H has d_e' > d_e then
16:                 Compute the maximum k-core W' in W̃;
17:                 if |W'| ≥ i + 1 and v ∈ W' then
18:                     return W' − {v};
19: return ∅;
```

mization strategies are proposed in [199] to reduce the computation cost. Interested readers are referred to [199] for details.

6.3 GEO-SOCIAL k-COVER GROUP SEARCH

In this section, we introduce another type of geo-social group search based on *spatial containment*, called *Geo-Social K-Cover Group* (GSKCG) query, which is proposed by Li et al. [123, 124]. Intuitively, given a set of spatial query points and an underlying social network, a GSKCG query finds a minimum user group in which the members satisfy certain social relationship and their associated regions can jointly cover all the query points. In the following, we present the problem formulation and the corresponding algorithms.

6.3.1 PROBLEM STATEMENT

A GSKCG query is defined over a location-based social network (LBSN) $G = (V, E)$, where each user $u \in V$ has an associated region denoted by $u.R$. Such an LBSN can be easily derived by combining the location and social data collected from real-life applications.

Definition 6.3.1 (GSKCG Query) *Given an* LBSN $G = (V, E)$, *a GSKCG query is defined as a 2-tuple* $Q = (k, P)$, *where k is a positive integer, indicating the social acquaintance constraint, and*

$P = \{p_1, p_2, \ldots, p_m\}$ *is a set of query points, indicating the spatial coverage constraint, and returns a set of users* $V' \subseteq V$ *such that:*

1. $P \subset \bigcup_{u \in V'} u.R$,

2. *the subgraph* $G[V']$ *of* G *is a* k-*core, and*

3. *the cardinality of* $G[V']$ *is minimum.*

Figure 6.7 shows an example of GSKCG query. In the spatial layer, every node is associated with a region. Assume that the query point set is $\{p_1, p_2, p_3, p_4\}$ and $k = 3$. Then there are two 3-cores, i.e., $\{v_3, v_5, v_7, v_8\}$ and $\{v_1, v_2, v_3, v_4, v_5, v_7, v_8\}$ cover all the query points. Since $|\{v_3, v_5, v_7, v_8\}| < |\{v_1, v_2, v_3, v_4, v_5, v_7, v_8\}|$, $\{v_3, v_5, v_7, v_8\}$ is the final result.

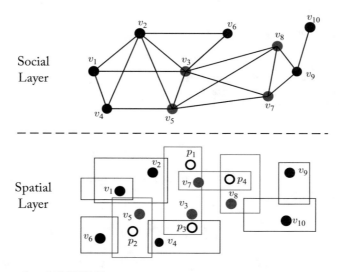

Figure 6.7: An example of GSKCG query.

As formally defined in Definition 6.3.1, a GSKCG query finds a set of users that satisfy the given spatial and social constraints. For ease of presentation, a user group is said to be *valid* if it satisfies both Conditions 1 and 2 in Definition 6.3.1. Next, the complexity of the GSKCG query problem is analyzed.

Theorem 6.3.1 *GSKCG query is NP-hard.*

Proof. The hardness is established by a reduction from a classical NP-hard problem, namely the minimum set cover (MSC) problem. An instance of the MSC problem consists of a universe $U = \{e_1, e_2, \ldots, e_n\}$ and a set of sets $S = \{S_1, S_2, \ldots, S_m\}$, where $S_i \subset U$. The question is to decide if there exists a subset S' of S such that all the elements in U are fully covered by S' and the size of S' is minimum.

Algorithm 6.28 KCGFinder (Query points P, Integer k, LBSN G)

1: $S \leftarrow$ The set of users in G that each covers at least one point in P;
2: $U^k \leftarrow$ The set of users belonging to S that may appear in a k-core;
3: $H \leftarrow$ All connected components of $G[U^k]$ that each fully covers P;
4: $M \leftarrow \max_{V^k \in H} |V^k|$;
5: **for** s from $k+1$ to M **do**
6:     **for** each V^k in H **do**
7:        **if** $|V^k| \geq s$ **then**
8:           $V^k_s \leftarrow$ GetOptimalGroup(V^k, k, s, P);
9:           **if** $V^k_s \neq \emptyset$ **then**
10:              **return** V^k_s;
11: **return** $\emptyset$;

Given an instance of MSC, we construct an instance of a GSKCG query $Q = (k, P)$ on a set of users. Each element e_i in U corresponds to a spatial query point in P, each set S_i corresponds to a user u_i's associated region $u_i.R$, and the elements in S_i corresponds to the spatial points in u_i's associated region $u_i.R$. We consider the restricted case of GSKCG query when $k = 0$. It can be seen that there exists a solution to the MSC problem if and only if there exists a solution to Q (i.e., find a minimum set of users such that all given query points are fully covered by their associated regions).

Suppose we have a polynomial-time algorithm A that returns the query answer $G' = \{u'_1, u'_2, \ldots, u'_m\}$ to a GSKCG query Q. If P is fully covered by the associated regions of G', then $\{S'_1, S'_2, \ldots, S'_m\}$ fully covers U and its size m is minimum. This implies that a polynomial-time solution to the MSC problem is found, which is impossible unless P = NP. $\square$

6.3.2 ALGORITHMS

To efficiently process GSKCG queries, an optimal solution that has short response time is proposed in [123]. This is mainly achieved by a set of effective pruning strategies and a new index structure.

Basic Algorithm

To satisfy the minimum cardinality requirement of a GSKCG query, a basic algorithm, called KCGFinder, is to process the user groups in increasing order of group size and return the current group as soon as it is found to be valid.

Algorithm 6.28 gives the pseudo code of KCGFinder. Before performing a search on the input LBSN $G = (V, E)$, the algorithm first conducts two filtering operations: spatial filtering and social filtering. In spatial filtering, it uses an R-tree to get the users whose associated regions cover at least one query point $p \in P$ (line 1). In social filtering, it adopts the core decomposition algorithm to identify the user set U^k in which the users belonging to S may appear in a k-core,

---

Algorithm 6.29 GetOptimalGroup (Component G, Integer k, Integer s, Query points P)

1: **for** each size-s user group V_s of G **do**
2:     **if** the number of edges of $G[V_s] \geq k(k+1)/2$ **then**
3:         **if** $G[V_s]$ is k-core and $P \subseteq \bigcup_{u \in V_s} u.R$ **then**
4:             **return** V_s;
5: **return** $\emptyset$;

---

and invokes a depth-first search (DFS) to find the set of connected components H of $G[U^k]$ that each fully covers P (lines 2–3). In line 4, it computes the maximum cardinality M of the components in H, which gives the upper bound of the size of the returned user group. By definition, the cardinality of a k-core is no less than $k + 1$. Thus, the algorithm enumerates user groups in increasing order of size from $k + 1$ to M. Given a size s, for each component V^k with size $\geq s$, the algorithm invokes the GetOptimalGroup function (see Algorithm 6.29) to find a size-s user group V_s^k whose joint regions fully cover P and which is a k-core. If V_s^k is not empty, it is returned as the final optimal answer to the GSKCG query.

It can be observed that the main complexity of KCGFinder comes from the GetOptimalGroup function (Algorithm 6.29). Its general idea is to enumerate all size-s user groups and check whether they are valid. For a systematic enumeration of all candidate user groups, the *branch and bound* technique is employed. By the definition of k-core, a user group V_s can be pruned out if the number of edges in $G[V_s]$ is less than $k(k + 1)/2$ (line 2). In addition, a set of pruning strategies are devised to speed up the branch and bound search [123].

Enhanced SaR-Tree-Based Algorithm

The SaR-tree has been introduced in Section 6.2 to model both spatial and social relationships. Unfortunately, the SaR-tree structure cannot directly support GSKCG queries. The main reason is that the method of computing CBRs assumes that each user is associated with a spatial point, whereas in our problem each user has an associated region. This fact significantly complicates the problem and calls for a new method to construct CBRs.

Li et al. [123] propose a new index structure, called enhanced SaR-tree, to address this problem. To construct an enhanced SaR-tree over an LBSN, a standard R-tree *rtree* is constructed and then the CBR for each entry in *rtree* is computed. To compute the CBR of an entry, a user's CBR should be built first. The basic idea of constructing a user's CBR includes two steps. First, as the users' associated regions may intersect with each other, it calculates the user's internal CBR (see Definition 6.3.2). Second, given the user's internal CBR, it expands CBR to obtain the corresponding external CBR (see Definition 6.3.3), from which the user's CBR will be selected. The formal definitions of these two types of CBRs are given below. For ease of exposition, a k-core containing a user u is denoted by $k(u)$.

Definition 6.3.2 *(Internal CBR) Given a k value, a user u's internal CBR $iCBR_{u,k}$ is a rectangle that is inside $u.R$ and that does not contain a $k(u)$.*

Algorithm 6.30 SaRBasedKCGFinder (Query points P, Integer k, Enhanced SaR-Tree *rtree*, LBSN G)

1: $MBR(P) \leftarrow$ The minimum rectangle containing all points in P;
2: Initialize H with the root of *rtree*;
3: **while** H has non-leaf entries **do**
4:     $e \leftarrow$ The first non-leaf entry in H;
5:     **for** each child entry e' of e **do**
6:         **if** $MBR(P) \cap e'.MBR \neq \emptyset$ and $cn(e') \geq k$ and $MBR(P) \not\subset CBR_{e',k}$ **then**
7:             $H.push(e')$;
8: $V_H \leftarrow$ The set of users represented by the entries in H;
9: **return** KCGFinder$(P, k, G[V_H])$;

Definition 6.3.3 *(External CBR) Given a user u's internal CBR $iCBR_{u,k}$, the corresponding external CBR $eCBR_{u,k}$ is defined as a rectangle that: (1) contains this $iCBR_{u,k}$, (2) is inside the MBR of u's parent in rtree, and (3) does not contain a $k(u)$.*

Based on the enhanced SaR-tree, the integrated algorithm SaRBasedKCGFinder is developed. Generally, the algorithm consists of two steps: (1) filter impossible users based on the enhanced SaR-tree and (2) feed the remaining users to KCGFinder.

The details of SaRBasedKCGFinder are given in Algorithm 6.30. It first calculates the minimum rectangle containing all query points in P (i.e., the coverage of P), denoted by $MBR(P)$. SaRBasedKCGFinder iteratively prunes impossible users in G by traversing the enhanced SaR-tree *rtree*. Note that, for the same G, *rtree* just needs to be constructed once and thereafter can be used for all GSKCG queries. At each entry e of *rtree*, SaRBasedKCGFinder compares $MBP(P)$ with e's MBR and CBR and checks the core number of e in order to prune out the users that cannot appear in the final result (line 6). Finally, SaRBasedKCGFinder feeds the subgraph of G that contains the users represented by the entries in H to KCGFinder and returns its output.

It is easy to extend the algorithm to support the case where each user has multiple associated regions. For each associated region of a user u, u and this associated region are indexed one time in the Enhanced SaR-tree. Thus, the number of associated regions of u corresponds the times of u being indexed. In spatial filtering, if a user u appears more than one time, it is simply combined together. The branch and bound search process remains the same as for the case where each user has exactly one associated region.

6.4 GEO-SOCIAL GROUP SEARCH BASED ON MINIMUM COVERING CIRCLE

6.4.1 PROBLEM STATEMENT

This section introduces the geo-social groups query using another spatial constraint, namely minimum covering circle (MCC) proposed by Fang et al. [64]. The notion of MCC has been widely adopted in the literature to achieve high spatial compactness for a set of spatial objects. It requires the locations of all the spatial objects being in a minimum covering circle with the smallest radius. Correspondingly, the geo-social group search based on MCC is termed as spatial-aware community (SAC) search [64]. The MCC and the SAC search are formally defined as follows.

Definition 6.4.1 (MCC) *Given a set of vertices S, the MCC of S is the spatial circle with the smallest radius that covers the spatial locations of all the vertices in S.*

Problem 6.4.1 (SAC Search) *Given a graph G, a positive integer k, and a vertex $q \in V$, return a subgraph $G_q \subseteq G$ such that the following properties hold:*
  *1. **Connectivity**. G_q is connected and contains q;*
  *2. **Structure cohesiveness**. G_q is a k-core;*
  *3. **Spatial cohesiveness**. Among all subgraphs $G'_q \subseteq G$ satisfying properties 1 and 2, the MCC of G_q has the smallest radius.*

Using the dataset in Figure 6.1 again, assume that v_3 is the query vertex and $k = 3$. The social layer in Figure 6.8 shows three feasible 3-cores containing v_3, i.e., $C1, C2, C3$. The spatial layer in Figure 6.8 depicts the corresponding MCCs of the 3-cores. Since the MCC formed by v_1, v_2, v_3, v_4, and v_5 is minimum, $C2$ is the optimal spatial-aware community.

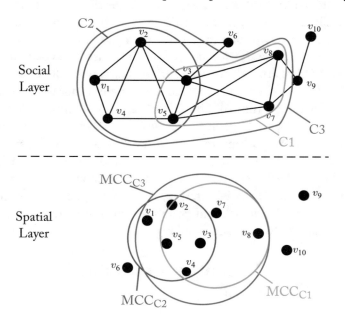

Figure 6.8: An example of SAC.

6.4.2 ALGORITHMS

The solutions of fast SAC search follow a two-step framework: (1) find a community S of vertices, based on an existing community search algorithm, e.g., Global-Core [157]; and (2) find a subset of S that satisfies both structure and spatial cohesiveness. Step (2) is computationally challenging; a naive approach is to enumerate all possible subsets of S, and then choose the one that satisfies the two criteria of SAC and has an MCC with the smallest radius. In the above example, $S = \{v_1, v_2, v_3, v_4, v_5, v_7, v_8\}$; a SAC is then chosen from the $2^7 - 1 = 127$ subsets of S. In the following, we discuss a basic exact algorithm and an approximate algorithm which avoids the exponential blowup of the naive algorithm. We use $|u, v|$ to denote the Euclidean distance between vertices u and v.

Basic Exact Algorithm

As mentioned before, a k-core contains at least $k + 1$ vertices. When $k=1$, the algorithm can simply return the subgraph, induced by q and its nearest neighbor, as the result. Next, we consider the case $k \geq 2$. We first present a useful lemma about MCC:

Lemma 6.4.1 *[62] Given a set $S(|S| \geq 2)$ of vertices, its MCC can be determined by at most three vertices in S which lie on the boundary of the circle. If it is determined by only two vertices, then the line segment connecting those two vertices must be a diameter of the circle. If it is determined by three vertices, then the triangle consisting of those three vertices is not obtuse.*

By Lemma 6.4.1, there are at least two or at least three vertices lying on the boundary of the MCC of the target SAC. The vertices lying on the boundary of an MCC are termed *fixed* vertices. So a straightforward method of SAC search can follow the two-step framework directly. It first finds the k-core containing q, which is the same as what Global-Core [157] does, and then returns the subgraph achieving both the structure and spatial cohesiveness by enumerating all the possible combinations of three vertices in the k-core. The procedure is detailed in Algorithm 6.31. First, the list X of vertices of the k-core are found and sorted according to their distances to q (lines 1–2). Then, for each of the three-vertex combinations, it verifies whether there is a k-core in the MCC fixed by it, and finally returns the one with the smallest radius (lines 4–14). The time complexity of this algorithm is $O(|E(G)| \cdot |V(G)|^3)$.

Approximation Algorithms

The major limitation of the exact algorithm is its high computational cost, which makes it impractical for large spatial graphs with millions of vertices. To alleviate this issue, more efficient approximation algorithms are developed in [64].

A 2-Approximation Algorithm. The first approximation algorithm is AppInc, which has an approximation ratio of 2. The key observation is that, the optimal solution Ψ is usually very close to q. As such, AppInc considers the smallest circle, denoted by $\odot(q, \delta)$, which is centered at q and contains a feasible solution, denoted by Φ. Let the radius of the MCC covering Φ

Algorithm 6.31 Query algorithm: `Exact`

1: Find the vertex list X of the k-core containing q;
2: Sort vertices of X;
3: Initialize $r \leftarrow +\infty$, $\Psi \leftarrow \emptyset$;
4: **for** $i \leftarrow 3$ to $|X|$ **do**
5:     **for** $j \leftarrow 1$ to $i-2$ **do**
6:         **for** $h \leftarrow j + 1$ to $i-1$ **do**
7:             Compute the MCC mcc of $\{X_i, X_j, X_h\}$;
8:             **if** $mcc.radius < r$ **then**
9:                 $R \leftarrow$ a set of vertices in mcc;
10:                 **if** exist a k-core with q in $G[R]$ **then**
11:                     $r \leftarrow mcc.radius$, $\Psi \leftarrow$ this k-core;
12:     **if** $|q, X_i| > 2r$ **then**
13:         **break**;
14: **return** Ψ;

Algorithm 6.32 Query algorithm: `AppInc`

1: Initialize $Queue$, $S \leftarrow \emptyset$, $T \leftarrow \emptyset$, $\Phi \leftarrow \emptyset$;
2: $Queue$.add(q);
3: **while** $|Queue| > 0$ **do**
4:     $p \leftarrow Queue$.poll();
5:     S.add(p);
6:     **for** $v \in nb(p)$ **do**
7:         **if** $\deg_G(v) \geq k$ **then**
8:             **if** $|v, q| \leq |p, q|$ **then**
9:                 S.add(v);
10:         **else if** $v \notin T$ **then**
11:             $Queue$.add(v); T.add(v);
12:     **if** $|S \cap nb(q)| \geq k \wedge |S \cap nb(p)| \geq k$ **then**
13:         **if** exist a k-core containing q in $G[S]$ **then**
14:             $\Phi \leftarrow$ this k-core; **break**; //stop
15: **return** Φ;

---

be γ ($\gamma \leq \delta$). Note that, γ can be obtained by computing the MCC containing Φ by a linear algorithm. `AppInc` finds Φ in an incremental manner. Specifically, it examines the vertices close to q one by one incrementally, and checks whether there exists a feasible solution when a new vertex is examined. It stops once a feasible solution is found.

Algorithm 6.32 describes the procedure of `AppInc`. It starts by initializing four variables $Queue$, S, T, and Φ: $Queue$ is a priority queue of vertices, in which the vertices are sorted in an ascending order of their distances to q; S is the set maintaining the vertices close to q incrementally; T is a set for recording the vertices added to $Queue$; and Φ is the approximated SAC. Then, the algorithm adds q to $Queue$ (line 2). In the while loop (lines 3–14), it first gets the nearest vertex, p, from $Queue$, and adds p to S (lines 4–5); next, it considers p's neighbors

Algorithm 6.33 Query algorithm: `AppFast`

1: Find the vertex list X of the k-core, Λ, containing q;
2: Initialize l, u using Eq. (6.2);
3: **while** $u > l$ **do**
4:    $r \leftarrow \frac{l+u}{2}$;
5:    $S \leftarrow$ vertices in $\odot(q, r)$;
6:    $\Lambda' \leftarrow$ the k-core containing q in $G[S]$;
7:    **if** $\Lambda' \neq \emptyset$ **then**
8:       $\Lambda \leftarrow \Lambda'$;
9:       **if** $r - l \leq \alpha$ **then**
10:          **return** Λ;
11:       $u \leftarrow \max_{v \in \Lambda} |q, v|$;
12:    **else**
13:       **if** $u - r \leq \alpha$ **then**
14:          **return** Λ;
15:       $l \leftarrow \min_{v \in \Lambda \wedge v \notin S} |q, v|$;

one by one (lines 6–11). For each neighbor $v \in X$, if it is in $\odot(q, |p, q|)$, we add it to S directly; otherwise, v is put into *Queue*. Note that in any feasible solution, each vertex should have at least k neighbors. Thus, if both p and q have at least k neighbors in S, it checks whether there exists a SAC in $G[S]$. If there does, then `AppInc` returns this SAC as the result (lines 12–15). The time complexity of this algorithm is $O(|E(G)| \cdot |V(G)|)$.

$(2 + \epsilon_F)$-Approximate Algorithm. With a quadratic time complexity, `AppInc` is much faster than the exact algorithm. Yet it is still inefficient for large graphs. This section introduces another fast approximation algorithm, called `AppFast`, which has a more flexible approximation ratio, i.e., $2 + \epsilon_F$, where ϵ_F is an arbitrary non-negative value.

Instead of finding the circle $\odot(q, \delta)$ in an incremental manner, `AppFast` approximates the radius δ by performing binary search. This is based on the observation that, the lower and upper bounds of δ, denoted by l and u, can be stated by Eq. (6.2):

$$l = \max_{v \in KNN(q)} |q, v|, \quad u = \max_{v \in X} |q, v|, \tag{6.2}$$

where X is the list of vertices of the k-core containing q, and $KNN(q)$ contains the K nearest vertices in $X \cap nb(q)$ to q. Hence, the radius of the circle $\odot(q, \delta)$ can be approximated by performing binary search within $[l, u]$, until the gap $|u - l|$ is less than α, a predefined threshold.

Algorithm 6.33 describes the procedure of `AppFast`, where Λ denotes the returned SAC and ϵ_F is an input parameter. By following the two-step framework, it first computes the k-core (line 1), and then finds Λ from the k-core (lines 2–15). At the beginning, the variables l and u are initialized (line 2). In the while loop (lines 3–15), it first finds a SAC Λ' from $\odot(q, r)$ using breadth-first search (BFS). If Λ' does exist, it updates Λ and checks whether the gap, i.e., $r - l$, is smaller than α. If it is not larger than α, Λ is returned; otherwise, it updates u as the maximum distance from q to the vertices in Λ. This ensures that the feasible solution found later has at least one less vertex than Λ. If Λ' does not exist, Λ is returned if the gap, i.e., $u - r$, is small enough; otherwise, it updates l as the minimum distance from q to the vertices in Λ but not in S, so that the set S in the next iteration has at least one more vertex than the current S.

If α is set as $\frac{r \times \epsilon_F}{2 + \epsilon_F}$, AppFast achieves an approximation ratio of $(2 + \epsilon_F)$. Regarding the time complexity, AppFast has $O(\min\{mn, m \log \frac{1}{\epsilon_F}\})$ if $\epsilon_F > 0$, or $O(mn)$ if $\epsilon_F = 0$, where $m = |E(G)|$ and $n = |V(G)|$.

Continuous SACs

Besides static SACs, Fang et al. [67] further study the problem of continuous SAC (CSAC) search, which aims to find the SACs of a query vertex q that can move as time goes by. The CSAC search can be applied to many social applications that wish to offer recommendations based on users' latest communities. For example, when a user moves to a new place, it would be more relevant to offer event recommendations based on geo-social groups found using her/his current location.

A simple method of tackling the CSAC search problem is to invoke a SAC search algorithm upon every location update, which however is very inefficient. To handle frequent location updates, more efficient algorithms are needed. To this end, an interesting observation is that although a user's SACs may change frequently, they often share some vertices and are spatially close or overlapped. Based on this observation, several fast algorithms with theoretical accuracy guarantees are developed in [67].

CHAPTER 7

Datasets and Tools

Research on community search is motivated by real-world applications. The availability of datasets from such applications, or real-world datasets that closely resemble them, is important to validate the models about how communities are formed in practice under a variety of conditions.

This chapter introduces a number of publicly available datasets with ground-truth communities that have been used by researchers in this field. The pointers to specific instances of such datasets are also provided. Then, we describe the models of query generation and evaluation metrics for testing communities. Finally, we briefly outline packaged software that researchers have developed. Such software and demo systems are beneficial to researchers and users for further study.

7.1 REAL-WORLD DATASETS

In the following, we introduce five types of real-world graph datasets with ground-truth that can be used to evaluate research ideas on community search, as well as one new type of real-world public-private graph datasets with DBLP that will be helpful for further study of community search on public-private networks. The first one is structural networks with ground-truth communities. The second one is attributed graphs with ground-truth communities. The third one is individual's social networks, i.e., ego-networks with ground-truth social circles. The fourth one is geo-social networks. The last one is public-private collaboration networks.

7.1.1 NETWORKS WITH GROUND-TRUTH COMMUNITIES

We present six real-world networks with ground-truth communities, which are frequently used in experiments and publicly available from the Stanford Network Analysis Project [116]. All networks are treated as undirected graphs. The network statistics are shown in Table 7.1. Below we briefly describe each of the networks and their ground-truth communities.

1. The *Amazon* network was collected from the Amazon website. It is based on *Customers Who Bought This Item Also Bought* feature of the Amazon website. If a product i is frequently co-purchased with product j, the graph contains an undirected edge between i and j. Product categories provided by Amazon define ground-truth communities.

2. The *DBLP* network is a co-authorship network that was constructed from the research papers published in computer science from DBLP. Two authors are connected if they publish

at least one paper together. Publication venues, e.g, journal or conference, define individual ground-truth communities; authors who published in the same journal or conference form a community.

3. The last four networks are online social networks: *Youtube video-sharing social network, LiveJournal blogging community, Orkut social network,* and *Friendster online gaming network.* Users can create explicit functional groups which others then join and share contents. Groups are created based on specific topics, hobbies, interests, and geographical regions. For example, LiveJournal categorizes groups into the following types: technology, entertainment, fandom, life/style, gaming, and so on. Each such an explicit interest group is treated as a ground-truth community.

Table 7.1: Network statistics of graphs with ground-truth communities (K = 10^3 and M = 10^6) [180]

Network	$|V_G|$	$|E_G|$	#Communities
Amazon	335 K	926 K	151,037
DBLP	317 K	1 M	13,477
Youtube	1.1 M	3 M	8,385
LiveJournal	4 M	35 M	287,512
Orkut	3.1 M	117 M	6,288,363
Friendster	65 M	1,806 M	957,154

A user can belong to zero, one, or more ground-truth communities, indicating that ground-truth communities can overlap. All these networks also provide 5,000 top-quality ground-truth communities. The largest dataset of these social networks is Friendster, which has 65 million nodes, 1.8 billion edges, and 957,154 ground-truth communities.

7.1.2   ATTRIBUTED GRAPHS WITH GROUND-TRUTH COMMUNITIES

We present four datasets of attributed graphs with ground-truth communities. The network statistics are summarized in Table 7.2.

The first dataset is PPI network, *Krogan,* from the BioGRID database, where the PPI data are related to the yeast Sacchoromyces cerevisiae [85]. Each protein has three kinds of attributes: biological processes, molecular functions, and cellular components. There are 255 known protein complexes for Sacchromyces cerevisiae in the MIPS/CYGD [85], which can be regarded as ground-truth communities.

The second dataset is *Facebook* ego-networks [116]. For a given user id X in Facebook network G, the ego-network of X, denoted ego-facebook-X, is the induced subgraph of G by

Table 7.2: Network statistics of attributed graph with ground-truth communities ($K = 10^3$ and $M = 10^6$). $\bar{\tau}(\emptyset)$ is the largest value of edge trussness in graphs.

Network	$|V|$	$|E|$	d_{max}	$\bar{\tau}(\emptyset)$	$|\mathcal{A}|$	$|attr(V)|$
Krogan	2.6 K	7.1 K	140	16	3,064	28,151
Facebook	1.9 K	8.9 K	416	29	228	3,944
Cornell	195	304	94	4	1,588	18,496
Texas	187	328	104	4	1,501	15,437

X and its neighbors. This dataset contains 10 ego-networks indicated by its ego-user X, where $X \in \{0, 107, 348, 414, 686, 698, 1684, 1912, 3437, 3890\}$. Vertex attributes were collected from real profiles and anonymized, e.g., political leaning, age, education, etc. Each ego-network has several overlapping ground-truth communities, called friendship circles [117]. Note that the statistics of Facebook in Table 7.2 are results averaged over 10 networks. Each ego-network can be taken as an attributed graph and each social circle as a ground-truth community.

The third and fourth datasets are the web graphs gathered from universities—Cornell and University of Texas, Austin, respectively.[1] The webpages are partitioned into five groups including course, faculty, student, project, and staff. Vertex attributes are unique words frequently present in the webpages. There is a README file that provides detailed information on these two datasets.

In addition, to conduct experimental studies on more attributed graphs with ground-truth communities, one way is to leverage the six graph datasets in Table 7.1. Recall that each network of Amazon, DBLP, Youtube, LiveJournal, Orkut, and Friendster contains 5,000 top-quality ground-truth communities. Since the vertices on these networks have no attributes, one may synthetically generate an attribute set consisting of $|\mathcal{A}| = 0.005 \cdot |V|$ different attribute values in each network G. The average number of attribute/vertex $\frac{|\mathcal{A}|}{|V|} = 0.005$ is less than the proportion of attributes to vertices in datasets with real attributes (e.g., the value of 0.12 in Facebook) in Table 7.2. A smaller attribute pool $\mathcal{A}$ makes homogeneity of synthetic attributes in different communities more likely, which stress tests attributed community search algorithms. Therefore, the setting of $|\mathcal{A}| = 0.005 \cdot |V|$ gives significant challenges for attributed community models for detecting exact answers.

7.1.3 EGO-NETWORKS WITH GROUND-TRUTH SOCIAL CIRCLES

McAuley and Leskovec [117] release three ego-networks and ground-truth social circles from three social network sites: Facebook, Google+, and Twitter [116]. The statistics of the three datasets are shown in Table 7.3. The Facebook network contains 4,039 vertices, 88,234 edges,

[1]https://linqs-data.soe.ucsc.edu/public/lbc/WebKB.tgz

and 10 ego-networks, which consist of 193 ground-truth circles. The ground-truth circles to which Facebook friends belonged were manually identified by a survey of ten users. On average, users identified 19 circles in their ego-networks, with an average circle size of 22 friends. Such examples of circles include students studying in common universities and classes, relatives, sports teams, and so on [117]. On the other hand, the other two datasets, Google+ and Twitter, were obtained from publicly accessible data. The Google+ dataset contains 107,614 vertices, 13,673,453 edges, and 133 ego-networks with 479 ground-truth circles. The Twitter network contains 81,306 vertices, 1,768,149 edges, and 1,000 ego-networks with 4,869 ground-truth circles. The vertex size of ego-networks ranges from 10–4,964.

Table 7.3: Network statistics of ego-networks with ground-truth circles [116, 167]. (K = 10^3 and M = 10^6.)

Network	$|V|$	$|E|$	#Ego-Networks	#Circles
Facebook	4 K	88 K	10	193
Google+	107 K	13.6 M	133	479
Twitter	81 K	1.77 M	1,000	4,869

7.1.4 GEO-SOCIAL NETWORKS

This section presents five real-world datasets of geo-social networks where each vertex's location is collected from real geo-social services. All these datasets are used and evaluated in the research studies of geo-social group search [64, 199]. The network statistics are summarized in Table 7.4.

Table 7.4: Network statistics of geo-social networks. d_{avg} is the average degree.

Network	$|V|$	$|E|$	d_{avg}
Gowalla [199]	107,092	456,830	9.18
Dianping [199]	2,673,970	922,977	5.18
Brightkite [64]	51,406	197,167	7.67
Flickr [64]	214,698	2,096,306	19.5
Foursquare [64]	2,127,093	8,640,352	8.12

The first two datasets of Gowalla and Dianping are used in [199]. Gowalla dataset was collected from the location-based social network Gowalla (available on http://snap.stanford.edu/data/loc-gowalla.html). The Dianping dataset was crawled from a Chinese restaurant review site (available on https://goo.gl/uUV4Wg). For both datasets, the users with no check-ins are removed and the first check-in position of each user is selected as his/her location. As a result, the preprocessed Gowalla dataset has 107,092 nodes (users) and 456,830 edges (friend relations), while the preprocessed Dianping dataset has 2,673,970 nodes and 922,977 edges [199].

The other three datasets of Brightkite, Flickr, and Foursquare are used in [64]. The Brightkite dataset [116] contains a collection of check-in data shared by users of Brightkite service. There are 4,491,143 check-ins collected during the period of April 2008–October 2010 on 772,783 distinct places. In the Flickr dataset,[2] a user is marked with a location if he/she has taken a photo there. The Foursquare dataset[3] is collected from the Foursqaure website. The location of each user is the position of his/her hometown. For the Brightkite, Flickr, and Foursquare datasets, the users without locations are ignored [64].

7.1.5   PUBLIC-PRIVATE COLLABORATION NETWORKS

In many online social networks (e.g., Facebook, Google+, Twitter, and Instagram), users prefer to hide their partial relationships, which makes such private relationships not visible to public users or even friends [92]. This leads to a new graph model called public-private networks, where each user has her/his own perspective of the network including the private connections [48].

Huang et al. present public-private networks from real-world DBLP records, called PP-DBLP [92]. To date, five PP-DBLP datasets have been publicly released.[4] The intuition of generating PP-DBLP is that the information of an accepted paper available in *public* is usually later than the information of co-author collaboration which may have really happened in *private*. In addition, such collaborations (prior to publication) are always only known to the authors themselves, and are not known to others. Thus, collaboration relationships in the published papers are taken as public edges, and collaboration relationships in the ongoing works are regarded as private edges. Moreover, motivated by widely existing attributed graphs, the corresponding attributed PP-DBLP datasets with attributes are also generated from the rich keywords of paper titles on DBLP records so that the vertices have not only private edges but also private attributes. The numbers $|V|$ and $|E|$, respectively, represent the number of vertices and edges in the public graph, and the numbers $|V_{private}|$ and $|E_{private}|$, respectively, represent the number of private vertices and private edges in all private graphs. Note that $E_{private} \cap E = \emptyset$, and each edge present in different private graphs only counts once in the private edge set $E_{private}$. For an attributed public-private graph $\mathcal{G}$, $\delta(\mathcal{G})$ measures the average overlapping ratio between public attributes and private attributes over all private graphs. Table 7.5 reports the statistic $\delta(\mathcal{G})$ for all PP-DBLP datasets.

---

[2]https://www.flickr.com
[3]https://archive.org/details/201309_foursquare_dataset_umn
[4]https://github.com/samjjx/pp-data

Table 7.5: **PP-DBLP** network statistics

Network	$|V|$	$|E|$	$|V_{private}|$	$|E_{private}|$	$\delta(\mathcal{G})$
PP-DBLP-2013	2,221,139	5,432,667	1,265.175	6,007,245	0.107
PP-DBLP-2014	2,221,139	6,186,831	1,150,642	5,322,474	0.108
PP-DBLP-2015	2,221,139	7,012,003	1,018,652	4,518,645	0.110
PP-DBLP-2016	2,221,139	7,864,133	870,054	3,628,517	0.112
PP-DBLP-2017	2,221,139	8,794,753	690,588	2,658,750	0.116

7.2   QUERY GENERATION AND EVALUATION

7.2.1   QUERY GENERATION

It is natural for users to issue the community search queries they are interested over graphs. However, to comprehensively evaluate the quality of communities found by community search algorithms, a large number of queries are needed. We suggest generating queries for different tasks as follows. For a ground-truth community $\hat{C}$ in structural graphs, we may randomly pick a set of query vertices from the community as the query vertices. For a ground-truth attributed community $\hat{C}$, we may randomly pick a set of query vertices and then select a set of common query attributes from the query vertices. For an **ego-network** with social circles, the query vertex is the center vertex (i.e., "ego" itself).

7.2.2   EVALUATION METRICS

To evaluate the quality of communities found by the algorithms, we suggest two evaluation metrics to handle different outcomes of queries in community search, i.e., single ground-truth community and multiple ground-truth communities.

For a query with a single ground-truth community, we can measure the F1-score reflecting the alignment between a discovered community C and a ground-truth community $\hat{C}$. Specifically, $F1$ is defined as

$$F1(C, \hat{C}) = \frac{2 \cdot prec(C, \hat{C}) \cdot recall(C, \hat{C})}{prec(C, \hat{C}) + recall(C, \hat{C})}, \qquad (7.1)$$

where $prec(C, \hat{C}) = \frac{|C \cap \hat{C}|}{|C|}$ is the precision and $recall(C, \hat{C}) = \frac{|C \cap \hat{C}|}{|\hat{C}|}$ is the recall.

For a query with multiple ground-truth communities, let us denote the discovered communities as $\mathcal{C} = \{C_1, \ldots, C_i\}$, and the ground-truth communities as $\overline{\mathcal{C}} = \{\overline{C}_1, \ldots, \overline{C}_j\}$. We may still use the $F1$ score to measure the alignment between a discovered community C and a ground-truth community $\overline{C}$. But since we do not know the correspondence between communities in $\mathcal{C}$ and $\overline{\mathcal{C}}$, we can compute the optimal match via linear assignment [117] by maximizing

$$\max_{f:\mathcal{C}\to\overline{\mathcal{C}}} \frac{1}{|f|} \sum_{C\in dom(f)} F1(C, f(C)), \tag{7.2}$$

where f is a (partial) correspondence between $\mathcal{C}$ and $\overline{\mathcal{C}}$ and the denominator $|f|$ is $\min\{i, j\}$.

7.3   SOFTWARE AND DEMO SYSTEMS

In this section, we introduce publicly available software tools and demo systems for assisting further study of community search.

VizCS [101] is an online query processing system for searching and visualizing communities for one query vertex in graphs. This demo system integrates two community models of Triangle-Connected-Truss [89] and (α, γ)-OCS [54]. The system architecture of VizCS is illustrated in Figure 7.1. VizCS generates a community exploration wall by offering interactive community visualization, which facilitates in-depth understanding of the data. In particular, to offer direct, simplified, intuitive, and human-friendly images to help users understand the overview of query results, VizCS employs graph visualization tool to depict communities (see Figure 7.2 for an example).

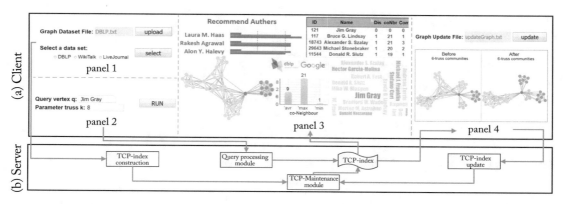

Figure 7.1: System architecture of VizCS.

Another useful demo system is C-Explorer developed by Fang et al. [66] to assist users in extracting, visualizing, and analyzing communities. Figure 7.3 shows the community search and visualization in C-Explorer system. C-Explorer implements the ACC method to allow a user to view her interested graphs, indicate her required vertex q, and display the communities to which q belongs in an attributed graph. The vertices in the generated communities are structurally and semantically related. Additionally, C-Explorer reports the detailed statistics of discovered communities (see Figure 7.4a), and compares ACC with different community models (e.g., Local-Core [55]) (see Figure 7.4b).

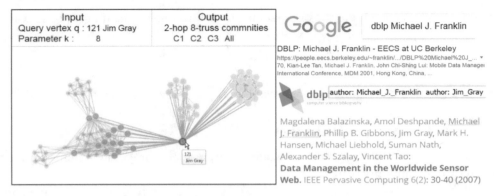

Figure 7.2: Community visualization in *Community Exploration Wall* of VizCS.

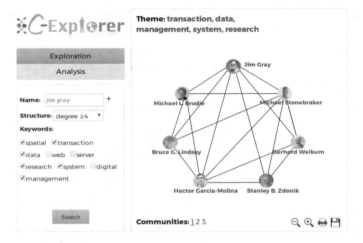

Figure 7.3: Community search and visualization in C-Explorer.

The source code of **QDC** [180], which finds the query-biased densest subgraph, can be found from `https://github.com/YubaoWu/LCD`. In addition, for social circle discovery in ego networks, code for the machine learning approach proposed in [117] is available at `https://cseweb.ucsd.edu/~jmcauley/code/code_nips2012.tar.gz`.

7.4   SUGGESTIONS ON DENSE SUBGRAPH SELECTION FOR COMMUNITY MODELS

In the preceding chapters, we have discussed several models of community search and several notions of dense subgraphs. An important question facing practitioners is which dense subgraph

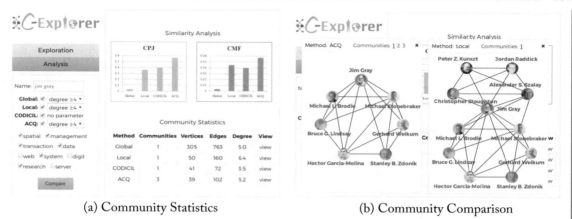

(a) Community Statistics   (b) Community Comparison

Figure 7.4: Community analysis in C-Explorer.

community model they should explore and when. Based on the theoretical analysis and experimental results in Chapter 2 (Section 2.6), we make the following observations and suggestions.

1. Even though k-clique has the best quality in terms of community density and cohesiveness, it can be expensive to apply for community search in large-scale networks. Furthermore, large communities are less likely to be perfect cliques. These considerations motivate relaxing the notion of k-clique.

2. Dense subgraph models based on k-core, k-ecc, and k-truss are appropriate for community search. However, a direct application of these models may lead to low-quality communities in terms of graph size, diameter, and density, as shown in in Table 2.2. Additional constraints are necessary in order to develop a community search paradigm based on these models.

3. If a balance between quality and efficiency is desired, the k-truss model not only achieves higher cohesiveness but also reasonable efficiency on moderate-to-large graphs.

4. If efficiency is more important, the k-core and k-ECC models are more appropriate since they can be computed more efficiently than the k-truss. The efficiency comes at a price of quality compared with k-truss.

5. For triangle-based networks with high clustering coefficient, e.g., social networks, the k-truss model is generally more preferable than other models.

6. For some special graphs without any triangles, e.g., bipartite graphs, the triangle-based k-truss model should not be used.

CHAPTER 8

Further Readings and Future Directions

This chapter first lists the community search models that are not detailed in the previous chapters. We then conclude the book by discussing future directions and open problems for further research in community search over large graphs.

8.1 FURTHER READINGS

Many new studies on community search have been published during our writing of this book, showing the hot trend of this research area. Due to space limitations, we briefly introduce these works to readers, but without much elaboration. Readers are encouraged to consult the relevant papers for more details. In the following, we categorize these works according to the dense subgraph models they adopt.

8.1.1 CLIQUE-BASED COMMUNITY SEARCH

Lee and Lakshmanan [114] investigate the query-driven maximum quasi-clique (QMQ) search, which aims to find the largest λ-quasi-clique containing a given query node set S. Efficient approaches for overlapping community search based on the (α, γ)-OCS model is studied in [151] and [152]. Xu et al. [184] study the personalized influential community search to find communities with the largest influence score over large social networks. The community model is based on a novel subgraph of pk-clique. Li et al. [120] investigate the most influential community search problem to find the kr-clique community that influences the largest number of vertices under a given diffusion model.

8.1.2 CORE-BASED COMMUNITY SEARCH

Bi et al. [23] improve the work of [122] with an instance-optimal and progressive algorithm for online search of top-k influential communities. Li et al. [121] apply the classical skyline idea on community search. Zhang et al. [190] study the community search problem using a novel cohesive subgraph model, named (k, s)-core, which requires each user to have at least k familiars or friends (not just acquaintances) in the subgraph. Zheng et al. [195] discover k-core-based communities in weighted graphs, w.r.t. the highly cohesive structure and the semantics of intimate connections. Li et al. [121] find skyline communities in multi-valued networks where each vertex has multiple numerical attributes (i.e., h-index, diversity, PageRank, similarity score, etc.). Skyline communities are not dominated by other communities in terms of numerical attributes. In contrast to existing attributed community search models of ACC [65] and ATC [93] that require the input of query vertices to find dense community structure, Zhang et al. [194] study attributed community search using only query keywords but no query vertices. The discovered communities have cohesive structure and are most relevant to query keywords over the whole network. Wang et al. [172] study the directed attribute community query (DACQ) to effectively retrieve k-core-based communities in directed attributed graphs.

8.1.3   TRUSS-BASED COMMUNITY SEARCH

Akbas and Zhao [8] propose a novel space-efficient and truss-preserving index structure named EquiTruss for speeding up the k-truss community search [89]. Katunka et al. [104] develop a linear-time algorithm to find the top-r k-truss communities [89] with the largest k containing a query vertex in large graphs. Chen et al. [41] study the maximum co-located community search in large-scale social networks, based on by incorporating spatial proximity constraint in k-truss search. Zheng et al. [196] find k-truss-based communities in large weighted networks.

8.1.4   PLEX-BASED COMMUNITY SEARCH

Wang et al. [171] find k-plex-based communities for query vertices in graphs. Conte et al. [52] apply small-diameter k-plexes to discover communities in massive graphs.

8.1.5   OTHERS

Besides the above classical community search models, there are a number of other works worthy of attention.

Hollocou et al. [82] review and evaluates multiple approaches to local community detection. Huang et al. [91] overview the studies on attributed community analysis in terms of global and ego-centric views. Chang et al. [36] study the problem of efficiently computing the steiner component with maximum connectivity. That is, given a set of query vertices Q in a graph G, one aims to find the maximum induced subgraph g of G containing Q with the maximum connectivity. Hu et al. [86] study the minimum subgraph containing the given query nodes with the largest connectivity, and develops Expand-Refine algorithms to improve the efficiency. Yin et al. [189] propose a Motif-based Approximate Personalized PageRank (MAPPR) algorithm to find communities containing a query node with minimal motif conductance in directed graphs.

While many works focus on finding a single densest subgraph, a few studies focus on finding several dense subgraphs with limited overlapping. Balalau et al. [16] find at most k subgraphs with maximum total aggregate density, while satisfying an upper bound on the pairwise Jaccard coefficient between the sets of nodes of the subgraphs. Ruchansky et al. [147] study a novel problem of finding a minimum Wiener connector, that is, given a connected graph G and a set of query vertices Q, find a subgraph H of G that connects all query vertices and has minimum Wiener index, i.e., the sum of all pairwise shortest-path distances between its vertices. Shang et al. [153] propose an attribute-based community search method with graph refinement techniques using topology similarity and attribute similarity. Cai et al. [33] study the k-hop community search based on local distance dynamics. Harenberg et al. [80] propose memory-efficient query-driven community detection with application to complex disease associations.

Moreover, Kuo et al. [109] develop a model of query-oriented graph clustering (QGC), that combines query-oriented normalized cut and the cluster balance constraint. Huang et al. [90] study subspace clustering in multi-valued attributed networks. Jabbour et al. [99] study the problem of triangle-driven community detection in graphs. Chang et al. [35] present a pSCAN approach for structural graph clustering to assign vertices to clusters and also identify hubs and outliers. Yan et al. [186] conduct local graph clustering using the techniques of multi-network random walk with restart. In addition, Aritra Mandal [13] proposes distributed algorithms on Apache Spark for k-core and k-truss decomposition of a graph. Truss decomposition algorithms for uncertain graphs is studied in [98] and [200]. Bonchi et al. [27] investigates the core decomposition algorithms for uncertain graphs.

Community search can be regarded as local query-dependent community detection. Random walk-based methods are promising to address such local community detection. Bian et al. [24] proposed a multi-walker chain (MWC) model, which utilizes a group of walkers to explore the graph. The walkers follow a sequential order to walk to be pulled back by all other walkers, thus, staying together as a group. A memory-based random walk model, MRW, is proposed to simultaneously identify multiple target local communities for a given set of query vertices [25]. In addition, graph convolutional network [181] is an interesting direction for exploring local community patterns for community search. There are a lot of yet other opportunities to explore in this interesting field of community search, utilizing the ideas of classical community detection approaches (e.g., modularity [135], normalized cut [155], low-conductance cuts [71, 111], personalized pagerank [12, 161], and spectral clustering [68]), machine learning approaches (e.g., generative models [187, 188, 191]), and deep neural networks [193], for locally identifying communities.

8.2 FUTURE DIRECTIONS AND OPEN PROBLEMS

While significant progress has been made, research on community search is still in its infancy, and there are many opportunities for further research. In the following, we highlight some of the promising directions.

8.2.1 QUERYING COMMUNITIES ON HETEROGENEOUS INFORMATION NETWORKS

Most of the current research on community search focuses on homogeneous networks. For real-world heterogeneous networks where nodes and relations are of different types [159], the problem of community search has not been sufficiently investigated. For example, in a healthcare network, nodes can be patients, doctors, medical tests, diseases, medicines, hospitals, treatments, and so on. On one hand, treating all the nodes as of the same type may miss important semantic information. On the other hand, treating every node as of a distinct type may miss the big picture. Such multiple types of objects, interconnected, forming complex, heterogeneous but often semi-structured information networks, bring new opportunities and challenges for community modeling and discovery [160].

8.2.2   SCALABLE ALGORITHMS FOR BIG GRAPHS

Scaling community search techniques to the massive and rapidly growing network datasets of the Big Data era is another important direction. Current graph processing techniques include I/O-efficient algorithms for k-core decomposition [165, 179] and k-truss decomposition [44], distributed graph computing (including Pregel [130]and Blogel [185]), and sketching [26, 49]. Techniques for processing community search queries and for handling community indexes in highly evolving graphs [89] and streaming graphs [15] are also avenues for future work.

8.2.3   PUBLIC-PRIVATE SOCIAL NETWORKS

Most existing works assume that the entire network structure is visible and assume unrestricted access to it. However, in real applications, due to privacy issues, social networks can be more complex than a simple fully visible graph. Social network providers allow users to control their privacy by controlling the information they are willing to share. For example, as reported in a recent study, 52.6% of 1.4 million New York City Facebook users hid their friends list [57]. Such privacy protection leads to a novel graph model, called *public-private* graphs [48]. It contains a public graph, in which each node is also associated with a private graph. The public graph is visible to everyone, and each private graph is visible only to the corresponding user. From each user's viewpoint, the social network is exactly the union of the public graph and its own private graph. Despite the long existence of such networks, they have started gaining attention from the research community very recently. Owing to the scale of the network and its associated idiosyncrasies, community search over such networks cannot be efficiently answered by traditional algorithmic tools and techniques, and remains largely unexplored. Publicly available public-private networks datasets PP-DBLP are introduced in Section 7.1.5.

8.2.4   COMMUNITY SEARCH ON PROBABILISTIC GRAPHS

A large number of real-world networks are associated with uncertainty, due to the data collection process, machine-learning methods employed at preprocessing, inherent uncertainty in link inference in biological networks, or privacy-preserving reasons. The discovery of communities in uncertain graphs can be beneficial for a wide range of application domains, e.g., in biology, identification of functional modules for helping critical clinical diagnosis of diseases such as cancer. Given the recent surge of interest in dense subgraphs such as k-core [27] and k-truss [98] in probabilistic graphs, an exciting question is how to generalize various community models [18, 65, 89, 96] and search techniques to probabilistic graphs. The challenge is to develop extensions that are widely useful and tractable.

Other open problems include community search over dynamic and evolving geo-social networks with moving locations, and also graph representation learning for community search.

8.2.5 APPLICATIONS AND CASE STUDIES

While a growing number of research papers report real-life applications and case studies, they are limited in scale and scope. We stress the need for work on large scale and industry strength applications and case studies in order to firmly anchor the utility of community search over networks.

8.3 CONCLUSIONS

Communities serve as basic structures for understanding the organization of many real-world networks such as social, biological, collaboration, and communication networks. Recently, community search over large graphs has attracted significant attention, from simple and static graphs to evolving, attributed, and location-based graphs. Different from the well-studied problem of community detection that finds all communities in an entire network, the problem of community search is to find the cohesive communities w.r.t. predicates consisting of query vertices (and possibly query attributes).

In this book, we surveyed the state-of-the-art of research on community search over various kinds of networks. Specifically, we discussed topics such as densely-connected community search, attributed community search, social circle discovery, and querying geo-social groups. We highlighted the challenges posed by the community search problem in its various flavors. We presented the principles, methodologies, algorithms, and applications, and provided a comprehensive comparison of the state-of-the-art techniques for community search. We also provided a summary of various publicly available datasets for supporting community search research and available software and tools. We finally concluded by offering future directions for research in this important and growing area.

Bibliography

[1] https://www.statista.com/statistics/264810/number-of-monthly-active-facebook-users-worldwide 4

[2] http://ibts.hkbu.edu.hk/one_show.php/coid_3.htm 3

[3] https://www.facebook.com/notes/facebook-engineering/visualizing-friendships/469716398919 3

[4] F. Adu-Oppong, C. K. Gardiner, A. Kapadia, and P. P. Tsang. Social circles: Tackling privacy in social networks. In *Symposium on Usable Privacy and Security*. 3

[5] S. Agrawal, S. Chaudhuri, and G. Das. Dbxplorer: A system for keyword-based search over relational databases. In *ICDE*, pages 5–16, 2002. DOI: 10.1109/icde.2002.994693 105

[6] Y.-Y. Ahn, J. P. Bagrow, and S. Lehmann. Link communities reveal multiscale complexity in networks. *Nature*, 466(7307):761–764, 2010. DOI: 10.1038/nature09182 3, 4

[7] E. M. Airoldi, D. M. Blei, S. E. Fienberg, and E. P. Xing. Mixed membership stochastic blockmodels. *Journal of Machine Learning Research*, 9(Sep):1981–2014, 2008. 130

[8] E. Akbas and P. Zhao. Truss-based community search: A truss-equivalence based indexing approach. *PVLDB*, 10(11):1298–1309, 2017. DOI: 10.14778/3137628.3137640 164

[9] A. Anagnostopoulos, L. Becchetti, C. Castillo, A. Gionis, and S. Leonardi. Online team formation in social networks. In *WWW*, pages 839–848, 2012. DOI: 10.1145/2187836.2187950 106

[10] R. Andersen and K. Chellapilla. Finding dense subgraphs with size bounds. In *International Workshop on Algorithms and Models for the Web-Graph*, pages 25–37, 2009. DOI: 10.1007/978-3-540-95995-3_3 21, 22

[11] R. Andersen, F. Chung, and K. Lang. Local graph partitioning using pagerank vectors. In *FOCS*, pages 475–486, 2006. DOI: 10.1109/focs.2006.44 4

[12] R. Andersen and K. J. Lang. Communities from seed sets. In *WWW*, pages 223–232, 2006. DOI: 10.1145/1135777.1135814 4, 165

[13] M. Aritra. Distributed graph decomposition algorithms on apache spark. Ph.D. thesis, Purdue University, Indianapolis, 2018. 165

[14] L. Backstrom, D. P. Huttenlocher, J. M. Kleinberg, and X. Lan. Group formation in large social networks: Membership, growth, and evolution. In *KDD*, pages 44–54, 2006. DOI: 10.1145/1150402.1150412 111

[15] B. Bahmani, R. Kumar, and S. Vassilvitskii. Densest subgraph in streaming and mapreduce. *PVLDB*, 5(5):454–465, 2012. DOI: 10.14778/2140436.2140442 9, 20, 21, 166

[16] O. D. Balalau, F. Bonchi, T. Chan, F. Gullo, and M. Sozio. Finding subgraphs with maximum total density and limited overlap. In *WSDM*, pages 379–388, 2015. DOI: 10.1145/2684822.2685298 164

[17] B. Balasundaram, S. Butenko, and I. V. Hicks. Clique relaxations in social network analysis: The maximum k-plex problem. *Operations Research*, 2009. DOI: 10.1287/opre.1100.0851 135

[18] N. Barbieri, F. Bonchi, E. Galimberti, and F. Gullo. Efficient and effective community search. *DMKD*, 29(5):1406–1433, 2015. DOI: 10.1007/s10618-015-0422-1 7, 10, 27, 34, 39, 42, 43, 51, 78, 79, 80, 87, 167

[19] V. Batagelj and M. Zaversnik. An o (m) algorithm for cores decomposition of networks. *ArXiv Preprint cs/0310049*, 2003. 9, 10, 12, 17, 19, 20, 24, 25, 57, 94

[20] V. Batagelj and M. Zaveršnik. Short cycle connectivity. *Discrete Mathematics*, 307(3–5):310–318, 2007. DOI: 10.1016/j.disc.2005.09.051 52

[21] N. Beckmann, H.-P. Kriegel, R. Schneider, and B. Seeger. The R*-tree: An efficient and robust access method for points and rectangles. In *ACM SIGMOD Record*, vol. 19, pages 322–331, 1990. DOI: 10.1145/93605.98741 140

[22] G. Bhalotia, A. Hulgeri, C. Nakhe, S. Chakrabarti, and S. Sudarshan. Keyword searching and browsing in databases using banks. In *ICDE*, pages 431–440, 2002. DOI: 10.1109/icde.2002.994756 105, 106

[23] F. Bi, L. Chang, X. Lin, and W. Zhang. An optimal and progressive approach to online search of top-k influential communities. *PVLDB*, 11(9):1056–1068, 2018. DOI: 10.14778/3213880.3213881 163

[24] Y. Bian, J. Ni, W. Cheng, and X. Zhang. Many heads are better than one: Local community detection by the multi-walker chain. In *ICDM*, pages 21–30, 2017. DOI: 10.1109/icdm.2017.11 165

[25] Y. Bian, Y. Yan, W. Cheng, W. Wang, D. Luo, and X. Zhang. On multi-query local community detection. In *ICDM*, pages 9–18, 2018. DOI: 10.1109/icdm.2018.00016 165

[26] P. Boldi, M. Rosa, and S. Vigna. HyperANF: Aproximating the neighbourhood function of very large graphs on a budget. In *WWW*, pages 625–634, 2011. DOI: 10.1145/1963405.1963493 166

[27] F. Bonchi, F. Gullo, A. Kaltenbrunner, and Y. Volkovich. Core decomposition of uncertain graphs. In *KDD*, pages 1316–1325, 2014. DOI: 10.1145/2623330.2623655 165, 166

[28] C. Borgs, M. Brautbar, J. Chayes, and B. Lucier. Maximizing social influence in nearly optimal time. In *SODA*, pages 946–957, 2014. DOI: 10.1137/1.9781611973402.70 43

[29] E. Boros and P. L. Hammer. Pseudo-Boolean optimization. *Discrete Applied Mathematics*, 123(1–3):155–225, 2002. DOI: 10.1016/s0166-218x(01)00341-9 129

[30] C. Bothorel, J. D. Cruz, M. Magnani, and B. Micenkova. Clustering attributed graphs: Models, measures and methods. *Network Science*, 3(03):408–444, 2015. DOI: 10.1017/nws.2015.9 107

[31] C. Bron and J. Kerbosch. Finding all cliques of an undirected graph (algorithm 457). *Communications of the ACM*, 16(9):575–576, 1973. 9, 10, 12, 13, 24

[32] R. S. Burt. Social contagion and innovation: Cohesion versus structural equivalence. *American Journal of Sociology*, 92(6):1287–1335, 1987. DOI: 10.1086/228667 111

[33] L. Cai, T. Meng, T. He, L. Chen, and Z. Deng. K-hop community search based on local distance dynamics. In *International Conference on Neural Information Processing*, pages 24–34, 2017. DOI: 10.1007/978-3-319-70139-4_3 165

[34] B. Cao, N. N. Liu, and Q. Yang. Transfer learning for collective link prediction in multiple heterogenous domains. In *ICML*, pages 159–166, 2010. 4

[35] L. Chang, W. Li, L. Qin, W. Zhang, and S. Yang. pSCAN: Fast and exact structural graph clustering. *IEEE Transactions on Knowledge and Data Engineering*, 29(2):387–401, 2017. DOI: 10.1109/icde.2016.7498245 165

[36] L. Chang, X. Lin, L. Qin, J. X. Yu, and W. Zhang. Index-based optimal algorithms for computing Steiner components with maximum connectivity. In *SIGMOD*, pages 459–474, 2015. DOI: 10.1145/2723372.2746486 164

[37] L. Chang and L. Qin. *Cohesive Subgraph Computation over Large Sparse Graphs: Algorithms, Data Structures, and Programming Techniques*. Springer, 2018. DOI: 10.1007/978-3-030-03599-0 57

[38] L. Chang, J. X. Yu, L. Qin, X. Lin, C. Liu, and W. Liang. Efficiently computing k-edge connected components via graph decomposition. In *SIGMOD*, pages 205–216, 2013. DOI: 10.1145/2463676.2465323 9, 22, 23, 24, 25

[39] M. Charikar. Greedy approximation algorithms for finding dense components in a graph. In *International Workshop on Approximation Algorithms for Combinatorial Optimization*, pages 84–95, 2000. DOI: 10.1007/3-540-44436-x_10 21

[40] J. Chen and Y. Saad. Dense subgraph extraction with application to community detection. *IEEE Transactions on Knowledge and Data Engineering*, 24(7):1216–1230, 2012. DOI: 10.1109/tkde.2010.271 20

[41] L. Chen, C. Liu, R. Zhou, J. Li, X. Yang, and B. Wang. Maximum co-located community search in large scale social networks. *PVLDB*, 11(9), 2018. DOI: 10.14778/3231751.3231755 164

[42] W. Chen, L. V. Lakshmanan, and C. Castillo. Information and influence propagation in social networks. *Synthesis Lectures on Data Management*, 5(4):1–177, 2013. DOI: 10.2200/s00527ed1v01y201308dtm037 2, 43

[43] H. Cheng, Y. Zhou, X. Huang, and J. X. Yu. Clustering large attributed information networks: An efficient incremental computing approach. *DMKD*, 25(3):450–477, 2012. DOI: 10.1007/s10618-012-0263-0 107

[44] J. Cheng, Y. Ke, S. Chu, and M. T. Özsu. Efficient core decomposition in massive networks. In *ICDE*, pages 51–62, 2011. DOI: 10.1109/icde.2011.5767911 9, 10, 12, 17, 20, 166

[45] J. Cheng, Y. Ke, A. W.-C. Fu, J. X. Yu, and L. Zhu. Finding maximal cliques in massive networks by H*-graph. In *SIGMOD*, pages 447–458, 2010. DOI: 10.1145/1807167.1807217 9, 12, 13

[46] X.-Q. Cheng and H.-W. Shen. Uncovering the community structure associated with the diffusion dynamics on networks. *Journal of Statistical Mechanics: Theory and Experiment*, 2010(04):P04024, 2010. DOI: 10.1088/1742-5468/2010/04/p04024 4

[47] N. Chiba and T. Nishizeki. Arboricity and subgraph listing algorithms. *SIAM Journal on Computing*, 14(1):210–223, 1985. DOI: 10.1137/0214017 60, 122

[48] F. Chierichetti, A. Epasto, R. Kumar, S. Lattanzi, and V. Mirrokni. Efficient algorithms for public-private social networks. In *KDD*, pages 139–148, 2015. DOI: 10.1145/2783258.2783354 157, 166

[49] E. Cohen. Size-estimation framework with applications to transitive closure and reachability. *JCSS*, 55(3):441–453, 1997. DOI: 10.1006/jcss.1997.1534 72, 166

[50] J. Cohen. Trusses: Cohesive subgraphs for social network analysis. *Technical Report*, National Security Agency, 2008. 9, 10, 12, 18, 19, 20, 52, 54, 55, 67, 94

[51] J. Cohen. Graph twiddling in a MapReduce world. *Computing in Science and Engineering*, 11(4):29–41, 2009. DOI: 10.1109/mcse.2009.120 20

[52] A. Conte, T. De Matteis, D. De Sensi, R. Grossi, A. Marino, and L. Versari. D2K: Scalable community detection in massive networks via small-diameter k-plexes. In *KDD*, pages 1272–1281, 2018. DOI: 10.1145/3219819.3220093 164

[53] T. H. Cormen, C. E. Leiserson, R. L. Rivest, and C. Stein. *Introduction to Algorithms*. MIT Press, 2009. DOI: 10.2307/2583667 113, 115, 116

[54] W. Cui, Y. Xiao, H. Wang, Y. Lu, and W. Wang. Online search of overlapping communities. In *SIGMOD*, pages 277–288, 2013. DOI: 10.1145/2463676.2463722 2, 4, 5, 7, 27, 30, 31, 32, 34, 54, 55, 63, 65, 78, 79, 80, 85, 105, 159

[55] W. Cui, Y. Xiao, H. Wang, and W. Wang. Local search of communities in large graphs. In *SIGMOD*, pages 991–1002, 2014. 7, 10, 27, 34, 38, 39, 51, 78, 79, 80, 85, 87, 159 DOI: 10.1145/2588555.2612179

[56] M. Danisch, O. Balalau, and M. Sozio. Listing k-cliques in sparse real-world graphs. In *WWW*, pages 589–598, 2018. DOI: 10.1145/3178876.3186125 24, 25

[57] R. Dey, Z. Jelveh, and K. Ross. Facebook users have become much more private: A large-scale study. In *IEEE International Conference on Pervasive Computing and Communications Workshops*, pages 346–352, 2012. DOI: 10.1109/percomw.2012.6197508 166

[58] B. Ding, J. X. Yu, S. Wang, L. Qin, X. Zhang, and X. Lin. Finding top-k min-cost connected trees in databases. In *ICDE*, pages 836–845, 2007. DOI: 10.1109/icde.2007.367929 105

[59] P. S. Dodds and D. J. Watts. Universal behavior in a generalized model of contagion. *Physical Review Letters*, 92:218701, 2004. DOI: 10.1103/physrevlett.92.218701 111

[60] N. Durak, A. Pinar, T. G. Kolda, and C. Seshadhri. Degree relations of triangles in real-world networks and graph models. In *CIKM*, pages 1712–1716, 2012. DOI: 10.1145/2396761.2398503 52

[61] J. Edachery, A. Sen, and F. J. Brandenburg. Graph clustering using distance-k cliques. In *Proc. of the 7th International Symposium on Graph Drawing*, pages 98–106, 1999. DOI: 10.1007/3-540-46648-7_10 9, 55

[62] J. Elzinga and D. W. Hearn. Geometrical solutions for some minimax location problems. *Transportation Science*, 6(4):379–394, 1972. DOI: 10.1287/trsc.6.4.379 149

[63] M. Fang, N. Shivakumar, H. Garcia-Molina, R. Motwani, and J. D. Ullman. Computing iceberg queries efficiently. In *VLDB*, 1999. 112

[64] Y. Fang, R. Cheng, X. Li, S. Luo, and J. Hu. Effective community search over large spatial graphs. *PVLDB*, 10(6):709–720, 2017. DOI: 10.14778/3055330.3055337 10, 131, 133, 147, 148, 149, 156, 157

[65] Y. Fang, R. Cheng, S. Luo, and J. Hu. Effective community search for large attributed graphs. *PVLDB*, 9(12):1233–1244, 2016. DOI: 10.14778/2994509.2994538 5, 7, 10, 83, 87, 89, 91, 103, 105, 127, 164, 167

[66] Y. Fang, R. Cheng, S. Luo, J. Hu, and K. Huang. C-explorer: Browsing communities in large graphs. *PVLDB*, 10(12):1885–1888, 2017. DOI: 10.14778/3137765.3137800 159

[67] Y. Fang, Z. Wang, R. Cheng, X. Li, S. Luo, J. Hu, and X. Chen. On spatial-aware community search. *IEEE Transactions on Knowledge and Data Engineering*, 2018. DOI: 10.1109/tkde.2018.2845414 152

[68] S. Fortunato. Community detection in graphs. *Physics Reports*, 486(3–5):75–174, 2010. DOI: 10.1016/j.physrep.2009.11.002 3, 4, 165

[69] H. N. Gabow and R. E. Tarjan. A linear-time algorithm for a special case of disjoint set union. In *STOC*, pages 246–251, 1983. DOI: 10.1145/800061.808753 42

[70] A. Gajewar and A. D. Sarma. Multi-skill collaborative teams based on densest subgraphs. In *SDM*, pages 165–176, 2012. DOI: 10.1137/1.9781611972825.15 105, 106

[71] G. Gallo, M. D. Grigoriadis, and R. E. Tarjan. A fast parametric maximum flow algorithm and applications. *SIAM Journal on Computing*, 18(1):30–55, 1989. DOI: 10.1137/0218003 4, 165

[72] M. R. Garey and D. S. Johnson. *Computers and Intractability: A Guide to the Theory of NP-Completeness*. W. H. Freeman, 1979. DOI: 10.1137/1024022 55, 67

[73] D. Gibson, J. Kleinberg, and P. Raghavan. Inferring web communities from link topology. In *Proc. of the 9th ACM Conference on Hypertext and Hypermedia: Links, Objects, Time and Space—Structure in Hypermedia Systems: Links, Objects, Time and Space—Structure in Hypermedia Systems*, pages 225–234, 1998. DOI: 10.1145/276627.276652 4

[74] D. Gibson, R. Kumar, and A. Tomkins. Discovering large dense subgraphs in massive graphs. In *VLDB*, pages 721–732, 2005. 24

[75] A. Goyal, F. Bonchi, and L. V. Lakshmanan. Learning influence probabilities in social networks. In *WSDM*, pages 241–250, 2010. DOI: 10.1145/1718487.1718518 43

[76] S. Günnemann, B. Boden, and T. Seidl. DB-CSC: A density-based approach for sub-space clustering in graphs with feature vectors. In *ECML/PKDD*, pages 565–580, 2011. DOI: 10.1007/978-3-642-23780-5_46 107

[77] J. Han, M. Kamber, and J. Pei. *Data Mining: Concepts and Techniques*, (3rd ed.). Morgan Kaufmann Publishers Inc., San Francisco, CA. 2011. 92

[78] J. Han, J. Pei, and Y. Yin. Mining frequent patterns without candidate generation. In *ACM SIGMOD Record*, vol. 29, pages 1–12, 2000. DOI: 10.1145/335191.335372 92

[79] M. S. Handcock, A. E. Raftery, and J. M. Tantrum. Model-based clustering for social networks. *Journal of the Royal Statistical Society: Series A (Statistics in Society)*, 170(2):301–354, 2007. DOI: 10.1111/j.1467-985x.2007.00471.x 130

[80] S. Harenberg, R. G. Seay, S. Ranshous, K. Padmanabhan, J. K. Harlalka, E. R. Schendel, M. P. O'Brien, R. Y. Chirkova, W. Hendrix, A. N. Choudhary, et al. Memory-efficient query-driven community detection with application to complex disease associations. In *SDM*, pages 1010–1018, 2014. DOI: 10.1137/1.9781611973440.115 165

[81] E. Hartuv and R. Shamir. A clustering algorithm based on graph connectivity. *Information Processing Letters*, 76(4–6):175–181, 2000. DOI: 10.1016/s0020-0190(00)00142-3 9, 55

[82] A. Hollocou, T. Bonald, and M. Lelarge. Multiple local community detection. *ACM SIGMETRICS Performance Evaluation Review*, 45(2):76–83, 2018. DOI: 10.1145/3199524.3199537 164

[83] V. Hristidis, L. Gravano, and Y. Papakonstantinou. Efficient IR-style keyword search over relational databases. In *PVLDB*, pages 850–861, 2003. DOI: 10.1016/b978-012722442-8/50080-x 105, 106

[84] V. Hristidis and Y. Papakonstantinou. Discover: Keyword search in relational databases. In *PVLDB*, pages 670–681, 2002. DOI: 10.1016/B978-155860869-6/50065-2 105, 106

[85] A. L. Hu and K. C. Chan. Utilizing both topological and attribute information for protein complex identification in PPI networks. *TCBB*, 10(3):780–792, 2013. DOI: 10.1109/tcbb.2013.37 84, 85, 103, 154

[86] J. Hu, X. Wu, R. Cheng, S. Luo, and Y. Fang. On minimal steiner maximum-connected subgraph queries. *IEEE Transactions on Knowledge and Data Engineering*, 29(11):2455–2469, 2017. DOI: 10.1109/tkde.2017.2730873 164

[87] X. Huang, H. Cheng, R.-H. Li, L. Qin, and J. X. Yu. Top-k structural diversity search in large networks. *PVLDB*, 6(13):1618–1629, 2013. DOI: 10.14778/2536258.2536272 5, 7, 109, 112, 118, 123

[88] X. Huang, H. Cheng, R.-H. Li, L. Qin, and J. X. Yu. Top-k structural diversity search in large networks. *The VLDB Journal*, 24(3):319–343, 2015. DOI: 10.14778/2536258.2536272 5, 109, 111, 112, 118, 123, 124

[89] X. Huang, H. Cheng, L. Qin, W. Tian, and J. X. Yu. Querying k-truss community in large and dynamic graphs. In *SIGMOD*, pages 1311–1322, 2014. DOI: 10.1145/2588555.2610495 3, 4, 5, 7, 10, 20, 27, 52, 58, 67, 78, 79, 80, 98, 99, 159, 164, 166, 167

[90] X. Huang, H. Cheng, and J. X. Yu. Dense community detection in multi-valued attributed networks. *Information Sciences*, 314:77–99, 2015. DOI: 10.1016/j.ins.2015.03.075 107, 165

[91] X. Huang, H. Cheng, and J. X. Yu. Attributed community analysis: Global and ego-centric views. *IEEE Data Engineering Bulletin*, 39(3):29–40, 2016. 164

[92] X. Huang, J. Jiang, B. Choi, J. Xu, Z. Zhang, and Y. Song. PP-DBLP: Modeling and generating attributed public-private networks with DBLP. In *IEEE International Conference on Data Mining Workshops (ICDMW)*, pages 986–989, 2018. DOI: 10.1109/icdmw.2018.00142 157

[93] X. Huang and L. V. Lakshmanan. Attribute-driven community search. *PVLDB*, 10(9):949–960, 2017. DOI: 10.14778/3099622.3099626 1, 5, 7, 10, 83, 85, 94, 97, 102, 104, 127, 164

[94] X. Huang, L. V. Lakshmanan, and J. Xu. Community search over big graphs: Models, algorithms, and opportunities. In *ICDE*, pages 1451–1454, IEEE, 2017. DOI: 10.1109/icde.2017.211 8

[95] X. Huang, L. V. Lakshmanan, and J. Xu. Tutorial slides: Community search over big graphs: Models, algorithms, and opportunities. http://www.comp.hkbu.edu.hk/~xi nhuang/publications/pdfs/ICDE-Tutorial17-April19.ppt, 2017. 3, 8

[96] X. Huang, L. V. Lakshmanan, J. X. Yu, and H. Cheng. Approximate closest community search in networks. *PVLDB*, 9(4):276–287, 2015. DOI: 10.14778/2856318.2856323 2, 5, 7, 10, 27, 52, 65, 72, 78, 79, 80, 85, 87, 94, 105, 167

[97] X. Huang, L. V. Lakshmanan, J. X. Yu, and H. Cheng. Approximate closest community search in networks. *ArXiv Preprint ArXiv:1505.05956*, 2015. DOI: 10.14778/2856318.2856323 72

[98] X. Huang, W. Lu, and L. V. S. Lakshmanan. Truss decomposition of probabilistic graphs: Semantics and algorithms. In *SIGMOD*, pages 77–90, 2016. DOI: 10.1145/2882903.2882913 165, 166

[99] S. Jabbour, N. Mhadhbi, B. Radaoui, and L. Sais. Triangle-driven community detection in large graphs using propositional satisfiability. In *AINA*, pages 437–444, 2018. DOI: 10.1109/aina.2018.00072 165

[100] M. Jalili, Y. Orouskhani, M. Asgari, N. Alipourfard, and M. Perc. Link prediction in multiplex online social networks. *Royal Society Open Science*, 4(2):160863, 2017. DOI: 10.1098/rsos.160863 4

[101] Y. Jiang, X. Huang, H. Cheng, and J. X. Yu. VizCS: Online searching and visualizing communities in dynamic graphs. In *ICDE*, 2018. DOI: 10.1109/icde.2018.00182 159

[102] V. Kacholia, S. Pandit, S. Chakrabarti, S. Sudarshan, R. Desai, and H. Karambelkar. Bidirectional expansion for keyword search on graph databases. In *VLDB*, pages 505–516, 2005. 105, 106

[103] M. Kargar and A. An. Discovering top-k teams of experts with/without a leader in social networks. In *CIKM*, pages 985–994, 2011. DOI: 10.1145/2063576.2063718 105, 106

[104] A. M. Katunka, C. Yan, K. B. Serge, and Z. Zhang. K-truss based top-communities search in large graphs. In *International Conference on Advanced Cloud and Big Data*, pages 244–249, IEEE, 2017. DOI: 10.1109/cbd.2017.49 164

[105] D. Kempe, J. Kleinberg, and É. Tardos. Maximizing the spread of influence through a social network. In *KDD*, pages 137–146, 2003. DOI: 10.1145/956750.956769 43, 44, 111

[106] S. Khuller and B. Saha. On finding dense subgraphs. In *ICALP*, pages 597–608, 2009. DOI: 10.1007/978-3-642-02927-1_50 9, 21

[107] G. Kortsarz and D. Peleg. Generating sparse 2-spanners. *Journal of Algorithms*, 17(2):222–236, 1994. DOI: 10.1007/3-540-55706-7_7 21

[108] L. Kou, G. Markowsky, and L. Berman. A fast algorithm for Steiner trees. *Acta Informatica*, 15(2):141–145, 1981. DOI: 10.1007/bf00288961 43

[109] L.-Y. Kuo, C.-K. Chou, and M.-S. Chen. Query-oriented graph clustering. In *PAKDD*, pages 749–761, 2017. DOI: 10.1007/978-3-319-57529-2_58 165

[110] H. Kwak, C. Lee, H. Park, and S. B. Moon. What is twitter, a social network or a news media? In *WWW*, pages 591–600, 2010. DOI: 10.1145/1772690.1772751 110

[111] K. Lang and S. Rao. A flow-based method for improving the expansion or conductance of graph cuts. In *International Conference on Integer Programming and Combinatorial Optimization*, pages 325–337, 2004. DOI: 10.1007/978-3-540-25960-2_25 4, 165

[112] T. Lappas, K. Liu, and E. Terzi. Finding a team of experts in social networks. In *KDD*, pages 467–476, 2009. DOI: 10.1145/1557019.1557074 105, 106

[113] E. L. Lawler. *Combinatorial Optimization: Networks and Matroids*. Courier Corporation, 1976. 21

[114] P. Lee and L. V. Lakshmanan. Query-driven maximum quasi-clique search. In *SDM*, pages 522–530, 2016. DOI: 10.1137/1.9781611974348.59 163

[115] C. Lei and J. Ruan. A novel link prediction algorithm for reconstructing protein—protein interaction networks by topological similarity. *Bioinformatics*, 29(3):355–364, 2012. DOI: 10.1093/bioinformatics/bts688 4

[116] J. Leskovec and A. Krevl. SNAP Datasets: Stanford large network dataset collection. http://snap.stanford.edu/data, June 2014. 153, 154, 155, 156, 157

[117] J. Leskovec and J. J. Mcauley. Learning to discover social circles in ego networks. In *NIPS*, pages 539–547, 2012. 4, 5, 7, 109, 110, 127, 128, 130, 155, 156, 159, 160

[118] C.-T. Li and M.-K. Shan. Team formation for generalized tasks in expertise social networks. In *IEEE International Conference on Social Computing*, pages 9–16, 2010. DOI: 10.1109/socialcom.2010.12 106

[119] G. Li, B. C. Ooi, J. Feng, J. Wang, and L. Zhou. Ease: An effective 3-in-1 keyword search method for unstructured, semi-structured and structured data. In *SIGMOD*, pages 903–914, 2008. DOI: 10.1145/1376616.1376706 105, 106

[120] J. Li, X. Wang, K. Deng, X. Yang, T. Sellis, and J. X. Yu. Most influential community search over large social networks. In *ICDE*, pages 871–882, 2017. DOI: 10.1109/icde.2017.136 43, 163

[121] R.-H. Li, L. Qin, F. Ye, J. X. Yu, X. Xiao, N. Xiao, and Z. Zheng. Skyline community search in multi-valued networks. In *SIGMOD*, pages 457–472, 2018. DOI: 10.1145/3183713.3183736 163

[122] R.-H. Li, L. Qin, J. X. Yu, and R. Mao. Influential community search in large networks. *PVLDB*, 8(5), 2015. DOI: 10.14778/2735479.2735484 5, 7, 10, 27, 35, 43, 44, 45, 50, 51, 78, 79, 80, 85, 87, 163

[123] Y. Li, R. Chen, J. Xu, Q. Huang, H. Hu, and B. Choi. Geo-social k-cover group queries for collaborative spatial computing. *IEEE Transactions on Knowledge and Data Engineering*, 27(10):2729–2742, 2015. DOI: 10.1109/icde.2016.7498399 7, 131, 133, 143, 145, 146

[124] Y. Li, R. Chen, J. Xu, Q. Huang, H. Hu, and B. Choi. Geo-social k-cover group queries for collaborative spatial computing. In *ICDE*, pages 1510–1511, 2016. DOI: 10.1109/icde.2016.7498399 7, 10, 133, 143

[125] Y. Li, C. Sha, X. Huang, and Y. Zhang. Community detection in attributed graphs: An embedding approach. In *AAAI*, 2018. 4

[126] Y. Li, Y. Zhao, G. Wang, F. Zhu, Y. Wu, and S. Shi. Effective k-vertex connected component detection in large-scale networks. In *International Conference on Database Systems for Advanced Applications*, pages 404–421, 2017. DOI: 10.1007/978-3-319-55699-4_25 22

[127] B. Lucier, J. Oren, and Y. Singer. Influence at scale: Distributed computation of complex contagion in networks. In *KDD*, pages 735–744, 2015. DOI: 10.1145/2783258.2783334 43

[128] D. J. MacKay and D. J. Mac Kay. *Information Theory, Inference and Learning Algorithms*. Cambridge University Press, 2003. DOI: 10.1108/03684920410534506 129

[129] A. Majumder, S. Datta, and K. Naidu. Capacitated team formation problem on social networks. In *KDD*, pages 1005–1013, 2012. DOI: 10.1145/2339530.2339690 106

[130] G. Malewicz, M. H. Austern, A. J. Bik, J. C. Dehnert, I. Horn, N. Leiser, and G. Czajkowski. Pregel: A system for large-scale graph processing. In *SIGMOD*, pages 135–146, 2010. DOI: 10.1145/1807167.1807184 166

[131] K. Mehlhorn. A faster approximation algorithm for the steiner problem in graphs. *Information Processing Letters*, 27(3):125–128, 1988. DOI: 10.1016/0020-0190(88)90066-x 78, 79

[132] R. J. Mokken. Cliques, clubs and clans. *Quality and Quantity*, 13(2):161–173, 1979. DOI: 10.1007/bf00139635 9, 10, 12, 14, 15

[133] M. E. Newman. Finding community structure in networks using the eigenvectors of matrices. *Physical Review E*, 74(3):036104, 2006. DOI: 10.1103/physreve.74.036104 4

[134] M. E. Newman. Spectral methods for community detection and graph partitioning. *Physical Review E*, 88(4):042822, 2013. DOI: 10.1103/physreve.88.042822 4

[135] M. E. Newman and M. Girvan. Finding and evaluating community structure in networks. *Physical Review E*, 69(2):026113, 2004. DOI: 10.1103/physreve.69.026113 4, 165

[136] M. E. Newman, D. J. Watts, and S. H. Strogatz. Random graph models of social networks. *PNAS*, 99(suppl 1):2566–2572, 2002. DOI: 10.1073/pnas.012582999 52

[137] J.-P. Onnela, A. Chakraborti, K. Kaski, J. Kertesz, and A. Kanto. Dynamics of market correlations: Taxonomy and portfolio analysis. *Physical Review E*, 68(5):056110, 2003. DOI: 10.1103/physreve.68.056110 2

[138] L. Page, S. Brin, R. Motwani, and T. Winograd. The pagerank citation ranking: Bringing order to the Web. *Technical Report*, Stanford InfoLab, 1999. 44

[139] G. Palla, I. Derényi, I. Farkas, and T. Vicsek. Uncovering the overlapping community structure of complex networks in nature and society. *Nature*, 435(7043):814–818, 2005. DOI: 10.1038/nature03607 1, 2, 3, 4, 27, 28, 29, 78

[140] R. Pastor-Satorras and A. Vespignani. Epidemic spreading in scale-free networks. *Physical Review Letters*, 86(14):3200, 2001. DOI: 10.1103/physrevlett.86.3200 111

[141] L. Qin, J. X. Yu, L. Chang, and Y. Tao. Querying communities in relational databases. In *ICDE*, pages 724–735, 2009. DOI: 10.1109/icde.2009.67 106

[142] E. Ravasz, A. L. Somera, D. A. Mongru, Z. N. Oltvai, and A.-L. Barabási. Hierarchical organization of modularity in metabolic networks. *Science*, 297(5586):1551–1555, 2002. DOI: 10.1126/science.1073374 2

[143] D. M. Romero, B. Meeder, and J. M. Kleinberg. Differences in the mechanics of information diffusion across topics: Idioms, political hashtags, and complex contagion on twitter. In *WWW*, pages 695–704, 2011. DOI: 10.1145/1963405.1963503 111

[144] M. Rosvall and C. T. Bergstrom. Maps of random walks on complex networks reveal community structure. *PNAS*, 105(4):1118–1123, 2008. DOI: 10.1073/pnas.0706851105 4

[145] C. Rother, V. Kolmogorov, V. Lempitsky, and M. Szummer. Optimizing binary MRFS via extended roof duality. In *CVPR*, pages 1–8, 2007. DOI: 10.1109/cvpr.2007.383203 130

[146] Y. Ruan, D. Fuhry, and S. Parthasarathy. Efficient community detection in large networks using content and links. In *WWW*, pages 1089–1098, 2013. DOI: 10.1145/2488388.2488483 107

[147] N. Ruchansky, F. Bonchi, D. García-Soriano, F. Gullo, and N. Kourtellis. The minimum Wiener connector problem. In *SIGMOD*, pages 1587–1602, 2015. DOI: 10.1145/2723372.2749449 164

[148] Y. Saad. *Iterative Methods for Sparse Linear Systems*, vol. 82, SIAM, 2003. DOI: 10.1137/1.9780898718003 73

[149] S. E. Schaeffer. Graph clustering. *Computer Science Review*, 1(1):27–64, 2007. DOI: 10.1016/j.cosrev.2007.05.001 77, 78

[150] J. Scott. *Social Network Analysis*. Sage, 2017. DOI: 10.1177/0038038588022001007 2

[151] J. Shan, D. Shen, T. Nie, Y. Kou, and G. Yu. An efficient approach of overlapping communities search. In *International Conference on Database Systems for Advanced Applications*, pages 374–388, 2015. DOI: 10.1007/978-3-319-18120-2_22 163

[152] J. Shan, D. Shen, T. Nie, Y. Kou, and G. Yu. Searching overlapping communities for group query. *World Wide Web*, 19(6):1179–1202, 2016. DOI: 10.1007/s11280-015-0378-5 163

[153] J. Shang, C. Wang, C. Wang, G. Guo, and J. Qian. An attribute-based community search method with graph refining. *The Journal of Supercomputing*, pages 1–28, 2017. DOI: 10.1007/s11227-017-1976-z 165

[154] H. Shen, X. Cheng, K. Cai, and M.-B. Hu. Detect overlapping and hierarchical community structure in networks. *Physica A: Statistical Mechanics and its Applications*, 388(8):1706–1712, 2009. DOI: 10.1016/j.physa.2008.12.021 4

[155] J. Shi and J. Malik. Normalized cuts and image segmentation. *Departmental Papers (CIS)*, page 107, 2000. DOI: 10.1109/cvpr.1997.609407 4, 165

[156] S. Soundarajan and J. Hopcroft. Using community information to improve the precision of link prediction methods. In *WWW*, pages 607–608, 2012. DOI: 10.1145/2187980.2188150 4

[157] M. Sozio and A. Gionis. The community-search problem and how to plan a successful cocktail party. In *KDD*, pages 939–948, 2010. DOI: 10.1145/1835804.1835923 5, 7, 10, 27, 34, 35, 36, 38, 51, 78, 79, 80, 85, 87, 105, 149

[158] V. Spirin and L. A. Mirny. Protein complexes and functional modules in molecular networks. *PNAS*, 100(21):12123–12128, 2003. DOI: 10.1073/pnas.2032324100 2

[159] Y. Sun and J. Han. Mining heterogeneous information networks: A structural analysis approach. *ACM SIGKDD Explorations Newsletter*, 14(2):20–28, 2013. DOI: 10.1145/2481244.2481248 2, 165

[160] Y. Sun, J. Tang, J. Han, M. Gupta, and B. Zhao. Community evolution detection in dynamic heterogeneous information networks. In *Proc. of the 8th Workshop on Mining and Learning with Graphs*, pages 137–146, 2010. DOI: 10.1145/1830252.1830270 166

182 BIBLIOGRAPHY

[161] S. A. Tabrizi, A. Shakery, M. Asadpour, M. Abbasi, and M. A. Tavallaie. Personalized pagerank clustering: A graph clustering algorithm based on random walks. *Physica A: Statistical Mechanics and its Applications*, 392(22):5772–5785, 2013. DOI: 10.1016/j.physa.2013.07.021 4, 165

[162] C. E. Tsourakakis, F. Bonchi, A. Gionis, F. Gullo, and M. A. Tsiarli. Denser than the densest subgraph: Extracting optimal quasi-cliques with quality guarantees. In *KDD*, pages 104–112, 2013. DOI: 10.1145/2487575.2487645 9, 10, 12, 13, 15

[163] J. Ugander, L. Backstrom, C. Marlow, and J. Kleinberg. Structural diversity in social contagion. *PNAS*, 109(16):5962–5966, 2012. DOI: 10.1073/pnas.1116502109 7, 109, 111, 122

[164] J. C. Valverde-Rebaza and A. de Andrade Lopes. Link prediction in complex networks based on cluster information. In *Brazilian Symposium on Artificial Intelligence*, pages 92–101, 2012. DOI: 10.1007/978-3-642-34459-6_10 4

[165] J. Wang and J. Cheng. Truss decomposition in massive networks. *PVLDB*, 5(9):812–823, 2012. DOI: 10.14778/2311906.2311909 9, 10, 12, 15, 18, 19, 20, 24, 25, 52, 54, 55, 56, 80, 99, 100, 166

[166] J. Wang, J. Cheng, and A. W.-C. Fu. Redundancy-aware maximal cliques. In *KDD*, pages 122–130, 2013. DOI: 10.1145/2487575.2487689 9, 12, 13

[167] M. Wang, W. Zuo, and Y. Wang. An improved density peaks-based clustering method for social circle discovery in social networks. *Neurocomputing*, 179:219–227, 2016. DOI: 10.1016/j.neucom.2015.11.091 156

[168] N. Wang, J. Zhang, K.-L. Tan, and A. K. H. Tung. On triangulation-based dense neighborhood graphs discovery. *PVLDB*, 4(2):58–68, 2010. DOI: 10.14778/1921071.1921073 12, 23

[169] Y. Wang, J. Fang, and F. Wu. Application of community detection algorithm with link clustering in inhibition of social network worms. *IJ Network Security*, 19(3):458–468, 2017. 4

[170] Y. Wang and L. Gao. An edge-based clustering algorithm to detect social circles in ego networks. *Journal of Computers*, 8(10):2575–2582, 2013. DOI: 10.4304/jcp.8.10.2575-2582 7, 109, 127

[171] Y. Wang, X. Jian, Z. Yang, and J. Li. Query optimal k-plex based community in graphs. *Data Science and Engineering*, 2(4):257–273, 2017. DOI: 10.1007/s41019-017-0051-3 164

[172] Z. Wang, Y. Yuan, G. Wang, H. Qin, and Y. Ma. An effective method for community search in large directed attributed graphs. In *International Conference on Mobile ad hoc and Sensor Networks*, pages 237–251, 2017. DOI: 10.1007/978-981-10-8890-2_17 164

[173] T. Waskiewicz. Friend of a friend influence in terrorist social networks. In *ICAI*, page 1, 2012. 4

[174] S. Wasserman and K. Faust. *Social Network Analysis: Methods and Applications*, vol. 8. Cambridge University Press, 1994. DOI: 10.1017/cbo9780511815478 52

[175] D. J. Watts and P. S. Dodds. Influentials, networks, and public opinion formation. *Journal of Consumer Research*, 34:441–458, 2007. DOI: 10.1086/518527 111

[176] D. J. Watts, P. S. Dodds, and M. E. Newman. Identity and search in social networks. *Science*, 296(5571):1302–1305, 2002. DOI: 10.1126/science.1070120 2

[177] D. J. Watts and S. H. Strogatz. Collective dynamics of small-world'networks. *Nature*, 393(6684):440, 1998. DOI: 10.1515/9781400841356.301 52

[178] D. Wen, L. Qin, X. Lin, Y. Zhang, and L. Chang. Enumerating k-vertex connected components in large graphs. *ArXiv Preprint ArXiv:1703.08668*, 2017. DOI: 10.1109/icde.2019.00014 22, 23

[179] D. Wen, L. Qin, Y. Zhang, X. Lin, and J. X. Yu. I/O efficient core graph decomposition at web scale. In *ICDE*, pages 133–144, 2016. DOI: 10.1109/icde.2016.7498235 166

[180] Y. Wu, R. Jin, J. Li, and X. Zhang. Robust local community detection: On free rider effect and its elimination. *PVLDB*, 8(7), 2015. DOI: 10.14778/2752939.2752948 5, 7, 27, 73, 74, 75, 76, 77, 78, 79, 80, 81, 87, 154, 160

[181] Z. Wu, S. Pan, F. Chen, G. Long, C. Zhang, and P. S. Yu. A comprehensive survey on graph neural networks. *ArXiv Preprint ArXiv:1901.00596*, 2019. 165

[182] J. Xiang, C. Guo, and A. Aboulnaga. Scalable maximum clique computation using MapReduce. In *ICDE*, pages 74–85, 2013. DOI: 10.1109/icde.2013.6544815 9, 12, 13

[183] J. Xie, S. Kelley, and B. K. Szymanski. Overlapping community detection in networks: The state-of-the-art and comparative study. *ACM Computing Survey*, 45(4):43, 2013. DOI: 10.1145/2501654.2501657 4

[184] J. Xu, X. Fu, L. Tu, M. Luo, M. Xu, and N. Zheng. Personalized top-n influential community search over large social networks. In *APWeb-WAIM*, pages 105–120, 2018. DOI: 10.1007/978-3-319-96890-2_9 43, 163

[185] D. Yan, J. Cheng, Y. Lu, and W. Ng.   Blogel: A block-centric framework for distributed computation on real-world graphs.   *PVLDB*, 7(14):1981–1992, 2014. DOI: 10.14778/2733085.2733103 166

[186] Y. Yan, D. Luo, J. Ni, H. Fei, W. Fan, X. Yu, J. Yen, and X. Zhang. Local graph clustering by multi-network random walk with restart. In *PAKDD*, pages 490–501, 2018. DOI: 10.1007/978-3-319-93040-4_39 165

[187] J. Yang and J. Leskovec.   Overlapping community detection at scale: A non-negative matrix factorization approach.   In *WSDM*, pages 587–596, 2013. DOI: 10.1145/2433396.2433471 4, 165

[188] J. Yang and J. Leskovec.   Overlapping communities explain core—periphery organization of networks.   *Proc. of the IEEE*, 102(12):1892–1902, 2014. DOI: 10.1109/jproc.2014.2364018 4, 165

[189] H. Yin, A. R. Benson, J. Leskovec, and D. F. Gleich. Local higher-order graph clustering. In *KDD*, pages 555–564, 2017. DOI: 10.1145/3097983.3098069 164

[190] F. Zhang, L. Yuan, Y. Zhang, L. Qin, X. Lin, and A. Zhou. Discovering strong communities with user engagement and tie strength. In *International Conference on Database Systems for Advanced Applications*, pages 425–441, 2018. DOI: 10.1007/978-3-319-91452-7_28 163

[191] G. Zhang, D. Jin, J. Gao, P. Jiao, F. Fogelman-Soulié, and X. Huang. Finding communities with hierarchical semantics by distinguishing general and specialized topics. In *IJCAI*, pages 3648–3654, 2018. DOI: 10.24963/ijcai.2018/507 4, 165

[192] Y. Zhang and S. Parthasarathy. Extracting analyzing and visualizing triangle k-core motifs within networks. In *ICDE*, pages 1049–1060, 2012. DOI: 10.1109/icde.2012.35 12, 20

[193] Z. Zhang, P. Cui, and W. Zhu. Deep learning on graphs: A survey. *ArXiv Preprint ArXiv:1812.04202*, 2018. 4, 165

[194] Z. Zhang, X. Huang, J. Xu, B. Choi, and Z. Shang. Keyword centric community search. In *ICDE*, pages 422–433, 2019. DOI: 10.1109/icde.2019.00045 164

[195] D. Zheng, J. Liu, R.-H. Li, C. Aslay, Y.-C. Chen, and X. Huang. Querying intimate-core groups in weighted graphs. In *IEEE International Conference on Semantic Computing*, pages 156–163, 2017. DOI: 10.1109/icsc.2017.80 163

[196] Z. Zheng, F. Ye, R.-H. Li, G. Ling, and T. Jin.   Finding weighted k-truss communities in large networks.   *Information Sciences*, 417:344–360, 2017. DOI: 10.1016/j.ins.2017.07.012 164

[197] R. Zhou, C. Liu, J. X. Yu, W. Liang, B. Chen, and J. Li.   Finding maximal k-edge-connected subgraphs from a large graph. In *EDBT*, pages 480–491, 2012. DOI: 10.1145/2247596.2247652 22

[198] Y. Zhou, H. Cheng, and J. X. Yu. Graph clustering based on structural/attribute similarities. *PVLDB*, 2(1):718–729, 2009. DOI: 10.14778/1687627.1687709 84, 107

[199] Q. Zhu, H. Hu, C. Xu, J. Xu, and W.-C. Lee.   Geo-social group queries with minimum acquaintance constraints. *The VLDB Journal*, 26(5):709–727, 2017. DOI: 10.1007/s00778-017-0473-6 3, 7, 10, 133, 135, 136, 138, 143, 156, 157

[200] Z. Zou and R. Zhu. Truss decomposition of uncertain graphs. *Knowledge and Information Systems*, 50(1):197–230, 2017. DOI: 10.1007/s10115-016-0943-y 165

Authors' Biographies

XIN HUANG

Xin Huang is an Assistant Professor in the Department of Computer Science, Hong Kong Baptist University. He received his B.Eng. in computer science from Xiamen University in 2010, and Ph.D. in systems engineering and engineering management from Chinese University of Hong Kong in 2014. During 2015–2016, he worked as a postdoctoral research fellow at University of British Columbia. His research interests include graph data management, big graph mining and visualization, and social network analysis.

LAKS V.S. LAKSHMANAN

Laks V.S. Lakshmanan is a Professor of Computer Science at the University of British Columbia, Vancouver, BC, Canada. His research covers a wide spectrum of topics in data management and mining, including advanced data models for novel applications, OLAP and data warehousing, data integration, data cleaning, semi-structured data and XML, information and social networks and social media, recommender systems, personalization, knowledge graphs, and fake news detection and mitigation. His publications appear in top-tier venues in these areas and he has served on the program and senior program committees of top-tier conferences in these areas, as well as on the editorial board of the *VLDB Journal*. He is an ACM Distinguished Scientist and currently serves on the editorial board of *Distributed and Parallel Databases* and *Information Systems*. His paper on concise representation and exploration of medical trajectories, in collaboration with colleagues, won the Best Research Paper Award at the IEEE International Conference on Data Science and Advanced Analytics (DSAA 2018).

JIANLIANG XU

Jianliang Xu is a Professor in the Department of Computer Science, Hong Kong Baptist University. He received his B.Eng. in computer science and engineering from Zhejiang University, Hangzhou, China and his Ph.D. in computer science from Hong Kong University of Science and Technology. He held visiting positions at Pennsylvania State University and Fudan University. His research interests include data management, blockchain, mobile computing, and data security and privacy. He has published more than 200 technical papers in these areas, most of which appeared in leading journals and conferences including SIGMOD, VLDB, ICDE, *TODS*, *TKDE*, and *VLDBJ*. He has served as a program co-chair/vice chair for a number of major international conferences including IEEE ICDCS 2012, WAIM 2016, and IEEE MDM 2019. He has been an Associate Editor of *IEEE Transactions on Knowledge and Data Engineering (TKDE)* and *Proceedings of the VLDB Endowment (PVLDB)*.

Printed in the United States
by Baker & Taylor Publisher Services